ALTERED READING

LEVINAS AND LITERATURE

JILL ROBBINS

THE

UNIVERSITY

OF CHICAGO

PRESS

CHICAGO &

LONDON

JILL ROBBINS is associate professor of English and comparative literature at the State University of New York at Buffalo. She is the author of *Prodigal Son/Elder Brother: Interpretation and Alterity in Augustine, Petrarch, Kafka, Levinas*, also published by the University of Chicago Press.

The University of Chicago Press, Chicago 60637
The University of Chicago Press, Ltd., London
© 1999 by The Unversity of Chicago
All rights reserved. Published 1999
Printed in the United States of America
08 07 06 05 04 03 02 01 00 99   1 2 3 4 5
ISBN: 0-226-72112-4 (cloth)
ISBN: 0-226-72113-2 (paper)

Library of Congress Cataloging-in-Publication Data

Robbins, Jill.
    Altered reading : Levinas and literature / Jill Robbins.
        p.   cm.
    Includes bibliographical references and index.
    ISBN 0-226-72112-4 (cloth : alk. paper). — ISBN 0-226-72113-2 (paper : alk. paper)
        1. Lévinas, Emmanuel.   2. Literature—Philosophy—History—20th century.
    I. Title.
    B2430.L484R63   1999
    194—dc21   98-37917
                                                                                        CIP

CONTENTS

ACKNOWLEDGMENTS

It is a pleasure to acknowledge the obligations that I have incurred during the writing of this book. A condensed version of Chapter 2 first appeared in Adriaan Peperzak, ed., *Ethics as First Philosophy* (London: Routledge, 1995), 173–83. A version of Chapter 3 was published in Arleen B. Dallery and Stephen H. Watson with Marya Bower, eds., *Transitions in Continental Philosophy* (Albany: State University of New York Press, 1993), 283–91. An earlier version of Chapter 4 appeared in *Yale French Studies* 79 (1991): 139–49, and again in a revised and expanded form in Cathy Caruth and Deborah Esch, eds., *Critical Encounters: Reference and Responsibility in Deconstructive Writing* (New Brunswick: Rutgers University Press, 1995), 275–98. A condensed version of Chapter 5 appeared in *L'Esprit Créateur* 35 (1995): 66–79. Permission to reprint is gratefully acknowledged.

An American Council of Learned Societies Fellowship in 1992–93 gave me free time and financial assistance. I would like to thank the Department of Philosophy at the University of Toronto who welcomed me as a Visiting Scholar that same year, and the staff of the John P. Robarts Research Library. The first three chapters of this book reproduce the rhythm of the Second Annual Lecture Series in Philosophy and Literature which I delivered at the University of Notre Dame in 1992. Special thanks are due to Gerald Bruns for this invitation and his encouragement. Portions of this book were given at the Society for Phenomenology and Existential Philosophy, the International Association of Philosophy and Literature, the Collegium Phaenomenologicum, Johns Hopkins University, Emory University, Loyola University at Chicago, DePaul University, McMaster University, University of King's College, University of

Oregon, University of California, Berkeley, and University of California, Santa Barbara.

Karsten Harries and Paul de Man guided this work in its earliest stages. Geoffrey Hartman provided valuable advice throughout the course of the project. Among many persons in the field of Levinas research who shared their knowledge with me, Robert Bernasconi, John Llewelyn, Tina Chanter, Catherine Chalier, and Adriaan Peperzak deserve special mention. I also would like to thank my colleagues at the State University of New York at Buffalo, especially Carol Jacobs, Henry Sussman, and Rodolphe Gasché, and my students for providing an environment in which this book could be written. Benjamin Friedlander generously gave his time and help. Marcus Coelen assisted with the translation that appears in the appendix. Aaron Alter provided technical support. I thank Lila Weinberg for her patient and expert editing. I would like to thank Derek Attridge and Elizabeth Weber, who advised me on the completed manuscript. Finally, I owe special thanks to Cathy Caruth and Lewis Fried, whose support of and critical response to this work were indispensable.

ABBREVIATIONS

WORKS BY EMMANUEL LEVINAS

BPW *Basic Philosophical Writings*, ed. Adriaan T. Peperzak, Simon Critchley, and Robert Bernasconi (Bloomington: Indiana University Press, 1996).

CPP *Collected Philosophical Papers*, trans. Alphonso Lingis (Dordrecht: Martinus Nijhoff, 1987).

DDVI *Of God Who Comes to Mind*, trans. Bettina Bergo (Stanford: Stanford University Press, 1998). *De Dieu qui vient à l'idée* (Paris: Vrin, 1982).

DF *Difficult Freedom*, trans. Seán Hand (Baltimore: Johns Hopkins University Press, 1990). *Difficile liberté* (Paris: Albin Michel, 1976 [1963]).

EDE *En découvrant l'existence avec Husserl et Heidegger* (Paris: Vrin, 1974 [1967]).

EE *Existence and Existents*, trans. Alphonso Lingis (The Hague: Martinus Nijhoff, 1978). *De l'existence à l'existant* (Paris: Vrin, 1947).

EI *Ethics and Infinity*, trans. Richard Cohen (Pittsburgh: Duquesne University Press, 1985).

EP "Enigma and Phenomenon," in CPP. "Enigme et phénomène," *Esprit* 33 (1965) 1128–42; reprinted in EDE, 203–17.

FC "Freedom and Command," in CPP. "Liberté et commandment," *Revue de Métaphysique et de Morale* 58 (1953).

IR *Is It Righteous to Be? Interviews*, ed. Jill Robbins (Stanford: Stanford University Press, 1999).

JW "Jean Wahl: Neither Having nor Being," trans. Michael Smith, *Outside the Subject* (Stanford: Stanford University Press, 1993). *Jean*

Wahl et Gabriel Marcel, ed. Jeanne Hersch (Paris: Beauchesne, 1976).

LB   "Lévy-Bruhl et la philosophie contemporaine," *Revue Philosophique de la France et de l'Étranger* 147 (1957): 556–69; reprinted in *Entre nous* (Paris: Grasset, 1991).

LR   *The Levinas Reader,* ed. Seán Hand (Oxford: Blackwell, 1989).

NI   "No Identity," in *CPP.* *L'Ephémère* 13 (1970): 27–44; reprinted in *Humanisme de l'autre homme* (Montpellier: Fata Morgana, 1972).

NP   *Proper Names,* trans. Michael Smith (Stanford: Stanford University Press, 1996). *Noms propres* (Montpellier: Fata Morgana, 1976).

OB   *Otherwise than Being or Beyond Essence,* trans. Alphonso Lingis (The Hague: Martinus Nijhoff, 1981). *Autrement qu'être ou au-delà de l'essence* (The Hague: Martinus Nijhoff, 1987).

OP   "The Other in Proust," in *LR* and *NP.* "L'autre dans Proust," *Deucalion* 2 (1947).

RO   "Reality and Its Shadow," in *CCP.* "La réalité et son ombre," *Les Temps Modernes* 38 (1948); reprinted in *Les imprévus de l'histoire* (Montpellier: Fata Morgana, 1994).

SMB *On Maurice Blanchot,* trans. Michael Smith, in *NP.* *Sur Maurice Blanchot* (Montpellier: Fata Morgana, 1975).

T   "The Trace of the Other," trans. Alphonso Lingis, in *Deconstruction in Context,* ed. Mark C. Taylor (Chicago: University of Chicago Press, 1986). "La trace de l'autre," 1963; reprinted in *EDE,* 187–202.

TA   *Time and the Other,* trans. Richard Cohen (Pittsburgh: Duquesne University Press, 1985). *Le temps et l'autre* (Montpellier: Fata Morgana, 1979 [1947]).

TI   *Totality and Infinity,* trans. Alphonso Lingis (Pittsburgh: Duquesne University Press, 1969). *Totalité et infini* (The Hague: Martinus Nijhoff, 1961).

TW   "The Transcendence of Words," trans. Seán Hand, in *LR.* "La transcendance des mots," *Les Temps Modernes* 44 (1949); reprinted in *Hors sujet* (Montpellier: Fata Morgana, 1987).

OTHER WORKS

A   Jacques Derrida and Pierre-Jean Labarrière, *Altérités* (Paris: Éditions Osiris, 1986).

AD   Jacques Derrida, *Adieu* (Paris: Galillée, 1997).

ATM Jacques Derrida, "At This Very Moment in This Work Here I

Am," trans. Ruben Berezdivin, in *RRL*. "En ce moment même dans cet ouvrage me voici," in *TEL*.

CME Jean Wahl, *Le choix, le monde, l'existence* (Paris: Arthaud, 1947).

CT Jean Wahl, "Introduction," *Crainte et tremblement*, trans. Pierre Tisseau (Paris: Aubier, 1935).

D Jacques Derrida, "Différance," in *Margins of Philosophy*, trans. Alan Bass (Chicago: University of Chicago Press, 1982). *Marges* (Paris: Minuit, 1972).

DI Jean-François Lyotard, *The Differend: Phrases in Dispute*, trans. Georges Van Den Abbeele (Minneapolis: University of Minnesota Press, 1988). *Le différend* (Paris: Minuit, 1983).

EFP *Ethics as First Philosophy*, ed. Adriaan Peperzak (London: Routledge, 1995).

EK Jean Wahl, *Études Kierkegaardiennes* (Paris: Aubier, 1938).

EPE Georges Bataille, "From Existentialism to the Primacy of Economy," trans. Jill Robbins (see Appendix, this vol.). "De l'existentialisme au primat de l'économie," *Critique* 3 (1947–48); reprinted in *Oeuvres complètes*, vol. 11 (Paris: Gallimard, 1988).

ET Jean Wahl, *Existence humaine et transcendance* (Neuchâtel: La Baconnière, 1944).

FF *Face to Face with Levinas*, ed. Richard A. Cohen (Albany: State University of New York Press, 1986).

IC Maurice Blanchot, *The Infinite Conversation*, trans. Susan Hanson (Minneapolis: University of Minnesota Press, 1993). *L'entretien infini* (Paris: Gallimard, 1969).

JG Jean-François Lyotard, *Just Gaming*, trans. Wlad Godzich (Minneapolis: University of Minnesota Press, 1985). *Au juste* (Paris: Christian Bourgois, 1979).

KV *Kierkegaard vivant*, ed. Jean Wahl (Paris: Gallimard, 1966).

LL Jean-François Lyotard, "Levinas's Logic," in *FF*.

PPP Jean Wahl, *Poésie, pensée, perception* (Paris: Calmann-Lévy, 1948).

PRX Joseph Libertson, *Proximity: Levinas, Blanchot, Bataille and Communication* (The Hague: Martinus Nijhoff, 1982).

RRL *Re-Reading Levinas*, ed. Robert Bernasconi and Simon Critchley (Bloomington: Indiana University Press, 1991).

SH Jean Wahl, *A Short History of Existentialism*, trans. Forrest Williams and Stanley Maron (New York: Philosophical Library, 1949). *Petite histoire de "l'existentialisme": Suivie de "Kafka et Kierkegaard: Commentaires"* (Paris: Club Maintenant, 1947).

SL Maurice Blanchot, *The Space of Literature*, trans. Ann Smock (Lincoln: University of Nebraska, 1982). *L'espace littéraire* (Paris: Gallimard, 1955).

TEL   *Textes pour Emmanuel Levinas*, ed. François Laruelle (Paris: Jean-Michel Place, 1980).

VM   Jacques Derrida, "Violence and Metaphysics," in *Writing and Difference*, trans. Alan Bass (Chicago: University of Chicago Press, 1978). "Violence et métaphysique," in *L'écriture et la différence* (Paris: Seuil, 1967).

WD   Maurice Blanchot, *The Writing of the Disaster*, trans. Ann Smock (Lincoln: University of Nebraska Press, 1986). *L'écriture du désastre* (Paris: Gallimard, 1980).

INTRODUCTION

Within recent Continental philosophy, Emmanuel Levinas has decisively renewed the question of the ethical. In a manner somewhat analogous to Heidegger's retrieval of the forgotten question of being, Levinas repeats and revisits an entire philosophical tradition from the vantage point of the forgetting of the ethical. The tradition, he argues, habitually suppresses alterity, subordinating it to the totality. Interpreting the other as a necessary moment of the same, that is, in an all too dialectizable manner, it would reduce the absolutely other to the other *of* the same. Although Levinas's critical retrieval of the ethical is not as systematic as Heidegger's "destruction" of the history of ontotheology, the status of the two descriptions is similar. Just as Heidegger through the existential analytic of Dasein had offered an analysis of the ontological structures constitutive of existence, so too Levinas describes the ethical structures which are constitutive of existence.

Ethics, as Levinas describes it in his mature philosophy, represented by the 1961 *Totality and Infinity*, denotes the putting into question of the self by the infinitizing mode of the face of the other *(le visage d'Autrui)*. The self's habitual economy is invariably totalizing. But this habitual (and, ultimately, murderous) tendency is interrupted by the face of the other which commands me, "Thou shalt not kill." Levinas describes the nonhabitual, ethical response to the face as generosity and language. (The term *responsibility* does not actually appear until his later work.)

The impact of the phenomenological traditions of Husserl and Heidegger is apparent in Levinas's account of the encounter with the other, which occurs on a level more originary than the empirical. Jacques Derrida alludes to the transcendental motif in Levinas's philosophy when in his 1963 essay, "Violence and Metaphysics," he proposes that Levinas gives us not *an* ethics but an "ethics of ethics" (VM, 111). Unlike the a priori structures of the Kantian transcendentals, however, the Levinasian "transcendentals" are not determining. They are closer to Heidegger's "finite" or "immanent" transcendentals, structures of the understanding of being which may or may not be taken up by Dasein. The term *quasitranscendental*, used by Rodolphe Gasché with reference to the conditions of possibility *and* impossibility that Derrida inquires into, can indeed be extended to Levinas.[1] For example, while *Totality and Infinity* asserts that generosity puts into question the self's "joyous possession of the world" (TI, 75–76) and that "the rupture with the totality" is achieved as language (TI, 39), the status of the ethical "event" that Levinas describes is precarious. At the limit, it is not clear that this gift *is*, that it even performs anything. Nor is it clear that the primordial ethical language, which Levinas elaborates as a form of speech which is first of all interpellative and interlocutionary, is something that one could ever claim to be taking up. Even if this gift and this ethical language are conceived, in very general terms, along the lines of what J. L. Austin described as the performative dimension of language, namely, an utterance that does not constate or describe what is the case but is the doing of an action, it is not necessarily the case that such a performative would be free of all contamination by the constative, or by what Levinas calls the language of ontology.

Levinas's later work, represented by the 1974 *Otherwise than Being*, takes up this problematic more or less explicitly. It seeks to describe ethics in a language that would depart from an ontological language. Levinas's effort is to discursively pass over to what is other than being, even if such an effort always risks falling into a being otherwise, that is, into a modality of being. The later work not only has a distinctive idiom, a different terminology predominates as well: trauma, wound, passivity, hostage, persecution, responsibility. Ethical language is described there in terms of the operative distinction between the Saying and the Said, which corresponds roughly to the difference between the kind of speech that foregrounds the relation to its addressee, and a denotative speaking that absorbs alterity into thematization. The major difference between the mature and the later work can be stated as follows. While *Totality and Infinity* sought to put into question the self and its totalizing tendency, *Otherwise than Being* seeks to put into question the very closure of the philosophical discourse itself. Whereas *Totality and Infinity* described the

---

1. See Rodolphe Gasché, *The Tain of the Mirror: Derrida and the Philosophy of Reflection* (Cambridge, MA: Harvard University Press, 1986), 316–17.

putting into question of the self in the presence of the other, *Otherwise than Being* describes the self as always already worked over, traumatized and dispossessed by the other. In the later work, ethics does not happen to a self or subject. The conception of responsibility and ethics that emerges is nonvoluntaristic and nonvolitional. Responsibility does not emanate from the initiative of a subject; it chooses me before I choose it. That is why it is on the basis of the thinking of a certain impossibility that the ethical becomes legible in Levinas. One might add that because of the often violent or, as Maurice Blanchot would say, "disastrous," terminology in his later work, and because of the consistent emphasis throughout his work, on an original *in*equality with the other, ethics, as Levinas describes it, is distinctly not a "feel-good" experience. "It's not pleasant, it is good," he states in a 1986 interview with François Poirié (*IR*).

Levinas's biography, which he recounts in the essay "Signature," and in a much more detailed fashion in interviews, draws attention to the specific points of reference that inform his work. He was born in Lithuania in 1906 in a cosmopolitan and assimilated Jewish milieu. His father owned a bookstore. During the Russian Revolution, his family, like other Jews from the Pale of Settlement, was expelled from "the border zone that Lithuania was" (*IR*), and Levinas's family moved to the Ukraine for three years. Upon his return, Levinas went to a Russian gymnasium. He attended university at Strasbourg, where he met Maurice Blanchot who became a lifelong friend. His most important teachers at Strasbourg were Maurice Halbwachs, Maurice Pradines, Charles Blondel, and Henri Carteron. In 1924–25 he studied with Husserl and Heidegger in Freiburg, which was decisive for his subsequent philosophical work. During the war he served in the French army and was subsequently incarcerated for four years in a labor camp in Hanover, Germany, for French Jewish prisoners of war. When he returned from captivity, he learned that his family in Lithuania, including his parents, his maternal and paternal grandparents, and his two younger brothers, had been murdered by the Nazis. The question of the way in which these experiences are reflected in his ethical philosophy, beyond an all too general level, is a complex one. As in the case of the related question of the way in which Levinas's ethical thought is linked to Judaism, the explanatory power of calling Levinas a post-Holocaust or a Jewish philosopher may be at once too great and, at the same time, lacking.

Although Levinas came from a part of Lithuania famous for its rabbinical academies, his childhood instruction was limited to learning Hebrew and reading scripture. Levinas did not begin the study of the rabbinical texts that traditionally accompany the reading of scripture until after the war, when he met a brilliant and unusual teacher, Shoshani, who was also the teacher of Elie Wiesel.[2] It is Shoshani whom Levinas credits with opening up the world of the Talmud to him. Subsequent to his studies with Shoshani, during which time he was also the director of a professional Jewish organization, a branch of the Alliance Israélite Universelle, Levinas published four books of commentary on talmudic exegesis. He offered philosophical readings of the Talmud which uncover its hidden intelligibility. These "talmudic readings," originally given at the annual Colloquium of French Jewish Intellectuals, form part of what Levinas calls his nonphilosophical or his "confessional" writings. He keeps them separate from his philosophical texts, as the difference between an exegetical adherence and a phenomenological inquiry aware of its own presuppositions. In my view, and in the way I read Levinas, the distinction between the philosophical and the nonphilosophical writing is not absolute. It breaks down, in any case, after 1975 with the publication of *Of God Who Comes to Mind*. Even before 1975, there are decisive indications in his philosophical work that his ethical thought takes inspiration from the Hebrew tradition. Conversely, even his earliest "confessional" writings register the ethical preoccupations characteristic of his philosophical texts.

The Levinas I emphasize is in a certain relation of proximity to the work of Maurice Blanchot, Georges Bataille, and Jacques Derrida. This is not only because they are arguably part of the same constellation, but because my presentation registers the impact of the readings of Levinas that each has produced. The responses to Levinas by Blanchot, Bataille, and Derrida are concerned with aesthetic as well as ethical issues. The three explore and exploit the "literary" dimensions of Levinasian thought more acutely and sympathetically than most other commentators do, and they do so in ways that are not at all reductive. Blanchot's *The Infinite Conversation* (1962) takes up Levinas's emphasis on language as a nontotalizing relation to the other. This asymmetrical relation is characterized by a distance so radical that the terms *myself* and the *other* are not limitrophe to the relation. The Blanchotian *parole* or speech is not a dialogue, with the reciprocity and comprehension that implies. In Blanchot's plangent inflection, this strange speech "is beyond the reach of the one who says it as much as of the one who hears it. It is between us, it holds itself between [*se tient entre*] and the conversation [*entretien*] is the approach on the basis of this between" (*IC*, 212). As Blanchot elaborates it,

---

2. See Salomon Malka, *Monsieur Chouchani: L'énigme d'un maître du XXᵉ siècle* (Paris: Editions Jean-Claude Lattès, 1994); and Elie Wiesel, *One Generation After* (New York: Random House, 1970), 120–25.

the response-ability of ethical language in Levinas lies precisely in its refusal to return to a discredited humanism. Blanchot's 1980 *Writing of the Disaster*, initially published in 1975 as "Exercises de la patience" with the reading of Levinas at its core, was one of the first critical texts to attend seriously to the style and claims of Levinas's later work.

In 1947 Georges Bataille produced a review essay on Levinas entitled "From Existentialism to the Primacy of Economy." (I provide a translation of this little-known essay in this book's Appendix.) The essay allowed Bataille to formalize the conceptual as well as terminological convergence between Blanchot, Levinas, and himself around the thinking of the *il y a* (the "there is"), the return of presence in negation. Joseph Libertson describes this convergence as the simultaneous discovery in the late forties of all three thinkers of a "weakness" in the Hegelian negative (*PRX*, 208). Bataille's edgy and engaged response to Levinas, written in a vocabulary heterogenous to Levinas's, brings out commonalities and differences between their two ways of contesting Hegel. It offers a very different understanding of the term *poetry*. Ultimately, there is between Levinas and Bataille rather than an affinity something more like an allergy. Levinas's ethical thought seems, no doubt, temperamentally averse to the philosophical climate of Bataille's speculations on cruelty, sacrifice, and expenditure. Hence, despite the "communication" that may ensue between their philosophies, Levinas and Bataille seem to have held each other at arm's length.

The first of Derrida's major essays on Levinas, "Violence and Metaphysics" (1963), decided and determined to a large extent the reception of Levinas's thought, particularly among English-speaking readers. There Derrida formulates the problem of Levinas's ethical thought in terms of the oppositions philosophy/nonphilosophy, philosophy/theology, philosophy/empiricism, and most influentially "Greek" and "Hebrew." "Greek" means a philosophical language Levinas is constrained to "speak," even when he would indicate a "Hebrew" tradition of ethical thought from which he draws inspiration. "Language" refers here in the broad sense to the conceptuality that we inhabit and the limits of what we can think. Hence these usages of "Greek" and "Hebrew" are not primarily historical. As Heidegger puts it: philosophy is Greek to the extent that philosophy "first appropriated the Greek world, and only it, in order to unfold itself."[3]

---

3. Martin Heidegger, *What Is Philosophy?* trans. William Kluback and Jean T. Wilder (New Haven, CT: College and UP, 1956), 28–31. Derrida cites and discusses this passage in VM, 81n.4.

Derrida is the first of Levinas's readers to call attention not just to the problem of the language that Levinas can speak but also to the use of metaphor in his writing, which "shelters within its pathos the decisive movements of his discourse" (VM, 84n.7). But this question of metaphor, to which I will return, is linked, in Derrida's text, as a footnote to the "necessarily partial" reading of Levinas that Derrida proposes. In other words, it arises in the context of a larger hermeneutical problem of what can be called "the ethics of interpreting Levinas." Would not a "partial" reading be more adequate to the hermeneutical demands of Levinas's nontotalizing thought? But in thus attempting to be faithful to the hermeneutic demands of Levinas's ethical thought—which states that the generosity of the work should go out to the other without return, should be received in ingratitude—must one not be unfaithful? The implicit interpretive prescription of Levinas's work, "Thou shalt not totalize," produces a consequent double bind.

Derrida's 1980 "At This Very Moment in This Work Here I Am" is devoted largely to exploring this ethico-hermeneutical double bind. The essay is written "in the second person," that is, in the very interlocutionary mode that for Levinas characterizes ethical discourse. Here again the question of the ethics of interpreting Levinas is linked to the question of "how he writes his works." How is it that Levinas not only describes the interruptive encounter he calls ethical, but he also staves off the necessary risk that the interruption be reabsorbed by discourse? How is Levinas's text *self*-interruptive? Derrida identifies the importance of a certain syntax, a linking, in Levinas's writing, and in particular a certain seriality, the repetition of a phrase after an interval: "[T]he first in the series which forms the element of reappropriation is obligated or interrupted by the second" (ATM, 22). The tying together of cut threads, the knotting of interruptions, characterizes Levinas's writing.

Suffice it to say that the crossing of Derrida's and Levinas's work has always been apparent, in "Violence and Metaphysics," where Levinas's attempt to think a "Hebrew" ethics in a "Greek" language was interpreted by Derrida as an attempt to "undo" the Greek language. Similarly, the differential structures of trace, gift, and anachronism in Levinas are consonant with structures that Derrida has also elaborated. At the limit, not only can deconstructive questioning be said to respond to an ethical demand when, seeking out suppressed alterities, it interrupts the totalities of a discourse. But also, when Levinas in the later work exposits the self(-same) as internally bordered by the other, ethics entails precisely the deconstruction of a secure and self-sufficient self. Derrida's reading marks the distance between Levinas's ethical thought and the philosophemes of traditional philosophical ethics, which invariably make reference to concepts such as the ego, consciousness, conscience, the subject, freedom. Derrida's 1997 *Adieu*, a series of texts delivered since Levinas's death on December 25, 1995, takes in the intertwined topics of hospitality, the host, and the hostage, beginning with *Totality and Infinity*. He elaborates further on Levinas's distinctive conception of transcendence, a "transcendence within immanence," or, in Levinas's phrase, an *au-delà-dans*, a "beyond-within" (*AD*, 138).

Jean-François Lyotard is one of Levinas's most attentive readers, certainly the most uncompromising in his respect for ethical alterity and its demands. For example, in "Levinas's Logic," the reader of Levinas's ethical message is denied the self-satisfaction or self-coincidence of being ethical toward it. This "hermeneutic of persecution" (LL, 118) emerges in Lyotard's willingness to relay the Levinasian ethical discourse through speculative dialectics and analytic deontics. In *The Differend* and *Just Gaming*, Lyotard elaborates on the radicality of the language game of ethics in Levinas and demonstrates its heterogeneity to ordinary philosophical vocabulary. He also links it with the uncovering of a specifically Judaic intelligibility.

In the interview with Poirié, to the question "What led you to philosophy," Levinas answered, "I think that it was first of all my reading in Russian, specifically Pushkin, Lermontov, and Dostoevsky, above all Dostoevsky. Books shot through with anxiety . . . but readable as a search for the meaning of life" (*IR*). Levinas's answer to Poirié that Russian literature "led him" to philosophy seems to presuppose a translatability or equivalence between literature and philosophy and, ultimately, a subsumption of literature by philosophy. Perhaps the form of the interviewer's question is at fault; it is too developmental or progressistic; it predetermines the answer. But in another interview from the same time period, Levinas himself proposes a similar formulation for the relationship between literature and philosophy in his work. In answer to Myriam Anissimov's question "Did you read Russian novels," he says: "The Russian novel was my preparation for philosophy."[4] Levinas's answer again seems to presuppose a secondarization of literature in relation to philosophy. The translatability between and subordination of literature to philosophy would seem to depend on conceiving of literature (not to mention philosophy) as something that happens primarily on a denotative

---

4. If philosophical questioning took the form of Russian novels, that was because in the Russian gymnasium, philosophy was not part of the ordinary curriculum. The tremendous investment in Russian letters, among *haskalah* or enlightenment Jews is also at issue.

level. Here one may anticipate Levinas's tendency throughout his work to use literature to *illustrate* a philosophical argument. Here again, Levinas's generous and well-meaning answer to his interviewers that literature was a preparation for philosophy in fact covers up the specificity of the literary, and the real question of Levinas and the literary. It perpetrates a domestication of literature at the hands of philosophy, even philosophy in the post-Heideggerian context in which Levinas is writing, which does not necessarily separate what is said from the way in which it is said, even philosophy in the surprising other way in which Levinas reinscribes it when he gives to think the ethical.

Much depends here on how one conceives of literature (not to mention philosophy). Literature need not be conceived solely in terms of a hermeneutic model of meaning and reference. Formalist literary theoretical accounts—such as Roman Jakobson's—stress the work's very suspension of reference and of the communicative function of language. Derrida states that "if the question of literature obsesses us . . . this half-century since the war . . . in its Sartrian form ('What is literature?') or the more 'formalist' but just as essentialist form of 'literarity,' " this is precisely because literature troubles the very regimes of essence and truth.[5] The hypostatization of literature and philosophy would be itself a form of subordination.[6] In short, we no more can take for granted *the literary* than we can *philosophy*.

Any approach to the question of the relationship of Levinas's philosophy to literature has also to deal with the incommensurability between Levinas's ethics and the discourse of literary criticism. Literary criticism, whether it is conceived as the determination of a work's meaning or as an analysis of its formal structures, would be derivative upon Levinas's more originary question of the ethical, part of what Heidegger calls a regional ontology. Hence Levinas's philosophy cannot function as an extrinsic approach to the literary work of art, that is, it cannot give rise to an application. Of course, much will depend on what one means by literary criticism. If literary criticism is conceived as a more originary questioning of the nature and the conditions of literature and poetic experience, as in the case of Maurice Blanchot, or as a study of the operations of tropes and figures within what Paul de Man calls the rhetorical dimension of

5. Derrida, *Acts of Literature*, ed. Derek Attridge (London: Routledge, 1992), 48.

6. Gasché, "A Relation Called 'Literary,'" ASCA, Brief 2, Amsterdam School for Cultural Analysis, Theory and Interpretation, University of Amsterdam, 1995, 17–19. Rather than thinking of the relationship of philosophy and literature as dyadically related entities, one might think of them as differential codeterminants of each other, Gasché suggests.

language, this incommensurability may prove to be only apparent. Finally, an approach to the question of Levinas and literature has to take into account that Levinas speaks rather rarely about the literary, and that when he does it is almost always in dismissive terms, as when he mentions his dislike of Heidegger's "exegeses" of Hölderlin (*EI,* 42). Levinas's theoretical discourse on the aesthetic most often asserts an unbridgeable chasm between art and ethics.

The range and resonances of the term *literature* in Levinas's work require comment. In interviews he uses it in the sense of "the national literatures" (*EI,* 21), that is, as specific literary historical traditions. He thus refers to it as a genre *of* art rather than the more essential, phenomenologically based descriptions, prior to genre distinctions, that are found in the 1948 "Reality and Its Shadow" and in *Totality and Infinity*. In these texts, the operative term is *poetry,* and it functions as the name for everything that Levinas finds bad about art. Indeed, in the 1951 "Is Ontology Fundamental?" *literature* is a term of opprobrium, when Levinas speaks of the achievement of Heidegger's fundamental questioning (which he will criticize for other reasons) as an approach to philosophy that, at least, "goes beyond literature and its pathetic problems."[7] (The question arises: What is literature's purchase on pathos?) Levinas argues that art produces in its audience a reversion to what in mythical mentality Lucien Lévy-Bruhl calls *participation,* an affective relation to collective representations that blurs the distinction between the natural and the supernatural worlds and that is in direct tension with the liability that Levinas terms *ethical.* He writes in *Totality and Infinity,* "The establishing of the primacy of the ethical . . . a primacy upon which all other structures rest (and in particular all those which seem to put us primordially in contact with an impersonal sublimity, *aesthetic or ontological*), is one of the objectives of the present work" (*TI,* 79; emphasis mine).

Finally, a less-usual use of the term *literature* can be found in *Difficult Freedom,* where Levinas assimilates it to the "literature" of the Bible: "To admit the action of literature on men, that is perhaps the ultimate wisdom of the West in which the people of the Bible will recognize itself" (*DF,* 53). While the ease with which Levinas conflates secular and sacred literature here may be surprising (Is not the Bible at once more and less than literature?), his perception of their common hermeneutical approach to the text is not. It is no accident that this reference occurs in the essay

---

7. "Is Ontology Fundamental?" trans. Simon Critchley with Peter Atterton and Graham Noctor, in *BPW,* 2. "L'ontologie est-elle fondamentale?" *Revue de Métaphysique et de Morale* 56 (1951).

"Identity Papers," where the documents in which Jewish identity is inscribed are the biblical and rabbinic texts. He describes the approach to these texts as "a one-way movement, steep: to the sources, to the old books which are forgotten and difficult, in a strenuous, laborious, and severe study" (*DF*, 52).

The gravitational pull of "Hebrew" texts on the one hand and "Greek" (Russian, French, German, English) texts on the other, which merits a separate discussion, is not my concern in the pages that follow. My concern is with the pull of text as such, in Levinas's work, and especially within the recurrent instances of citation and allusion in his writing. From the perspective of literary criticism, that close reading would be a form of respect is something of an article of faith. Some of the questions that guide this research are: Can Levinas's readings of literature be said to indicate the respect for and attentiveness to the letter of the text that characterizes his approach to scripture? In the terms of the double bind that governs the reception of the gift in Levinas's (and Derrida's) analyses in their pertinence to the reading of texts, does literary criticism require an ingratitude in order to be responsible? Are Levinas's own readings of literary texts grateful or ungrateful? To what extent is reading itself interruptive? What would it mean to extend the insights of Levinas's philosophy in the direction of hermeneutics and rhetorical reading?

This book offers an internal reading of the work of Levinas that will be attentive to the terms of his texts and the intrinsic organization of his work. The first part of this book, entitled "Literature *in* Levinas" (for what is problematic about the conjunction, literature *and* Levinas, has already been established), offers in its first two chapters a detailed critical exposition of ethical language as Levinas conceives it, and an examination of the differential structure of the trace as the other's distinctive mode of signification. The third chapter broaches the question of whether the face can be a figure, in particular a prosopopoeia. The subsequent chapter takes this up in the context of a detailed account of Levinas's murder analysis and the relationship between speech and murder. This part of the book is predominantly concerned with Levinas's mature philosophy: texts from the 1950s, *Totality and Infinity* (1961), and two subsequent essays on the trace, from 1963 and 1965, key transitional essays already in the style of the later works.

The second part of the book, entitled "Levinas and the Aesthetic," tracks and confronts Levinas's implicit and explicit attitude toward art throughout his career. Chapter 5 considers Levinas's explicit theoretical discussions of art from the late 1940s through *Totality and Infinity*, and examines in particular his readings of Marcel Proust and Michel Leiris as well as his polemic against Lévy-Bruhl's concept of participation. Chapter 6 examines the conceptual figure of the *il y a*, as developed in Levinas's early phenomenological works from the 1940s, and the *il y a*'s intrication in the ontology of the work of art. It also explores, by way of an extended reading of Bataille's "From Existentialism to the Primacy of Economy," Levinas's interpretive encounter with Søren Kierkegaard. Chapter 7 explores Levinas's oblique allusions to the poet Arthur Rimbaud in *Totality and Infinity*, and in major texts from the later work, "No Identity" (1970) and *Otherwise than Being* (1974). Chapter 8 discusses Levinas's intertextual engagements with S. Y. Agnon, Fyodor Dostoevsky, and Maurice Blanchot.

Throughout the book's second part I attend to the way in which Levinas not only constates his relationship to literature but also performs it. I hesitate to call this dimension of the work the "Saying" (the operative distinction within Levinas's theory of language in the later work), because I do not think that we should presuppose that we know what the Saying is. Levinas performs his relationship to literature by biblical and literary allusions and citations and a certain etiological play on words. The purview of the book's second part is everything that gets referred to, often confusedly, as "style" in a philosophical work. It is here that the way emerges in which Levinas needs the resources of the literary to say his philosophy.

At several junctures in this book's argument, the analysis pauses over the question of examples for the ethical. The (contentless) ethical language that Levinas describes—which most resembles what Roman Jakobson calls the conative dimension of language, oriented toward the addressee—finds its closest grammatical equivalent in the vocative and the dative. Composed entirely of vocatives and datives, such a language cannot have a syntax. It stammers "you, you, you." But in his philosophical works and in interviews, Levinas does provide some, albeit very few, examples of the primordial ethical language: "Bonjour" (*IR*), "Aprèsvous, monsieur" (*OB*, 117; *IR*), "Thou shalt not kill" (*TI*, 199), "Here I am [*hineni*]" (*OB*, 114, 146). But it is no more clear that one can ever claim to be exemplifying this ethical language than that one can be in the presence of the Saying. Similarly, there are very few examples for the ethical given in Levinas's work, as if it could not be translated into empiricism. Specific ethical prescriptions (all from the later work) include taking the bread from one's own mouth and giving it to the other (*OB*, 55), assuaging thirst or giving to drink, giving the coat from one's shoulders to the other (*OB*, 55), clothing the naked and feeding the hungry (*IR*), sheltering the shelterless (*IR*), turning one's cheek to the smiter (*OB*, 11; *NI*, 146). Several of these prescriptions use the resources of the biblical diction, by way of citation or the narrative expansion of a biblical verse. Finally, the face faces, Levinas warns, "without any metaphor" (*EDE,* 186). Because metaphor would be derivative upon the more originary summons to responsibility that Levinas calls *face,* caution is required before comparing Levinas's descriptions to figural and tropological operations such as prosopopoeia, synecdoche, or metonymy. But what is Levinas's reader to make of the obvious metaphoricity of "The face is a hand, an open hand,"[8] or, "The whole body—a hand or a curve of the shoulder—can express as a face" (*TI,* 212), which even suggest a transfer between synecdochic figures for the human?

This book's title, *Altered Reading,* has already been alluded to when I asked about the ethics of interpreting Levinas and the hermeneutical demands of a nontotalizing thought. The book's reading practice has been altered in this sense by Levinas's work. The title comprises, of course, the project of bringing to bear the insights of close reading on the alterity that Levinas terms *ethical.* "Alterity" in Levinas is neither a concept nor a category; perhaps its very name betrays it.[9] Ethical alterity would seem to have a specificity that excludes alteration in general. "It is an irrefutable logic that pure alterity should not be compatible with the logic of alteration," Derrida says (*A,* 31). Hence, the title asks whether Levinas himself might be altered—in a sense yet to be determined—by his reading of literary texts. It is not my intention to propose that a text has alterity in the same way that the other person does. My goal is to explore the ways in which reading alters—or interrupts—the very economy of the same that the other interrupts. In this way, literary criticism, as a response to this textual interruption, might be said to have an ethical content.

8. "The Paradox of Morality," in *The Provocation of Levinas,* ed. Robert Bernasconi and David Wood (London: Routledge, 1988), 169.

9. Derrida writes: "We would have to examine patiently what emerges in language when the Greek conception of *heteron* seems to run out of breath when faced by the *alter-huic;* what happens when the *heteron* seems to become incapable of mastering what it alone, however, is able to precomprehend by concealing it as alterity (other in general) and which, in return, will reveal to *heteron* its irreducible center of meaning (the other *as* other *[autrui]*). We would have to examine the complicity of the concealment and the precomprehension which does not occur within a conceptual movement, for the French word *autrui* does not designate a category of the genre *autre*" (*VM,* 105).

PART I

LITERATURE
IN LEVINAS'S
ETHICAL
PHILOSOPHY

[1] ON CALL FROM THE OTHER

ETHICAL LANGUAGE IN *TOTALITY AND INFINITY*

DISCOURSE AND GIFT

In *Totality and Infinity*, section I.B., entitled "Separation and Discourse," Levinas writes: "Language which does not touch the other, even tangentially, reaches the other by calling upon him [*en l'interpellant*] or by commanding him or by obeying him, with all the straightforwardness [*droiture*] of these relations" (*TI*, 62). Readers of Levinas will readily acknowledge the special privilege given to language in *Totality and Infinity* as a nontotalizing means of relating to the other: an exception, within the habitual economy, a realization of ethical possibility, an interruption the shock of which *waits* to be absorbed by thought.[1] Before elaborating on what Levinas means by language, and the language relation to the other, and before speculating on the force of this term, *droiture*, translated as straightforwardness, I would like to detail the ordinary state of affairs within which this extraordinary language event, this exception, arises.

The "I" (*le moi*) in Levinas is characterized as identification. This means that the I consists in "recovering its identity throughout all that happens to it" (*TI*, 36), and this includes losing itself, ennui, repugnance, self-aversion, and all the seeming extremes of self-alienation. All these are recuperable by the I. In the terms of Levinas's "The Trace of the Other," the putting into question of consciousness gets recuperated as a

---

1. See Blanchot's formulation about the prophetic dimension of Levinas's "waiting" in *WD*, 25n.8.

consciousness of being put into question. Or as Levinas describes the I's recuperative capacity in *Totality and Infinity:* "The I is identical in its very alterations, it represents them to itself, and thinks them" (*TI,* 36). The I in identification absorbs alterity *into* its identity as thinker or possessor; it draws everything into the play of the same. An Odyssean journey to be sure, in which all the seemingly unforeseeable adventures are but an accident of the return home. This homecoming paradigm and this economy are in fact a habitual economy in which the I never encounters the other.

It is a spurious alterity or, more accurately, a finite alterity to which the I is in relation. Identification denotes not an abstract representation of self by self but a concrete relationship between an I and a world. Levinas calls it "the primordial work of identification" (*TI,* 37). It is not anything that one would want to do away with.[2] The examples that he gives are dwelling, sojourning, being at home (*chez soi*). The "at home" is not, says Levinas, a container. It is a site where I can (*je peux*). The verb *pouvoir* in Levinas's usage conveys "ability" (and alludes to the Heideggerian description of the world as a space of possibilities for Dasein); it also slides into the notion of power. And whether I'm "at home in the world" or not, I will have been always already sojourning, for "everything is caught up in advance with the primordial occupying of a site" (*TI,* 37). This is what Levinas calls the "reversion of the alterity of the world to self-identification," which is the very way of the same.[3]

Strictly speaking, Levinas does not wish to contest this state of affairs (although one will find in his work a powerful indictment of what he calls the "imperialism of the same," as well as the philosophies in the West which underwrite it, "remaining indifferent to the other and to others" [T, 347]). He would simply take a step back to a situation prior to the totality, a situation where, as he states in the book's preface, "the totality breaks up, a situation which conditions the totality itself. That situation is the gleam of exteriority or transcendence in the face of the other *[le visage d'Autrui]*" (*TI,* 24). In Levinas's descriptions, the other who faces is absolutely or infinitely other. To the other, the I is in a relation not of lack or need but desire, which relates to a surplus and which is characterized by distance. The other is other with a radical remoteness which

2. As Adriaan Peperzak suggests, the egological life in Levinas is simply a relative—as opposed to an absolute—good. *To the Other* (West Lafayette, IN: Purdue University Press, 1993), 24.

3. On Levinas's (problematic) conflation of *ipse* (self) and *idem* (same), see Derrida, VM, 107–17.

permits of neither contact, nor vision, nor any form of the theoretical relation. The infinitely other is situated with reference to me in a dimension of height—elsewhere referred to by Levinas as a "curvature of space," "a curvature of intersubjective space," formulations that "inflect distance into elevation" (*TI*, 291) and that underscore the radical asymmetry between me and the other.

How to think the infinity of transcendence in relation to the other, to *autrui*? Strictly speaking, one does not *think* this relation, or talk about the same and the other as if one were observing two entities from the outside. My relation to the other cannot be viewed as a system from the outside; it cannot be totalized. The other and I, writes Levinas, "do not form a number. The collectivity in which I say 'you' or 'we' is not a plural of the 'I' " (*TI*, 39). No pluralism will suffice to think this relation. Nor can we take for granted such concepts as community or dialogue—at least in the ordinary sense of these terms. There is violence in the very unity of the concept, even in the unitary conception of the other. To approach the other armed with a concept such as community or dialogue (or any other humanistic platitude) would destroy the alterity of the other in the very guise of respecting him or her. Levinas writes: "Neither possession nor the unity of number nor the unity of concepts link me to the Stranger, the Stranger who disturbs the being at home with oneself *[le chez soi]*. But the Stranger also means the free one. Over him I have no power *[je ne peux pouvoir]*. He escapes my grasp by an essential dimension . . . He is not wholly in my site" (*TI*, 39). Recall the description of the "at home" as a site where I can (*je peux*). Over the other, *je ne peux pouvoir*; I have neither ability nor power. (In a subsequent passage Levinas will say that the face's expression defies my very power of power *[mon pouvoir de pouvoir]*.) With reference to the other I have no initiative, nothing that would proceed from the ego. (Ultimately in relation to the other, I am not I.) And it is from this singular situation of *in*ability, in which the subject has been altogether called into question, that responsibility, or ethics—in Levinas's reinscribed sense—may arise.[4] He writes: "We name this calling into question of my spontaneity by the presence of the other, ethics" (*TI*, 43). (And one might pause to note the distance between this sense of ethics—as an interruption on a primordial and originary level—and its derivative and used-up senses of right conduct, a set of moral precepts, or any particular morality. Prior to the

---

4. Ann Smock speaks of the *in*ability in responsibility in "Disastrous Responsibility," *L'Ésprit Créateur* 24 (1984), 5–20.

elaboration of all moral precepts, the interruption *opens* ethics, is its up-surge.)[5]

Let us examine closely how this interruption comes about. For Levinas vision is emblematic of the habitual economy and its tendency to grasp and possess. Vision is a violence and a form of adequation. But in the encounter with the face, the avaricious gaze undergoes a transformation. The habitual economy is checked, "arrested," in much the same way as when the face is said to paralyze my *pouvoir de pouvoir*. Levinas writes:

> For the presence before the face, my orientation toward the other can lose the avidity of the gaze only by turning into generosity, incapable of approaching the other with empty hands. This relationship, established over the things hereafter possibly common, that is, susceptible of being said, is the relationship of discourse *[discours]*. The way in which the other presents himself, exceeding the idea of the other in me, we here name face. (*TI,* 50)

This transformation of the gaze, which is a form of adequation, into generosity and language, forms of nonadequation, is preeminently *ethical* in the sense that Levinas gives that term. Note that the interruption, the cessation of power and possibility, can be described positively, indeed, has its positive production in generosity, what Levinas calls "the possession of a world I can bestow as a *gift* on the other," and in language. Generosity and language are the only *non*totalizing modes of relating to the other that are suggested in *Totality and Infinity.*

Why is generosity so important for Levinas? Why would I want—in Levinas's phrase—to *give* the world to the other?[6] He writes: "It is in generosity that the world possessed by me—the world open to enjoyment—is apperceived from a point of view independent of the egoist position . . . The presence of the other is equivalent to this calling into question of my joyous possession of the world" (*TI,* 75–76). It is as if, in generosity, the blind spot of the habitual economy were brought into view. The self's habitual economy, its tendency toward possession and *pouvoir*, is called into question by the other. But this calling into question, which will not be absorbed into an *awareness* of being called in question,

5. On Levinas's opening of the question of the ethical, especially in relation to the philosophies of Heidegger and Derrida, see Robert Bernasconi, "Deconstruction and the Possibility of Ethics," in John Sallis, ed., *Deconstruction and Philosophy: The Texts of Jacques Derrida* (Chicago: University of Chicago Press, 1987), 122–39.

6. "The *giving [le donner]* is in some way the original movement of spiritual life . . . the relation with the other will always be an offering and a gift, not an 'empty-handed' approach" (*DF,* 62).

must straightaway become generosity, or what Levinas also calls "the welcome of the expression of the face." One can only recognize the face in giving: "To recognize the other is to give. But it is to give to the master, to the lord, to him whom one approaches as 'You' *['Vous']*, in a dimension of height" (*TI*, 75).

Generosity preserves, for Levinas, the radical and absolute asymmetry between myself and the other. In "The Trace of the Other," he describes it as a one-way movement, irreversible, a departure without return that he associates with Abraham (*T*, 349). He writes: "A work conceived in its ultimate nature requires a radical generosity of the same who in the work goes unto the other. It then requires an *ingratitude* of the other. Gratitude would in fact be the *return* of the movement to its origin" (*T*, 349). This is a generosity that must be thought outside the balanced economy of reciprocal exchange, outside all economies of deficits and compensations, outside all accountable operations. Levinas conceives of language, similarly, as being able to meet the ethical requirements of asymmetry and separation, as being able to accomplish a nontotalizing and, ultimately, a just relation to the other. (Indeed, Levinas conceives of language *as* a gift, as speech-gift: "Language . . . offers things which are mine to the other" [*TI*, 76].) The only other exception (besides generosity) to the habitual economy, "language accomplishes a relation such that . . . the other, despite the relationship with the same, remains transcendent to the same" (*TI*, 39). It maintains the distance of infinite separation, "without this distance destroying this relation and without this relation destroying this distance, as would happen with relations within the same" (*TI*, 41). Language is "a relation in which the terms absolve [or loosen] themselves from the relation" (*TI*, 64).

That is why I do not *think* the infinity of the transcendence of *Autrui;* I *face* it, I *speak* it. In Levinas's descriptions I face the face in language, as when the avidity of the gaze turns into discourse. And the face, which has been defined as the way in which the other presents himself, exceeding the idea of the other in me, is described as that which presents itself *as* a phenomenon and also (already) exceeds or breaks out of the phenomenon. The face signifies as expression, a combination of glance and speech. Expression in Levinas is always about the way in which the face—not reducible to a plastic image—divests itself of its form. The face *(visage)* looks back, it intends me *(regarder ce qui . . . vous vise, c'est regarder le visage)* (*DF*, 8); it speaks. "The life of expression consists of undoing the form in which the existent, exposing itself as a theme, in this way dissimulates itself. The face speaks. The manifestation of the face is *already* discourse *[discours]*" (*TI*, 66). Thus as Alphonso Lingis formulates it, the face also faces *in* language.[7]

What does Levinas mean by language? And what—or how—would an ethical language be? The discourse that the face's expression invites is not a conversation between equals. The other is not on the same plane as myself (*TI*, 101). A conversation without reciprocity or recognition is not a dialogue or an exchange in any usual sense. Levinas calls it "a conversation *[entre-tien]* which proposes the world. This proposition is held over *[se tient entre]* two points which do not constitute a totality" (*TI*, 96). A conversation without commonality, "over the things henceforth possibly common," it makes commonality possible. It is a conversation *before* conversation. One would call it a founding conversation did it not take place over an abyss. "Language is spoken where community between the terms of the relationship is wanting" (*TI*, 73). And here it would seem that language does not bridge the gap; it deepens it.

Nor does this discourse involve any kind of exchange of information; it is prior to language conceived of as a system of signs. Of course, it is difficult to conceive of a presemiotic language. This is, we recall, a primordial language (and that is why, ultimately, this language cannot have any content). In any case, that is why Levinas insists on the face's distinctive mode of signification, as expression *kath 'auto*, "according to itself"— that which signifies only with reference to itself and thereby escapes the referrals inherent in sign systems, and thereby escapes the play of immanence. This is a mode of signification which he will later develop in the thought of the trace. (And one may note here that Levinas does not regard reference as any type of transcendence.)[8] This ethical language is pure apology, which Levinas defines as an inclination before the transcendent. He also intertwines it in a discursive chain with expression, revelation, teaching, and the discourse of the master.

The only content that Levinas ever gives the primordial conversation is negative, is a prohibition, and that is in his analysis of murder in section III.B of *Totality and Infinity* and in other early texts. There, the face speaks, and what it says is: "Thou shalt not kill." "Thou shalt not kill" refers primarily to the cessation of power and possibility in the encounter with

---

7. Alphonso Lingis, introduction to Levinas, *CPP*, xxx. See Lingis's subsequent accounts of Levinas in *Libido: The French Existential Theories* (Bloomington: Indiana University Press, 1985); and *Deathbound Subjectivity* (Bloomington: Indiana University Press, 1989).

8. This is in contrast to, for example, the understanding of the referential function of discourse proposed by Paul Ricoeur in *Discourse and the Surplus of Meaning* (Fort Worth: Texas Christian University Press, 1976), 1–23.

the face. Suffice it also to remark about this complex passage that as a citation of God's commandment, of God's word, this heteronomous utterance maintains the primordial inequality; it emphasizes that the two participants are not on the same plane. This would be one of the functions of biblical citation in Levinas's writing. In his later work the primordial utterance is also a biblical citation, this time a response *to* God by Abraham, Samuel, Isaiah, and others: "Here I am" *(hineni)*, denoting readiness, "at your service." In each of these cases, language is a speech with God.[9] And in the case of "here I am," the response to God is also, paradigmatically, the response of responsibility; it is "an aptitude for hearing a call."[10] And it dispossesses the subject altogether.

In "The Trace of the Other," published in 1963, two years after *Totality and Infinity*, Levinas writes: "A face is imposed on me without my being able to be deaf to its appeal nor to forget it, that is, without my being able to cease to be held responsible for its wretchedness. Consciousness loses its first place" (T, 352). The epiphany of the face as face interrupts the gaze and the habitual economy. The face as face commands me; yet it commands me, as Levinas makes clear, *in* its very misery and wretchedness. Because the face *is* a face, and not a mask, because it is without clothing or covering or attributes, because it divests itself of its form and signifies as expression, *kath 'auto*, as Levinas has said, having reference only to itself, it appears in the world as naked and destitute. In its extreme vulnerability, in the supplication of its gaze, it commands me. "It *calls* to me—or interpellates me *[il m'interpelle]*—and signifies an order to me by its very nudity, its denuding [or destitution] *[dénûment]*. Its presence is a summation to respond. The I does not simply become conscious of this necessity to answer, as if it were a matter of an obligation or duty which it would have to decide of" (T, 353). This response, the response of responsibility, does not proceed from a subject. Jean-François Lyotard aptly remarks, "Far from enriching me, from giving me the opportunity to grow and to enlighten my experience, the arrival of the other suppresses me as the subject of an experience" (DI, 113).

9. Blanchot notes that for Levinas "[a]ll true discourse is a discourse with God, not a conversation between equals" (IC, 56). There is a midrashic dimension of Levinas's use of biblical citation as well. It is as if the two primordial utterances were the entire lexicon and scripture, the world.

10. *L'aptitude à l'écoute d'un appel* is Jean-François Lyotard's phrase in *The Differend*. More often he calls it *une passibilité de l'autre*, that is, a liability for, from, or with regard to, the other. In any case, the question of obligation is "to know whether, when one hears something that might resemble a call, one is held to be held by it *[on est tenu d'être tenu par lui]*. One can resist it or respond to it, but it will first have to be received as a call" (DI, 107).

METAPHYSICAL ASYMMETRY

Metaphysical asymmetry means, for Levinas, "the radical impossibility of seeing oneself from the outside and of speaking in the same sense of oneself and of the others, and consequently the impossibility of totalization" (*TI*, 53). Most of the descriptions in *Totality and Infinity* avoid totalization, proceeding from me to the other or from the other to me. If the alterity of the other is not to be reduced, the other must not be made into a theme of my discourse. The other is an interlocutor. This relation to the other as interlocutor is the central thrust of Levinas's discussion of language. "In language," writes Levinas, "the essential is the interpellation, the vocative" (*TI*, 69). What is essential in this interpellation—this interruption by speaking—is not in any case a word or a content—but the fact of invocation itself. Levinas writes:

> The other is maintained and confirmed in his heterogeneity *as soon as one calls upon him [aussitôt qu'on l'interpelle]*, be it only to say to him that one cannot speak to him, to classify him as sick, to announce to him his death sentence. At the same time as grasped, wounded, outraged, he is "respected." The invoked is not what I comprehend. He is not under a category. He is the one to whom I speak. (*TI*, 69)

Levinas's point here is: the relation to the other as interlocutor is so fundamental, so primary, that any invocation—even of a violent sort, in the mode of refusal or domination—is preferable, is less violent and more "respecting" of the alterity of the other than the seemingly benign (i.e., the humanistic) modes of relating to the other: comprehension, recognition, and assimilation. These latter modes—because they are forms of adequation, or suggest objectifying cognition, or have a neutralizing element—are intrinsically violent. Announcing to the other his death sentence still "respects" (in quotation marks, one should note) the other's alterity because, as invocation, it maintains the asymmetry of the relation; it speaks *to* and not *about* the other. The worst violence, for Levinas, is to speak about the other in the third person. The other is a you, a *Vous*. He is addressed. The emphasis would be on sheer vocativity—and if this language of pure invocation is, indeed, nothing but a language of prayer, Levinas would not object to this characterization.[11] It would be an apologetic language, inclined and altogether oriented toward the addressee. Like the conative mode analyzed by Roman Jakobson, it would find its

---

11. In VM, Derrida asks if the nonviolent language Levinas describes can only be a language of prayer. Levinas's 1949 essay on Leiris refers to speech—a proffering speech—as a type of prayer.

closest grammatical analogues in the vocative and in the imperative.[12] It would be a language composed entirely of the vocative and the imperative. And the dative, case of the gift.[13] But even if the relationship to the other were reducible to a grammar, and Levinas makes it very clear that it is not, how would such a language—stripped of nominatives—be possible? How can one write in a way that calls upon the other?

It is possible to understand the force of Levinas's ethical language to be its irreducibly performative dimension. This is the working premise of Lyotard's—and somewhat differently, Derrida's—reading of Levinas. The rationale is: the ethical language that Levinas describes, as well as his own language about this ethical language, must not merely constate or describe the ethical, it must perform it. For Lyotard there is a resemblance between the "immediacy" of the performative phrase and the "immediacy" of the obligation addressed to me, which is straightaway obligation and is not mediated by any kind of cognition. Derrida, because he is engaged in thinking the Levinasian gift, and because he thinks together performative and gift (as archperformative), is able to keep in play the ethical demand for asymmetry between the two parties, addressor and addressee, and the rupture of a balanced economy of exchange.[14]

There is, however, a tension inherent in Levinas's language. It can be called a tension between its performative and constative dimension, that is, within the performative description—or it can be linked to the larger

12. According to Jakobson, the vocative and the imperative "syntactically, morphologically, and often even phonemically deviate from other nominal and verbal categories . . . The imperative cannot be challenged by the question 'Is it true or not?' " "Closing Statement: Linguistics and Poetics," in *Language in Literature* (Cambridge, MA: Harvard University Press, 1987), 67–68.

13. The relationship to the other is always "in the vocative" (*DF,* 7), or "in the dative" (*TI,* 69).

14. In this context, a separate question arises: Is the *inter*locutionary in Levinas indeed illocutionary, performative? Without addressing this question at length, several precautions would nonetheless have to be registered. First, the interlocutionary in Levinas is primordial and prior to what we think of as the utterance or a logic of speech *acts*. Second, the performative is *not*, strictly speaking, a relation to an addressee but to a set of conventions that allow the performative to be felicitously met. Consideration of the addressee would involve not the illocutionary but the perlocutionary realm. (This would be an area of performative that also would not be reducible to a grammar, code, or convention. It would belong to rhetoric, as Paul de Man has argued in *The Resistance to Theory* [Minneapolis: University of Minnesota, 1986].) Finally, the absolute asymmetry between addressor and addressee is not really implied in performative utterances. The asymmetry is between the utterance and other types of utterances in other cases and tenses, etc. In short, the resemblance is very general, but the performative model may still shed light on Levinas's ethical language as a nondenotative language that does not *constate* alterity but *gives* it.

problem of the language which is available to Levinas in order to speak the ethical. How can Levinas's work meet its own ethical requirements— say, to name one such requirement from "The Trace of the Other," that *the* work must not remain identical to itself but must go out to the other in a movement without return? Does this not produce a double bind? Levinas says that the work ought to be nonself-identical. But if his work is nonself-identical in the way that his work says that the work ought to be nonself-identical, then it is self-identical. In fact, if Levinas's work does not do what it says about the work, if his work is thus non- self-identical, then it does what it says about the work, and it is self- identical.

This double bind in which Levinas's work is caught also encircles his reader. For example, Lyotard asks how Levinas's reader is to read the talmudic wisdom of "doing before understanding," which Levinas articu- lates in a talmudic reading called "The Temptation of Temptation."[15] Doing before understanding refers to the reception of revelation, but it could as well apply to the Levinasian conversation where doing before understanding denotes a relation to the interlocuter that is not by way of comprehension. It is certainly typical of the way Levinas positions the ethical within the dominant conceptuality. In brief: according to the rabbinic reading that Levinas cites (*Shabbath* 88a–88b, at the foot of Mount Sinai, the people "did" the law before they heard it. After all, they did say, in scriptural verse Ex. 24:7, "All that the Lord has spoken we will do and we will hearken *[na'aseh venishmah]*." The verb *shema* means "hear, hearken, obey," and its sense can be extended to "understand." Thus the phrase translates, we will do and we will hear/understand. For the rabbinic commentators, the phrase's syntactical order signifies a temporal order, namely, the people did the law first, then they under- stood it or apperceived it. According to Levinas, this talmudic wisdom of "doing before understanding" inverts the philosophical priority given to theory over practice. It introduces a kind of originary practice or obli- gation (an adhesion to the law) prior to the very distinction between theory and practice. It suggests a way of actualizing without beginning with the possible. To claim that at the foot of Mount Sinai the people "did" the law, then heard it or understood it, is to suggest that they re- ceived this gift as a doing, not as a comprehension. A kind of folly per- haps, which certainly goes against the grain of the entire conceptuality

15. "The Temptation of Temptation," in *Nine Talmudic Readings*, trans. Annette Aron- owicz (Bloomington: Indiana University Press, 1990). *Quatre lectures talmudiques* (Paris: Minuit, 1968).

of the West. Doing before understanding is a paradigm for the ethical itself.

But how is Levinas's reader to receive this ethical wisdom of "doing before understanding"? Lyotard asks: "Is this not what the commentator is bound to do with this work, if he understands it" (LL, 118)? But if the reader understands, he has to do before understanding; he has not to understand. "As soon as one begins to speak about what one reads . . . is it not necessary that one place oneself back under the regimen of descriptives, under the temptation of knowledge?" (DI, 114). Thus, the performative dimension of the talmudic "doing before understanding" risks falling into a constative which neutralizes it and to which it is incommensurable. In fact, all of Levinas's ethical discourse can be seen to run precisely this risk of falling into a discourse *on* the ethical. A speaking to the other becomes a speaking about the other. How to speak about this ethical language without rendering its performative dimension constative, without returning it to the denotative language of the same? How can the reader possibly do it justice?

Lyotard reasons: "Levinas asks that the absolutely other be made welcome. The rule applies to any commentary on Levinas as well. So we will take care not to flatten the alterity of his work. We will struggle against assimilations and accommodations. This is . . . the hermeneutic— discourse of good faith. But good faith is never enough, or the request for alterity is never satisfied . . . the best way in answering it is to reinforce the difference between work and commentary" (LL, 117). That is to say, if the reader does not want "to flatten the alterity" of Levinas's work, he *has* to flatten the alterity of the work ("discourse of ambivalence").[16] From here it is only a short step to realizing that the best way for the commentator to respect Levinas's work is not a straightforward exposition. The best way to respect the work is to read it deviously, to misunderstand it entirely. For if the guiding principle of Levinas's work is "that thou shall never be 'I,'" Lyotard continues, "since you ask for it . . . , I will not treat you as my similar, but as my dissimilar. I can do you justice only by mistreating you. Indeed, if in your view to be just is to court alterity, the only way to be just towards your discourse of justice is to be unjust about it" (LL, 118). At the limit, then, the discourse of the ethical is *almost* indistinguishable from the discourse of persecution.

A similar problem emerges from Levinas's thinking of the gift. I begin with Derrida's speculation:

16. In his Afterword to Lyotard, *JG*, Samuel Weber discusses ambivalence as the other of prescription.

Suppose that I wish to *give* to him, to Emmanuel Levinas. Not to return something to him, an homage for example . . . but to give him something that
escapes from the circle of restitution, of the meeting *[rendez-vous]* . . . Beyond
any possible restitution, there would be a need for my gesture to operate beyond debt, in absolute ingratitude. The trap is that in such a case I render
homage, the only homage possible to his work, to what his work says about
the work . . . I will still be caught in the circle of debt and restitution . . . If
I restitute, if I restitute without fault, I am at fault. And if I don't restitute,
by *giving* beyond recognition, I risk being at fault. (ATM, 13–14)

To escape from the circle of the meeting (from the *rendez-vous*, the "render you"), from the contract, and from symmetry necessitates, as we recall, a radical ingratitude. But to be ungrateful is to conform to Levinas's
thinking of the structure of the gift; it is to be grateful. The fault in either
case is constitutive, originary. Derrida writes:

If someone says to you: do not render/return to me what I give you—you
are at fault even before he has finished speaking. It suffices that you hear/
understand *[entendre]* him, that you begin to understand and to recognize. You
have begun to receive his injunction, to render to yourself what he has said,
and the more that you will obey him by restituting nothing, the better you
will disobey him and will render yourself deaf to what he addresses to you.
(ATM, 14)

To receive the Levinasian gift of the gift, to hear its imperative, the reader
must do before understanding, must be deaf to Levinas's injunction (the
gift of the law of the gift must be received before all phenomenality,
within a certain nonmanifestation). The asymmetrical structure of the
gift necessitates an ingratitude so radical that it approaches ambivalence
and persecution.

But while these double binds look like paradoxes, they in fact indicate
a structure that is *prior* to formal logic. Derrida calls it "an incredible
logic, formal and nonformal" (ATM, 14). In other words, the double bind
is reducible neither to a logical deficiency nor to a trap in Levinas's discourse. "It is only felt as a trap," writes Derrida, "from the moment when
one would pretend to escape from absolute dissymmetry through a will
to mastery or coherence. It would be a way to acknowledge the gift in
order to refuse it. Nothing is more difficult than to accept a gift" (ATM,
14). How to receive the gift of Levinas's ethical thought? How to "affirm
and reaffirm" it? Beyond all restitution, this would require a radical ingratitude. But not just any ingratitude, "not the ingratitude that would

still belong to the circle of recognition and reciprocity," or to the economic sphere of the same (ATM, 15).[17]

Not just in the relations between work and reader but in the relations described *within* the work as well, Levinas's ethical prescription threatens to flip over into persecution. There are the repeated references to the other's being situated in a dimension of height, the figures of the other as master and teacher, the violent images of refusal and domination, where the other, even "wounded, injured," is still "respected." All are descriptions of a primordial metaphysical inequality. But is the metaphysical asymmetry also ontic? It often appears so. Blanchot notes the alternating images of the other as the destitute one, the powerless, the stranger and also as

> the obsession that afflicts me, that weighs down upon me, that separates me from myself—as if separation (which measured the transcendence from me to the other) did its work *within* me, *dis*-identifying me, abandoning me to passivity, leaving me without any initiative and bereft of present. And then, the other becomes rather the Overlord, indeed the Persecutor, he who overwhelms, encumbers, undoes me, he who puts me in his debt no less than he attacks me by making me answer for his crimes, by charging me with measureless responsibility which cannot be mine since it extends all the way to "substitution." So it is that . . . the relation of the other to me would tend to appear as sadomasochistic, if it did not cause us to fall prematurely out of the world. (*WD*, 19)

The "relations" which Levinas describes are not between already constituted entities. They "fall out of world" or are, if you will, at the origin of what we call world—they are relations between myself and the other before we are shaped into particular selves.[18] At the origin of world—this is in fact another meaning in Levinas of the other's destitution; that is his very strangeness, his exile from world. Hence the primordial inequality between myself and the other, which is not a relation between existents, should not be mistaken for a relationship of power. The other

17. In *Given Time* (trans. Peggy Kamuf [Chicago: University of Chicago Press, 1992]), Derrida elaborates on the aneconomic gift as that which interrupts economy and the system. This is a gift—conceived no longer in terms of exchange, reciprocity, symmetry, circulation, circularity—which has to be thought outside of all recognition, gratitude, or debt. As in ATM, such a gift produces a double bind, is impossible. Indeed, this gift precisely opens up a thinking of the impossible.

18. Blanchot writes: "I am at the same time pressed into a responsibility which not only exceeds me, but which I cannot exercise, since I cannot do anything and no longer exist as myself" (*WD*, 19).

who commands me in his or her very destitution "is not master . . . because he or she dominates the I, but because he or she *demands of* the I" (*DI,* 111).

But such a reading of the primordial inequality as ontic is, to a certain extent, inevitable because of the asymmetry and nonreversibility of the I/you relation. As Lyotard puts it: "The place of the one who speaks to me is never available to me to occupy" (*JG,* 39). It is inevitable because of the "immediacy" and noncomprehension that characterize obligation. Recall that "the other is affirmed in his heterogeneity *as soon as* one calls upon him" (*TI,* 69), namely, before all comprehension, by the very fact of invocation. Similarly, "the demand . . . is made of me by the other by the simple fact that he speaks to me" (*JG,* 22). And what is the effect of this demand that the other makes upon me? As Lyotard explains it, the revelation of the other expels the ego

> from the addressor instance from which it managed its work of enjoyment, power, and cognition . . . What gives rise to persecution is when the I is passively attached, against its will, and in its recurrent narcissism, which protests against this liability *[cette passibilité]* and does not accept exteriority. The return of the I in situation of *you* where he or she has been placed by the other turns the latter into a persecutor. (*DI,* 110–12)

The other in his demand displaces and disauthorizes the I as subject, for in prescribing "*you* shall not murder," the other turns the I into a *you.* Yet there is a certain return of the I which "tries to repossess itself through the understanding of what dispossesses it" (*DI,* 110).[19] Resenting its self-dispossession, the I blames the other, feels persecuted by the other. Responsibility feels like persecution, if it is not ethics. Derrida had also alluded to the dialectizable kind of ingratitude that Levinas's work seems to invite if one approaches it with a will to coherence or mastery. It is hard to think the lacerated, exposed, and self-dispossessed subjectivity that Levinas describes as responsibility to the other.

RHETORIC AND THE FACE

It still remains to speak about the *non*ethical language that Levinas identifies. This is of some pertinence to literary critics, when thinking about the impact of Levinas's work on literary interpretation and the nonappli-

---

19. Or as Geoffrey Bennington puts it, the I tries to return the prescriptive to cognition, to the primacy of cognition, to ground the prescription in a description. *Lyotard: Writing the Event* (New York: Columbia University Press, 1988), 137–38.

cability of Levinas's ethics to literature. In closing this chapter, I would like to offer a sketch of, and pose some questions about, Levinas's views on rhetoric.

"Not every discourse is a relation with exteriority"; he writes, "it is not the interlocutor our master whom we approach most of the time in our discourse" (*TI,* 70). First of all and most of the time, according to Levinas, our discourse is rhetoric, which he defines as "the position of him who approaches his neighbor with ruse" (*TI,* 70) and which he characterizes as "ruse, emprise, and exploitation" (*TI,* 72). The relationship to the other in discourse as rhetoric is, for Levinas, "preeminently violence and injustice . . . Justice coincides with the overcoming of rhetoric" (*TI,* 70). Ethical language, which is called the essence of language and which is said to accomplish the *droiture,* the straightforwardness or uprightness of the relation to the other, because of its maintenance of separation and asymmetry, is, as it turns out, an exception to the habitual economy.

Levinas's denigration of rhetoric—which he always, at least in the early work, understands in the sense of persuasion, as action upon others—is of the most classical sort.[20] It is continuous in his work with a certain phonocentrism, a privileging of oral discourse as "the plenitude of discourse" and expression as the other's "coming to his own assistance in the manifestation" or his "being behind the sign" (*TI,* 66, 96; VM, 101–2). But in this context my concern is less with Levinas's negative view of rhetoric as such than with the way in which he tropes it, within the terms of his ethics of the face. "Rhetoric approaches the other not to face him, but obliquely *[Elle aborde l'Autre non pas de face, mais de biais]*" (*TI,* 70). Rhetoric approaches the other from an angle. It means, if you will, *having an angle* on the other, approaching him with an agenda (which Levinas also calls "demagogy, psychagogy, pedagogy") (TI, 70). But this is not the only time in his work where Levinas refers us to the significance of the angle.

In an early version of the murder analysis, where the face is said to deliver its prohibition against murder, Levinas writes: "Violence consists in ignoring this opposition, ignoring the face of a being, avoiding the gaze, and *catching sight of an angle* whereby the *no* inscribed on a face by the very fact that it is a face becomes a hostile or submissive force. Violence is a way of acting on every being and every freedom by approaching

20. See, for example, the 1951 essay, "Freedom and Command," where, in a discussion of rhetoric and its violences, Levinas refers explicitly to Plato's denunciation of poetry in Book VIII of *The Republic.* This is one of many places where Levinas endorses Plato's view of rhetoric.

it from an *indirect angle [La violence est une façon d'agir sur tout être et toute liberté en l'abordant de biais]"* (FC, 19). Levinas is explaining that while murder is an ethical *im*possibility (insofar as the face brings about a cessation of power and possibility and insofar as murder is doomed in advance to a certain failure), it is of course a real possibility. He is describing a way of responding to the face—call it a misreading—which eventuates in murder. In Levinas's analysis, to which I will return in detail in Chapter 4, murder mistakes the other's resistance for a force. The mistake that is murder—the substitution of an infinity-target for infinity as a mode of revelation—comes from catching sight of the face from an angle; it comes from indirection. In another passage from Levinas's work, indirection is nothing less than criminal. He writes: "To approach someone from works is to enter into his interiority as though by burglary . . . Works signify their author, but indirectly, in the third person" (TI, 66). Thus to approach the other from an angle is to lose face (to lose the face of the other and always also to lose one's own face).

It is clear that when Levinas presents rhetoric in terms of the geometrical figure of the oblique he means avoiding the demand of the face-to-face. The angle of rhetoric is opposed to the face-to-face of "veritable conversation" (TI, 70). The bias or deviation that is the basis of rhetoric denotes for Levinas not an epistemological error but a moral one. Yet the figure of the oblique alludes to the dimension of language called "rhetorical" in the sense not just of persuasion but also of trope. In short, when Levinas figures rhetoric as the obliqueness of persuasion—as ruse, as inherently double, as two-faced, as we sometimes like to say—he alludes in a sense to another obliqueness, between a rhetorical figure and that to which it refers, to another duplicity of language, a duplicity *within* language (as in such oppositions as proper/improper, signifier/signified, sign/referent), which would also characterize rhetoric as trope.

Would ethical language be free of rhetoric in *this* sense? Levinas suggests that there is a language of the face—a language of the eyes, before all rhetoric, before the duplicity inherent in sign relations. He calls it *droiture* ("straightforwardness," "uprightness") and also *franchise* ("frankness"): "It is the frank presence of an existent that can lie, that is, disposes of the theme he offers, without being able to dissimulate his frankness as interlocutor, always struggling openly *[luttant toujours à visage découvert].* The eyes break through the mask—the language of the eyes, impossible to dissemble" (TI, 66). While Levinas makes clear that this frankness is prior to the alternative between truth and lying (TI, 202), he nonetheless suggests that there is an unmediated ethical language, which needs have recourse to neither the obliqueness, nor the duplicity, nor the arbitrariness inherent in sign relations.

It would be possible to show, in the purview of another discussion, that this distinction between ethical and rhetorical language, between the straight ahead, righteous language of "veritable conversation" and the obliqueness and deviation of rhetoric cannot be sustained. A classical deconstruction could show that the one possibility inhabits and contaminates another, that language—even the primordial and righteous language that Levinas describes will never be freed from intrinsic duplicity. But with reference to language as ethical possibility, in its extension to literary critical issues, and what I would draw attention to in closing, is: first, the special privilege of face and facing, of the frontal figure (both in space and exceeding space); and second, the certain figurality or rhetoricity of the face, a turning, within as well as toward face, even at the level of the opening of the question of the ethical, even at the level of an originary language-response to the other.[21] Concerning this response, Levinas writes: "The primordial sphere, which corresponds to what we call the same, *turns to* the absolutely other only *on call from* the other *[le même ne se tourne vers l'absolument autre que sur l'appel d'Autrui]*" (*TI*, 67). This is not a response I initiate (like pity). Nor is it a response to a call that I hear. Yet the demand comes *from* and the response goes *unto* the other, in the language-relation to the face, in the primordial stammering of ethical language. On call *from* the other. Ready before the fact to respond to a call that I will not have heard. Ready before the fact in a response that, anachronistically, precedes the call. In utter *in*ability. But where? When? Who? And will it have taken place?

21. In "The Ego and the Totality" (1954), Levinas writes that "the absolute status of the interlocutor . . . his modality of being and of manifesting himself consist in his *turning his face* to me, in being a face" (*CPP*, 33). Cf. *TI*, 75, "The face has turned to me *[le visage s'est tourné vers moi]*—and this is its very nudity."

[2] TRACING RESPONSIBILITY

ABSOLUTELY TOWARD THE FUTURE

In the final sentences of his essay "The Trace of the Other," Levinas writes: "The revealed God of our Judeo-Christian spirituality maintains all the infinity of his absence, which is in the personal order itself. He shows himself only by his trace, as in Exodus 33. To go toward Him is not to follow this trace which is not a sign; it is to go toward the others who stand in the trace" (T, 359). These sentences are the culmination of an argument which has proposed "trace"—namely, the mark of the effacement of a mark—as the specific manner in which the other signifies. In contrast to other forms of signification, such as the sign, which is constituted by referrals within immanence, "trace" denotes a referral to transcendence, a relationship with a certain absence not reducible to the opposition presence/absence and belonging to an immemorial past. The term *trace*, here introduced in an essay written two years after the publication of *Totality and Infinity*, announces the distinctive emphases and departures—stylistic and conceptual—that come to characterize all of Levinas's subsequent work. It is central to his thinking about ethics. In this chapter I will examine closely Levinas's presentation of the conceptual figure of the trace in the 1965 essay "Enigma and Phenomenon" as well as in "The Trace of the Other" from 1963. I will consider in particular the consequences, for ethics and theology respectively, of thinking responsibility to the other as a relation to the trace. I will also pursue the link between theological questions and the question of the ethical, indeed, the very intertwining of the question of God and the question of the other that these enigmatic sentences suggest.

In "The Trace of the Other" Levinas argues that the history of philosophy in the West is a philosophy of the same that ignores the other. (At stake is not a continuous history of philosophy but one solely from the perspective of the suppression of the question of the ethical. Robert Bernasconi calls it "a history of the face.")[1] Recall the analysis in *Totality and Infinity* of the self's habitual economy—its concrete dealings with the world—as a "reversion of the alterity of the world to self-identification" (*TI*, 38). Just as the self's habitual economy is for Levinas an economy of the self-same, so too the habitual mode of philosophical thought is that of an "allergy" to the other that remains other (T, 346). Philosophy in its essential project is an adventure, or a would-be adventure, which in the end discovers only itself, returns to itself. It relates to alterity by drawing it into itself, absorbing it, reducing it: "The God of the philosophers, from Aristotle to Leibniz, by way of the God of the scholastics, is a god adequate to reason, a comprehended god who could not trouble the autonomy of consciousness, which finds itself again in all its adventures, returning home to itself like Odysseus, who through all his peregrinations is only on the way to his native land" (T, 346). There is an "imperialism" of the philosophy which unfolds within this home-coming paradigm. An indiscretion about a philosophical enterprise which in its relentless orientation toward evidence, toward what is seen, toward what shows itself, insists on bringing everything into the light.

Yet there has also been, in Western philosophy, a movement of transcendence, "something as contradictory in its terms as a heteronomous experience" (T, 348). It was prefigured, in the history of philosophy, by the Platonic good beyond being, the Cartesian thought of infinity, and, as Levinas puts it in "Enigma and Phenomenon," "a God always absent from perception" (EP, 62). The heteronomous experience is an irreversible movement which goes out unto the other, a departure without return which he associates with the biblical Abraham: "To the myth of Odysseus returning to Ithaca, we wish to oppose the story of Abraham leaving his fatherland forever for a land yet unknown, and forbidding his servant to bring even his son to the point of departure" (T, 348). The one-way movement is exemplified by *goodness* and the *work*, according to the particular inflection he gives these terms.

The work, we will recall, requires a radical generosity. It is a gift that demands consequently the radical ingratitude of the other, as opposed to the cyclical movement of warm thanks, recognition, and gratitude,

---

1. Robert Bernasconi, "Levinas and Derrida: The Question of the Closure of Metaphysics," in *FF*, 195.

"return to origin" (T, 349). It also requires, and here Levinas introduces another key term that is very close to generosity, *patience*:

> The departure without return, which does not go forth into the void, would also lose its absolute goodness if the work sought for its recompense in the immediacy of its triumph, if it impatiently awaited the triumph of its cause. The one-way movement would be inverted into a reciprocity. The work, confronting its departure and its end, would be absorbed again in calculations of deficits and compensations, in accountable operations. It would be subordinated to thought. The one-way action is possible only in patience, which, pushed to the limit, means for the agent to renounce being the contemporary of its outcome, to act without entering the promised land. (T, 349)

The allusion is covert, at least compared to Levinas's naming of Abraham. The paradigmatic figure for patience is Moses, who, in Deuteronomy 32, sees but does not pass over into the promised land. Moses is denied the reciprocity, the compensation implied in the law that he himself taught, namely, "in the same day thou shalt give him his hire" (Deut. 24: 15), the principle of daily remuneration for labor.[2] Moreover, this denial of recompense is necessary. For the radicality of the one-way movement risks—fault of language, fault of what Levinas here refers to simply as "thought"—being reappropriated in a calculation, a reciprocity. Moses's not getting into the promised land thus *affirms* the one-way movement. It makes him the very figure for the nonself-contemporaneity, the nonself-coincidence, the nonself-presence that is patience.

To be patient means to be given over to the future, absolutely toward the future, a future that always belongs to the other. Levinas also will call it "liturgy," in the sense of "a profitless investment" (T, 349–50). Not to be confused with the time of personal immortality, to be patient, "to be for a time that would be without me," is to go beyond the horizon of my time, beyond the being unto death. It is "passage to the time of the other" (T, 349).

In its ordinary sense, patience refers to the capacity for calm endurance or for bearing delay. But as Levinas renews the term, there is nothing psychological or existential about it. "I" cannot "be patient." Blanchot glosses the word: "[P]atience has already withdrawn me . . . from my power *[pouvoir]* to be patient: if I *can* be patient then patience has not worn out in me that me to which I cling for self-preservation" (WD, 13). To be patient then is not a *pouvoir*, not *my* possibility; it is not an abil-

---

2. See *Deuteronomy Rabbah* 11:10; and the discussion by Esther Starobinski-Safran, *Le buisson et la voix: Exégèse et pensée juives* (Paris: Albin Michel, 1987), 47–64.

ity, nor is it anything that the subject could initiate. It is in a certain sense *impossible.*[3] Yet for Levinas the absolutely patient action is ethics itself.

THE FACE

"The relationship with the other," says Levinas, "puts me into question, empties me of myself . . . The I loses its sovereign coincidence with itself, its identification, in which consciousness returned triumphally to itself and rested on itself . . . The I is expelled from this rest" (T, 350–53). For Levinas ethics in the most general sense is this putting into question of self-sufficiency, the interruption *of* self—described variously as an obligation, an imperative, an imposition, a responsibility—that arises in the encounter with the face of the other *(le visage d'Autrui).*

The face *(le visage)* is "the concrete figure for alterity" *(IR).*[4] Although the word's Latin root, *visum,* suggests associations with the visual or even with the *visée* which intentional consciousness intends, the *visage* is not primarily a thing seen or intended. Again, as Levinas etiologizes the word, it is that which intends me *(Regarder ce qui . . . vous vise: c'est regarder le visage) (DF,* 8). In a singular reversal that has nothing symmetrical or reciprocal about it, the face looks back. Thus to encounter the face *as* a face is not to intend it with the look, for the gaze would "immobilize its object as a theme." Recall the encounter with the face described in *Totality and Infinity,* where, by a proto-ethical necessity, the avaricious gaze is checked and transformed, where vision, a violence and a form of adequation, *turns into* generosity and language, forms of nonadequation. Just as the definition of face there emphasized its nonadequating, infinitizing mode, "the way in which the other presents himself, exceeding the idea of the other in me, we here name face" *(TI,* 50), so too in "The Trace of the Other," the face's mode of presentation is described as an exceeding. Levinas writes:

> The manifestation of the other is . . . first produced in conformity with the way every signification is produced. The other is present in a cultural ensemble and illuminated by the ensemble, like a text by its context . . . The other is given in the concept of the totality to which he is immanent . . . But the epiphany of the other involves a signifyingness of its own, independently of

3. Paul Davies discusses patience in "A Fine Risk: Reading Blanchot Reading Levinas," in *RRL,* 214ff.

4. In *Totality and Infinity* Levinas first introduces the face as "the deformalization or concretization of the idea of infinity" *(TI,* 50).

this signification received from the world. The other does not only come to us out of a context, but comes without mediation; he signifies by himself . . . [the] mundane signification is found to be disturbed and shaken by another presence, abstract, not integrated into the world. His presence consists in coming towards us, *making an entry*. This can also be stated in this way: the phenomenon which is the apparition of the other is also a *face*. (T, 351)

In the terms that Levinas uses, the other is given first in a context, in a totality, in the light, in a world. But while the other is given in a world, he is also out of world. Signifying *in* a context, with its totalizing explanatory power, the other also signifies out of context. The other is given as a phenomenon but also as a face.

Note that in Levinas's descriptions the face is not hypostatized in any way. Here the face is defined as a disturbance between world and that which exceeds world, a shaking up of the mundane, a collision, as Levinas will also put it, between two orders. The significance of facing is approach; it is the other's coming toward me, a mobile orientation, an interpellation. The face is an active surplus over the plastic image that would enclose it. Levinas continues:

> Although the phenomenon is already an image, a captive manifestation of a plastic and mute form, the epiphany of the face is alive. Its life consists in undoing the form in which every entity, when it enters into immanence, that is, when it exposes itself as a theme, is already dissimulated . . . The other who manifests himself in the face as it were breaks through his own plastic essence . . . His presence consists in divesting himself of the form which, however, manifests him. His manifestation is a surplus over the inevitable paralysis of manifestation. (T, 351–52)

Inherent in manifestation is the threat of rendering the face "captive" or "mute," "paralyzing" it, negating its life, which is its mobility. The face is by definition always on the move, as is underscored by the active verbs Levinas's formulations employ: the face "undoes the form"; "it as it were breaks through its own plastic essence," "it divests itself of its form."[5]

How does this extraordinary event called *face* conserve its significance? How can the face *appear* without renouncing its alterity? In *Totality and Infinity* and in the works that precede it, the answer was found in the conceptual figure of facial expression, the face's distinctive mode of signification. Expression—a combination of glance and speech—is the concrete way in which the face accomplishes its breakthrough or divestiture

---

5. Cf. "The life of expression consists in *undoing* the form in which the existent, exposed as a theme, is thereby dissimulated. The face speaks" (*TI*, 66).

of form. "To speak is . . . to come from behind one's appearance," says Levinas (T, 352). In the 1951 essay "Freedom and Command," he writes:

> The way for a being to break through its form, which is its apparition, is concretely, its look, its aim. There is not first a breakthrough, and then a look, to break through one's form is precisely to look; the eyes are absolutely naked. A face has a meaning not by virtue of the relationships in which it is found, but out of itself, that is what expression is. (FC, 20–21)

To say that the face has a meaning "out of itself" and not by referral or relationship to something else is to say that in contradistinction to other forms of signification, facial expressions signify only themselves. They do not refer to something else, either to states of mind or feeling. Like the nonadequating ethical language into which the avaricious gaze transformed itself, the language of facial expression is conative and interlocutionary in its orientation, performative in its speech. Not denotative, not a bit of information, the language of facial expression is a command. Or it is a greeting.

> The expression does not speak about someone, is not information about a coexistence, does not invoke an attitude in addition to knowledge; expression invites one to speak to someone. The most direct attitude before a being *kath 'auto* is not the knowledge one can have about him, but is social commerce with him. (FC, 21)

Again, the "direct" language-attitude which the face speaks and with which I face the face is originary, prior to communication as an exchange of signs. For the sign entails indirection, an obliqueness between sign and referent.[6] This primordial language has, we recall, but a single utterance in its lexicon, the "thou shalt not kill" that brings to a halt the self's unbridled *pouvoir*.

Hence the face's expression signifies not like other signs; it has a unique autosignification which Levinas calls signification *kath 'auto*, "according to itself." In the primordial expression *kath 'auto*, there is "coincidence" of manifestation and the manifested. "In contradistinction to plastic manifestation or disclosure, which manifests something *as* something" (*TI*, 296), the other signifies, says Levinas, "without qualities or attributes"—by himself, according to himself (*TI*, 74). He does not even signify as himself; he signifies without benefit of the "as" structure.

---

6. While Levinas, in at least one place, uses a different tropology to refer to the sign/signified relation, namely, parallelism ("the simple parallelism of two orders that would be in a relationship of sign to signified," [EP, 67]), he invariably maintains that correlation, systematicity, and conjuncture destroy the unique signification of the trace.

(Strictly speaking I do not encounter the face *as* a face; the face *is* not, *as* a face.) In the writings subsequent to *Totality and Infinity*, the face of the other is also said to signify in a distinctive manner—again, without context, without mediation, "by himself." "The beyond from which a face comes," Levinas will assert, "signifies as a trace" (T, 355).

TRACING AN ABSOLUTE PAST IN LEVINAS AND DERRIDA

Levinas proposes the trace in contrast to dissimulation and disclosure, revelation and unveiling. Dissimulation and disclosure are modes proper to the phenomenon and being: they would absorb and reduce the other's alterity. The model of revelation—invariably conceived as a dialectic between hidden and manifest—would convert transcendence into immanence. The conceptual figure of the trace allows Levinas to think a relationship to the other which does not convert the other into the same, and a relationship to transcendence that is not convertible into immanence.

Recall the emphasis on face as that which presents itself as a phenomenon and also, through its expression, exceeds the phenomenon. Or, in "The Trace of the Other," the definition of face as a disturbance between the mundane and the extra mundane, a collision between two orders. In Levinas's terms, its presentation is enigmatic, namely, a "way the other has of seeking my recognition while preserving his incognito," a "way of manifesting himself without manifesting himself" (EP, 66). In "Enigma and Phenomenon" Levinas evokes the approach of the other and the disturbance in the order produced by "an expression, a face facing and interpellating, coming from the depths, cutting the threads of the context . . . expression faces and confronts in a face, approaches and disturbs absolutely" (EP, 64–65). It disturbs absolutely, but—and here one will wish to employ the singular syntax that is reminiscent of the Blanchotian diction—it disturbs *without* disturbing. Levinas writes: "Disturbance is a movement that does not propose any stable order in conflict or in accord with a given order. It is a movement that already carries away the signification it brought: disturbance disturbs the order without troubling it seriously. It enters in so subtle a way that unless we retain it, it has already withdrawn. It insinuates itself, withdraws before entering. It remains only for him who would like to follow it up" (EP, 66). Hence disturbance is a movement that is already in retreat; withdrawal is built into its presentation. Moreover, Levinas says, it withdraws before entering. In similar formulations (which also employ the trope of hysteron proteron, "the latter put as the former"), Levinas says that "the hand was thrown in before the game began; the disconnection took place before the connection" (EP, 65); the other "has left before having come" (EP, 68). Note the impossibility of ever coinciding with the other; with the other there is no recognition, no simultaneity, no meeting. This structure which Levinas calls "anachronism" is necessary because the disturbing alterity is not a difference visible to the gaze which always synchronizes the same and the other. In disturbance what is required is a present that, in Levinas's formulation, "destructures itself in its very punctuality" (EP, 68). Hence "alterity occurs as a divergency and a past which no memory could resurrect as a present, . . . [as] a past that has never been present" (EP, 68), or, as he also puts it, as "the trace of an irreversible past" (T, 345). Levinas asks, "How refer to an irreversible past that is a past which the very reference would not bring back . . . like memory which retrieves the past, like signs which recapture the signified? What would be needed would be an indication that would reveal the withdrawal of the indicated instead of a reference that rejoins it. Such is the trace" (EP, 65).

Ordinarily a trace is conceived as a residual phenomenon. Levinas gives the following examples: "A detective examines everything in the area where a crime took place, as revealing signs which betoken the voluntary or involuntary work of the criminal; a hunter follows the traces of the game, which reflect the activity and movement of the animal the hunter is after; a historian discovers ancient civilizations which form the horizon of our world on the basis of the vestiges left by their existence" (T, 356). In each of these examples, the trace is the *mark* of an absence of what previously was present, and is derivative of full presence. This kind of trace is a mark or imprint *in* the world, the effect of a cause in the same world.[7] Moreover, ordinary traces—the fingerprints left by a criminal, the tracks of an animal, the vestiges of ancient civilizations— can be taken as signs, as signifiers relating to signifieds, accessible to an interpreter—the detective, the hunter, the archaeologist, respectively— who would decode them. As indicative signs, they are for Levinas synchronous; "[T]hey reestablish a conjuncture, a simultaneity, between the indicating and indicated terms, thus abolishing depth" (EP, 65). Fingerprints, animal tracks, vestiges of civilizations are the empirical signs of an absence; they are signs of a departure. Because they mark the absence of something that was previously present, these trace-signs remain within the phenomenal order, in a world.

But the trace as Levinas understands it, the trace of the other, is other-

7. Levinas writes: "A cause and an effect, even separated by time, belong to the same world" (T, 358).

wise. *This* trace escapes not only phenomenal presence but the very conceptual opposition between presence and absence. It has to be understood as nonphenomenal, that is, Edward Casey comments, "as non-present (i.e. as *not* the empirical sign of an absence), yet not as fading presence either (i.e. as an evanescent sign), or even as sheer absence. We have to do, rather, with a form of absence that has inscribed itself in material presence in such a subtle manner as already to have eluded its own presentation."[8] Neither "presence," nor "indication," nor even "an indicated presence" (EP, 66) will be adequate for understanding the trace.

For this enigmatic trace is simultaneous with its effacing. Says Levinas: "Its original signifyingness is sketched out in, for example, the fingerprints left by someone who wanted to wipe away his traces and commit a perfect crime. He who left traces in effacing his traces did not mean to say or do anything by the traces he left *[Celui qui a laissé des traces en effaçant ses traces, n'a rien voulu dire ni faire par les traces qu'il laisse].* He has disturbed the order in an irreparable way. He has passed absolutely. To *be* qua *leaving a trace* is to pass, to depart, to absolve oneself" (T, 357). The trace, as Levinas defines it, leaves a trace by effacing its traces. Such a trace is not the mark of an absence (which could be conceived in relation to a past or modified presence). Rather, it is the mark of the effacement of a mark. As it is the mark of the effacement of a mark that was already the mark of an absence (or if you will, the effacement of the mark of effacement), it is a double effacement, a double erasure, a re-mark and a re-tracing *(un re-trait).* That is why Levinas says "it occurs by overprinting *[sur-impression]*" (T, 357). Belonging to an immemorial past and accessible to no present, this trace is outside the presence/absence dyad.[9] It is, as Levinas puts it, "the presence of that which properly speaking has never been there" (T, 358). It is an irreversible past; its presence is "the very *passing* toward a past more remote than any past" (T, 358).[10] That is why when the trace leaves a trace, it leaves.

What is the relation between the trace as Levinas exposits it and what

8. Edward Casey, "Levinas on Memory and the Trace," in *The Collegium Phaenomeno-logicum*, ed. J. C. Sallis, G. Moneta, and J. Taminiaux (Boston: Kluwer Academic Publishers, 1988), 243. My discussion of the manner in which the trace escapes phenomenology is indebted to Casey's essay.

9. Even if absence is the only possible representation of the trace within the realm of appearances, as Rodolphe Gasché observes in *The Tain of the Mirror,* 188.

10. Casey observes that the trace "insert[s] itself between present moments without ever becoming such a moment itself . . . it has entered into the time of the same in a 'strange' way that does not make present, cannot become present. And in this presentlessness it can be only a past." "Levinas on Memory," 250–51.

Jacques Derrida calls the arche-trace? The question necessitates a response, however brief and insufficient, not least because in his 1968 essay "Différance," Derrida *names* Levinas in connection with the thought of the trace (D, 21).[11] Moreover, there is a profound convergence between Levinas's destructuring and Derrida's deconstruction of pure punctuality, whereby "each element appearing on the scene of presence is related to something other than itself." Derrida writes: "An interval must separate the present from what it is not in order for the present to be itself, but this interval that constitutes it as present must, by the same token, divide the present in and of itself, thereby also dividing, along with the present, everything that is thought on the basis of the present, that is, in our metaphysical language, every being, and singularly substance or the subject" (D, 13). It is this interval that Derrida names the "arche-trace." Rodolphe Gasché explains the Derridean trace as "a minimal structure of a relation to alterity" without which no self could be self, and because of which no self can be itself.[12] The formulation helps to indicate a certain proximity between the two thinkers, namely, the always possible commerce between Derrida's general Other, *Autre*, and *the* Other, the specific otherness of the other, Levinas's *Autrui*. The interruptions and the alterities with which Derrida's work is concerned may be shown to have an ethical force.[13]

In the essay "Différance," Derrida explicitly models the radicality of his conception of the trace on the Heideggerian motif of the forgetting of the ontico-ontological difference, a forgetting of the trace of difference that is so profound that even this forgetting is forgotten, without a trace. Erasure belongs to the very structure of this trace. Derrida writes of the "erasure which constitutes it from the outset as a trace, which situates it as a change of site, and makes it disappear in its appearance . . . The erasure of the early trace *[die frühe Spur]* of difference is therefore the 'same' as its tracing in the text of metaphysics" (D, 24). In this reading, it is *insofar* as the ontico-ontological difference was forgotten that it made all the difference, that it determined the history of philosophy in the West. That is why the erasure of the trace is the "same" as its tracing in the text of metaphysics (and this structure of a tracing-erasure is bound

---

11. A similar naming of Levinas by Derrida can be found in *Of Grammatology*, trans. Gayatri Chakravorty Spivak (Baltimore: Johns Hopkins University Press, 1976), 70.

12. See Gasché's discussion of the arche-trace in *The Tain of the Mirror*, 186–94.

13. This is the argument advanced by Simon Critchley in "The Chiasmus: Levinas, Derrida and the Ethical Demand for Deconstruction," *Textual Practice* 3 (1989): 99; and in *The Ethics of Deconstruction: Derrida and Levinas* (Oxford: Blackwell, 1992), 30.

to recall Levinas's description of the trace's enigmatic "overprinting"). Derrida continues: "The paradox of such a structure, in the language of metaphysics, is an inversion of metaphysical concepts, which produces the following effect; the present becomes the sign of the sign, the trace of the trace. It is no longer what every reference refers to in the last analysis. It becomes a function in a structure of generalized reference. It is a trace, and a trace of the erasure of the trace" (D, 24). In Derrida's reading, the erasure of the trace is constitutive of presence. If every metaphysical concept thus retains the mark of what it has set aside—is traced by a structure of generalized reference to Other—this mark also divides and deconstitutes presence. What are ordinarily the terms of plenitude within metaphysics—for example, presence, self, God—become a function, an effect of the structure of generalized reference to other, a function or effect of the trace.

One should remark that Derrida's discourse of the trace is specifically oriented toward the Heideggerian undermining of the determination of being as presence in a way that Levinas's is not.[14] But nevertheless the convergence between Derrida's and Levinas's thinking of the trace is decisive and several consequences ensue. For example, as noted earlier, it is possible to make explicit in Derrida's work the ethical—in Levinas's sense of the word—significance that invests it, the ethical demand to which it responds. Derrida has acknowledged as much when he says there is a duty, an (ultra)ethical demand of posing questions of a deconstructive kind (A, 76–77). Reciprocally, Levinas's thought takes on a deconstructive potential, for in identifying something like an internal division or border within the same that opens the same to the other, it achieves as it were a deconstruction of self, of self-coincidence, by the relation to the other. This crossing of the Levinasian and Derridean projects was already evident in Derrida's reading of Levinas in "Violence and Metaphysics" where Levinas's certain departure from the dominant (Greek) conceptuality that ignores and represses the ethical was interpreted by Derrida as a challenge to and a deconstruction of that conceptuality. Would the difference between the two indeed be merely the difference of what Derrida has called

---

14. Derrida himself states this in *Of Grammatology*, 70. Robert Bernasconi points out that Derrida's concern is "to direct Levinas against the philosophy of presence rather than to do justice to Levinas's attack on the neutrality of philosophy," and that Levinas's indebtedness to and break with Heidegger is elsewhere. "The Trace of Levinas in Derrida," in *Derrida and Différance*, ed. David Wood and Robert Bernasconi (Evanston, IL: Northwestern University Press, 1988): 13–29.

"idiom," "signature?" (*A*, 74–75). Levinas's descriptions would indeed seem to offer a way of thinking about ethics that is, as Derrida would understand it, nonmetaphysical, nonlogocentric, not oriented toward the subject, consciousness, or any of the philosophemes of traditional ethics.

But what are the implications of such a nonmetaphysical, nonhumanistic ethics? What are the consequences of thinking responsibility to the other as a relation to the trace? First, the other to whom I am responsible cannot be said to *be there*. The trace by which the face of the other signifies is outside the presence and absence dyad, and thus the other cannot be conceived in terms of the metaphysics of presence (i.e., as another presence or as a subject). In fact, to presuppose the other in terms of the metaphysics of presence, with its phenomenalizing and adequating forms, as when, for example, I see, know, recognize, or comprehend the other, would be to deny and enclose the other. It would be another instance of the economy of the same. It is the interruption of all such closed systems that lets alterity be glimpsed. Derrida glosses Levinas, in a manner that suggests an ultraethical imperative: "To enter into a rapport with the other, interruption must be possible. The rapport must be a rapport of interruption. Here interruption does not interrupt the rapport with the other, it opens it" (*A*, 82).

A second consequence of thinking responsibility as a relation to the trace concerns the status of the interruption, the disturbance. The ethical event has an ontological insecurity because withdrawal is built into the trace's presentation. As Derrida puts it: "The trace is inscribed in being effaced and leaving the traced wake of its effacement in the *re*-treat or in what Emmanuel Levinas calls the 'overprinting.' " But such a structure is, as Derrida understands it, menaced "by its very rigor" (ATM, 37). Will the ethical event have happened? Can it be said to happen? Strictly speaking, it does not happen; nothing forces us to take up the obligation, the imperative of responsibility the face delivers; the imposition is altogether without force. But such is the risk, the necessary risk of a thought that does not presuppose the other, does not merely reconstitute the economy of the same. Without this risk, the alterity of the other drops out altogether. And this is the risk that Levinas's *theology* is willing to run when he asks in "Enigma and Phenomenon" whether religions do not come to us from a past that has never been present, and when he asserts, in the essay entitled "Un Dieu homme?" that "the trace . . . is the proximity of God in the face of the other."[15]

15. Levinas, "Un Dieu homme?" in *Exercices de la patience* 1 (1980): 72.

THE TRACE OF GOD

To what extent can the God of Exodus be said to reveal himself as a trace? In "Enigma and Phenomenon," Levinas will propose a very condensed reading of two scriptural passages which recount a theophany. The first is the call of Moses in Exodus 3:2, to which we briefly turn. Moses is tending his flock when he comes to the mountain of Horeb, and "the angel of the Lord appeared to him as a flame of fire from the midst of a bush." (This fire is a figure for God's presence here and at the Sinaitic revelation as well.)

> And Moses said, "I must turn aside that I may see this marvelous sight, why the bush does not burn up." When the Lord saw that he turned aside to see, God called to him from the midst of the bush saying, "Moses, Moses." He answered, "Here I am." He said, "Do not come any closer; take off your sandals from your feet, for the place where you are standing is holy ground." Then he said, "I am the God of your father, the God of Abraham, the God of Isaac, and the God of Jacob." And Moses hid his face, for he was afraid to look at God. (Ex. 3:3–6)

Brevard Childs comments: "What began as just another day doing the same old thing, turned out to be an absolutely new experience for Moses."[16] Called to his prophetic office, Moses puts himself at God's service with the words, "Here I am," words which echo those of pious ancestors and which, in Levinas's later work, are the paradigmatic response of responsibility, indeed the sole utterance in the primordial lexicon. The sequence follows another pattern, namely, the appearance of a deity, who, at a holy place, reveals himself by name.[17] After hearing the name formula which effectively renews a promise, Moses—in his "inexperience," in his "timidity"[18]—hides his face.

Levinas's comments on the biblical passage emphasize the missed recognition, the nonself-coincidence, and ultimately the nonself-presence inherent in this theophany:

> The great "experiences" of our life have, properly speaking, never been lived . . . To the voice that calls from the burning bush Moses answers "Here I am" but does not dare to lift up his eyes. The glorious theophany which makes so much humility possible will be missed because of the very humility which

16. Brevard S. Childs, *The Book of Exodus: A Critical, Theological Commentary* (Philadelphia: Westminster Press, 1974), 72. The following exegesis and discussion of the history of exegesis of these Exodus passages is indebted to Childs's commentary.

17. Childs, *The Book of Exodus*, 65.

18. Moshe Greenberg, *Understanding Exodus* (New York: Behrman House, 1969), 94, 32.

lowers the eyes. Later, on the rock of Horeb, the prophet ventures to know but glory is refused to the boldness that seeks it. As transcendence, as pure passage, it shows itself as past. It is trace. (EP, 68–69)

In midrashic fashion, Levinas draws together two scriptural places which recount a theophany, juxtaposing Moses's humility in Exodus 3—he hides his face, "afraid to look at God"—with his boldness in Exodus 33, where he seems precisely to want to look at God. Or at least he asks to see God's glory *(kabod)*. This term, sometimes rendered as "presence,"[19] seems to denote "that side of the divine nature that can be perceived by man through revelation."[20] It becomes associated with "face" when God refuses to comply in full with Moses's request, saying,

> "You cannot see my face, for no mortal man can see me and live." And the Lord said, "Look, there is a place beside me. Station yourself on the rock, and, as my glory passes by I will place you in a crevice of the rock, and shield you with my hand until I have passed by. Then I will remove my hand and you will see my back, but my face shall not be seen." (Ex. 33:20–33)

What is the meaning of this request and its refusal? The request to see—the glory or the face of God—is a desire to know God. (Notice how Levinas assimilates this particular project to the indiscretion of the mode of knowing in general, saying simply that "on the rock of Horeb the prophet ventures *to know*.") But God will not be known in his essence. In an anthropomorphic image, scripture asserts that Moses sees not God's face but his back—his hinder parts—after he has passed by. The image, as it has been interpreted by Jewish and Christian commentators alike, suggests the limits of man's knowledge of God. God will not be seen with a totalizing view but glimpsed partially in his passing from the back. He will not be known in his essence but (for medieval interpreters) through his attributes and through his works.[21] God's denial of Moses's request recalls his denial of Moses's earlier request in Exodus 3:14 to know God's name, another "vehicle of his essential nature."[22] There God's paronomastic answer is more like the evasion of an answer, with its circular *idem per idem* formula, *ehyeh asher ehyeh,* "I am that I am."[23]

19. JPS translation.

20. Childs, *The Book of Exodus,* 597.

21. This is one of the interpretations attached to the phrase in Exodus 33:19: "I will make all my goodness pass before you."

22. Childs, *The Book of Exodus,* 596.

23. The interpretation of this verse poses enormous questions in the history of exegesis. The formula *ehyeh asher ehyeh* was often interpreted as a statement of being by the Church fathers. Childs (85) refers to Etienne Gilson, *The Spirit of Medieval Philosophy* (New York:

Both in Exodus 3 and 33 God is a *deus absconditus*. But is not the statement that Moses saw God's back in contradiction with numerous places in scripture—"The Lord would speak to Moses face to face, as a man speaks to his friend" (Ex. 33:11); "No prophet has arisen in Israel like Moses, with whom God spoke face to face" (Deut. 34:10); "My servant Moses is at home in my House, I speak with him mouth to mouth, and he beholds the likeness of the Lord" (Num. 12:6)[24]—all of which assert, by means of the anthropomorphic image of facing, Moses's special intimacy with God. What *did* Moses see? One rabbinic reading, *Berakhot* 7b (cited by Levinas in the essay "Revelation in the Jewish Tradition"), says in effect: He saw neither face, *nor* back. He saw the *knot* of the *tephillin*, the phylacteries at the back of God's neck.[25] In the manner of the most negative of negative theologies, in a progressive dephenomenalization, a subtraction, the rabbinic comment proposes that Moses saw nothing (corporeal) of God. The whole question of seeing (or knowing) God is displaced, even by means of the anthropomorphic image of God praying. As Levinas understands it, the theophany is referred to the centrality of the prescriptive in Judaism, the ritual observance that teaches obligation to the neighbor.

Let us come back to the scriptural text. God says to Moses, "I will shield you with my hand until I have passed by . . . and you will see my back." If face or facing suggests approach, back suggests departure, would seem to be a sign of departure. The back of God would be like one of the ordinary traces to which Levinas refers, the sign-traces exemplified

---

Scribners, 1940), 51: "From this moment it is understood once and for all that the proper name of God is being and that . . . this name denotes His very essence." Paul Ricoeur points out (as have other commentators) that such a reading may be an illegitimate imposition of a Neoplatonic and Augustinian ontology onto the phrase. He suggests that in this instance the name of God "is not a name which defines God but one that signifies the act of deliverance." "Toward a Hermeneutic of the Idea of Revelation," trans. David Pellauer, in *Essays on Biblical Interpretation*, ed. Lewis S. Mudge (Philadelphia: Fortress Press, 1980), 94. This essay was originally given, along with Levinas's "Revelation in the Jewish Tradition," at a 1976 conference on revelation at the École des sciences philosophiques et religieuses des Facultés universitaires Saint-Louis à Bruxelles, and published in *La révélation*, ed. Paul Ricoeur et al. (Brussels: Facultés universitaires Saint-Louis, 1984), 34.

24. These scriptural instances are cited by André Neher, *Moïse et la vocation juive* (Paris: Seuil, 1956), 82.

25. Levinas, "Revelation in the Jewish Tradition," trans. Sarah Richmond, in *LR*. "La révélation dans la tradition juive," in *La révélation*, ed. Paul Ricoeur et al., 71; reprinted in Levinas, *L'au-delà du verset* (Paris: Minuit, 1982). Note that this rabbinic comment does not seek to resolve the contradiction between verses but rather to widen the gap.

by footprints, fingerprints, animal tracks, indicative signs which mark the absence of something that was previously present. For example, the back of God which denotes his works is a sign-trace, an effect of God within the phenomenal order. But what if the back of God were not a sign-trace but a veritable trace, another kind of absence? Moses sees God leaving, but what he sees is not a sign of departure. He sees a God who disappears *in* his appearance, a proximity in retreat,[26] an exteriority that is always already past. Levinas says in his comment on Exodus 33, "as transcendence, as pure passage, it [the theophany] shows itself as past. It is a trace" (EP, 69). He also states: "The revealed God of our Judeo-Christian spirituality maintains all the infinity of his absence . . . he shows himself only by his trace, as in Exodus 33" (T, 359).[27] This God is pure passage and has never been present. "The term *present*," says Levinas, "suggests both the idea of a privileged position in the temporal series and the idea of manifestation" (EP, 61). To think God as a trace is to think the invisibility of God outside the opposition manifestation/nonmanifestation. For Levinas this means an *enigmatic* mode of presentation whose retreat is inscribed in advance. Within this logic, the Sinaitic theophany (in Exodus 19 and 20) is rigorously indistinguishable from a thunderstorm.[28]

In summary, at the theophany at the bush, Moses hides his face, afraid to look at God, and he sees nothing. Later, he asks to see: "Pray, let me see thy glory." He requests it, not quite in the manner in which he *pleaded* with God to let him into the promised land (Deut. 3:23–25),[29] but this

26. The phrase is Marc Faessler's. See his "L'intrigue du tout-autre: Dieu dans la pensée de Levinas," in *Les cahiers de* La nuit surveillée: *Emmanuel Levinas*, ed. Jacques Rolland (Paris: Verdier, 1984), 119–45.

27. This statement, occurring at the close of "The Trace of the Other," in effect fulfills the promise Levinas makes earlier in the essay, that "a certain idea of God [would] become visible, as a trace, at the end of our analysis" (T, 350). On the economy of the promise and its relation to theological questions, see Mark C. Taylor, "Non-Negative Negative Atheology," *Diacritics* 20 (1990): 2–16.

28. Some examples of the way in which Levinas reads and plays on the naturalistic images of God's presence in scripture: "Once come into correlation, the divinity of God dissipates, like the clouds that served to describe his presence" (EP, 62). "A God was revealed on a mountain or in a burning bush, or was attested to in Scriptures. And what if it were a storm!" (EP, 66). It is as if the predominance of these naturalistic images confirms the *enigma* of biblical revelation.

29. The many midrashim on Deuteronomy 3:23–25 ("I pleaded with the Lord at that time, saying '. . . Let me, I pray, cross over'") extend and offer a narrative expansion of this pleading. In his collection and retelling of these midrashim, Louis Ginzberg proposes this dialogue:

Moses: "Lord of the world! Let me, I pray, enter into the Land, live there two or three years, and then die." God: "I have resolved that thou shalt not go there." Moses: "If I

time he wants to see. God answers: "You cannot not see my face" (Ex. 33: 20). There is a cryptic footnote in "Enigma and Phenomenon" in which Levinas refers to, but does not cite, a rabbinic comment on this verse from *Berakhot* 7a. It, too, emphasizes this persistent noncoincidence:

> A Tanna taught in the name of R. Joshua v. Ḳorḥah: The Holy One, blessed be He, spoke thus to Moses: When I wanted, you did not want [to see my face], now that you want, I do not want.[30]

We could take this as an instance of the Hebrew Bible's rhetoric of the double bind, a rhetorical pattern of cruel power which, as Harold Bloom reads it, is exemplified in God's telling Moses in Deut. 34:4: "This is the land which I promised to you and your ancestors, you may see it with your eyes but you may not cross over there." As Bloom summarizes this rhetoric: "[E]verything is given to us, and then what matters most is taken away from us."[31] But in the rabbinic interpolation of this interlocutionary utterance—when I wanted you did not want, now that you want, I do not want—is there not also a *structure* that, beyond psychological and existential despair and frustration, characterizes what Levinas under-

---

may not enter it in my lifetime, let me reach it after my death." God: "Nay, neither dead nor alive shalt thou go into the land." Moses: "Why this wrath against me?" God: "Because ye sanctified Me not in the midst of the children of Israel." (*The Legends of the Jews*, vol. 3 [Philadelphia: Jewish Publication Society, 1911], 419–29, esp. 424)

Deuteronomy Rabbah 11:10, to which we referred in note 2, reads:

> Moses said to God: "Master of the Universe, the labour and the pains which I have devoted to making Israel believe in Thy name are manifest and known to Thee, to what trouble have I gone with them in connection with the precepts in order to fix for them Torah and precepts. I thought, just as I witnessed the woe, so too will I behold their good fortune; but now that the good fortune of Israel has come, Thou sayest to me, 'Thou shalt not go over this Jordan' [Deut. 31:2]; lo, Thou givest the lie to thy Torah. Therein it is written, 'In the same day thou shalt give him his hire, neither shall the sun go down upon it, for he is poor, and setteth his heart upon it; lest he cry against thee unto the Lord, and it be sin in thee' [Deut. 24:15]. Is this the reward for the forty years' labour that I went through?" (*The Midrash Rabbah: Deuteronomy*, trans. H. Freedman and Maurice Simon [London: Soncino Press, 1977])

It is worth attending to these midrashim, so that we do not take for granted that we know what it means "to act without entering the promised land," so that we do not gloss over the distress inherent in Moses's renunciation and reduce it to platitudes such as "life is a task," so that we do not reduce the difficulty and the radicality of the one-way movement.

30. *The Babylonian Talmud*, trans. Isadore Epstein (London: Soncino Press, 1948).

31. Harold Bloom and David Rosenberg, *The Book of J* (New York: Grove Weidenfeld, 1990), 268–69. The other biblical passage which for Bloom exemplifies this rhetoric is Genesis 2:16: "Of every tree of the garden you are free to eat; but as for the tree of knowledge of good and evil, you shall not eat of it."

stands as the *enigma* of the revelation of the other: missed recognition, nonreciprocity, noncoincidence, nonself-presence? The theophany at the bush is the radical incognito of transcendence. Precisely because it *is* an experience of transcendence, it is missed; the experience is not one. In summary, Levinas's reading of both Exodus 3 and 33 makes quite explicit what is only implied in "Enigma and Phenomenon," namely, that the scriptural narrative, or the scriptural account of revelation, is itself exposed to interruption, that it is ethical, in his precise sense of the term.[32]

A final question concerns the relation of the trace of God to the trace of the other. Two passages already quoted suggest that they are intertwined, that the trace of God is given in the face of the other. "The trace . . . is the proximity of God in the face of the other."[33] And the passage with which we began, along with the sentences preceding it, the last paragraph of "The Trace of the Other": "The God who passed is not the model of which the face would be an image. To be in the image of God does not mean to be an icon of God, but to find oneself in his trace. The revealed God of our Judeo-Christian spirituality maintains all the infinity of his absence, *which is in the personal order itself.* He shows himself only by his trace, as in Exodus 33. To go toward Him is not to follow this trace which is not a sign; it is to go toward the others who stand in the trace" (T, 359; emphasis mine). These statements reveal an emphasis that has been present from Levinas's earliest work, namely, that in the revealed morality of Judaism there is an "internal and necessary" relationship between three terms, *God, man,* and *the neighbor.*[34] This is often asserted in *Difficult Freedom* and in the talmudic readings. Or, in *Totality and Infinity* and in other works, the law—God's law, the "thou shalt not kill"—is given in the other's face. Would the later assertions about God, the other, and the trace be simply a re-stating, albeit in a less anthropological way, of these earlier emphases?

To go toward (the trace of) God is to go toward the trace of the other. We can say what this does *not* mean. It does not mean that God is an ontological guarantor of ethical responsibility to the other. It does not mean that God left his mark on the interhuman, because God is (nothing) but trace. God *is* not, apart from trace. The trace *of* God means the trace

32. "The very linking of the Narrative is exposed to interruption *[l'enchaînement du Récit s'expose à l'interruption]*" (EP, 69). The capitalized word *Récit,* which usually refers to the (totalizing) philosophical narrative, may refer here to the narrative linking of scripture.

33. Levinas, "Un Dieu homme?" 72.

34. See Emil Fackenheim's description of Judaism in *Encounters between Judaism and Modern Philosophy: A Preface to Future Jewish Thought* (New York: Schocken Books, 1980), 48–49.

that is God. "And if God were an effect of the trace?" Derrida asks in "Violence and Metaphysics." "If the idea of divine presence (life, existence, parousia, etc.), if the name of God was but the movement of this erasure of the trace in presence?" (VM, 108). That is, the self-presentation of God would be the illusory halting of the chain of referrals of the archetrace, the figure of the one unerasable presence.[35] But only—and the qualifier is enormous—a God conceived within ontotheology as first being, presence, *causa sui*, etc. If God can be understood as "not contaminated by being," as Levinas puts it, that is, in accordance with what might be called a "Judaic"[36] *non*ontotheological theology, then perhaps the nonmanifestation of the revelation of God can be understood otherwise, as a differential constitution of (textual) traces, as the other-trace. Then perhaps we can begin to think God, in Levinas's work, as the *name*—unpronounceable if you like—for the difficult way in which we are responsible to traces.

35. This is how Gasché explains the relation between the question of God and the thought of the trace in Derrida's work. See his "God for Example," in *Phenomenology and the Numinous*, Fifth Annual Symposium of the Simon Silverman Phenomenology Center (Pittsburgh: Duquesne University Press, 1988), 43–66.

36. Here we can no longer take for granted that we know what we mean by "Judaic," since the "Judaism" in question is arrived at only after such a detour through ontotheology and the Greco-Christian conceptuality.

[3] FACING FIGURES

Titles seem to guarantee a certain access, but it is precisely the identity of the literary that will be one of our questions. Indeed, Levinas's relation to what we will variously call literature, figure, rhetorical language, constitutes a vexed area of research. There is an incommensurability between the more originary level of Levinas's ethical discourse and the discourse of literary criticism. This means that an extrinsic approach to the topic will lead nowhere, for it is not a matter in any case of applying Levinas's philosophy to the interpretation of literary texts. An intrinsic approach to the topic is then required, one that will take into account both what Levinas says about literature and how he says it; but this, too, may prove to be a somewhat unrewarding undertaking because Levinas speaks very rarely about the literary, and when he does it is almost always in dismissive terms.

One of the earliest of Levinas's postwar writings is a rather violent article on aesthetics, entitled "Reality and Its Shadow," published in 1948 in *Les Temps Modernes*. This article, to which I will refer in the course of this and subsequent chapters, discusses the work of art as a form of nonresponsibility, evasion, and, in the "theological terms" that he himself proposes, idolatry. Recall also Levinas's denigration of rhetoric in the 1961 *Totality and Infinity* and its description as "injustice." There rhetoric—conceived as ruse and persuasion—is figured as an *oblique* approach to the other; coming at the other with an agenda, *from an angle*, it thereby loses the ethical specificity of facing, the *droiture* of the face-to-face. Levinas's rejection of the literary and rhetorical properties of language is most dramatically in evidence in another essay from the postwar period—on which I will focus here—the 1950 "Persons or Figures." In that essay, which reviews a poetic commentary on the Old Testament by Paul Claudel, Levinas describes figuration itself—or the figural impulse—as ethically suspect. *Figure* is one of the terms in Levinas's lexicon that, especially in the early work, is negatively charged; other such terms include *poetry*, *drama*, and *play*.

Having said this, one must also observe that paradoxically this gesture of rejection and denigration of the literary, particularly in Levinas's philosophical writings from the postwar period, cannot altogether be separated from a certain celebration of it, in the form of *allusions* to Shakespeare, Dostoevsky, and others, and in the name of traditionally conceived enduring aesthetic values: genius, the masterpiece, and so on.[1] (This alternation between denigration and celebration may not be as paradoxical as it first seems: each may be an effort to defend against or defuse a perceived threat.) In these allusive instances, which serve generally to *illustrate* a philosophical argument, Levinas has a tendency to treat the literary work as if it were transparently denotative. It should be noted also that, during this same postwar period, Levinas wrote essays on Proust (1947) and Leiris (1949), as well as several reviews of literary works (including the Claudel piece in 1950). By 1956 he had written the first of his interpretive essays on the narrative prose of Maurice Blanchot. Finally, suffice it to remark—as John Llewelyn does in a concise discussion of Levinas's relation to art—that twenty years later the picture changed somewhat: one could find a more positive valuation of art, especially in his interpretive engagement with the literary writers Blanchot (1966, 1971, 1975), Laporte (1966), Celan (1972) and Agnon (1973).[2]

But most at issue here as concerns Levinas and the literary is a story of turning away, specifically a turning away from figure. What does it mean to turn, as Levinas does in "Persons or Figures," away from figure? If my approach to this guiding question is somewhat oblique, that is not solely due to the question's tropological nature. It is due to a detour within Levinas's own work, a doubleness there, which causes his discourse on the literary to be intertwined with his discourse on the Judaic. In "Reality and Its Shadow," which argues that all art is essentially plastic image, he says: "The proscription of images is truly the supreme com-

---

1. The Proust essay begins with this sentence: "The timeless qualities of a masterpiece do not in any way lift it out of time" (OP, 161).

2. John Llewelyn, *The Middle Voice of Ecological Conscience* (New York: St. Martin's Press, 1991), 98–113.

mandment of monotheism" (RO, 11). Other references to Judaism that we have encountered thus far in Levinas's work include biblical citations, allusions to Abraham and Moses which grant a philosophical significance to their itineraries, a recourse to the talmudic tradition, and the certain return to a Judaic model of revelation in the thought of the trace. To what extent can Levinas's conflicted attitude toward literary art be attributed to this Judaizing emphasis?

Levinas's interpretation of Claudel, we shall see, is inseparable from another project, namely, his hermeneutic of Judaism. The Judaic, in Levinas, is always a problem of language, of the language and the conceptuality that is available to us. There is no access to Judaism that does not take place in the "Greek" language, that does not first confront the dominant "Greco-Christian" conceptuality in order to disengage the specificity of the Judaic.[3] If Levinas's discourse on *the literary* is thus intertwined with his discourse on the Judaic, this means that the discourse on the literary necessarily passes through the very difference or the distinction between the "Judaic" and the "Christian." "Persons or Figures" provides the stage not just for Levinas's confrontation with figure but for his decisive confrontation with Christian imaginative literature as well.

THE CLAIMS OF FIGURAL INTERPRETATION

What, after all, is a figure? What's in a figure? What does it mean to be or to happen *in a figure*, as when Paul, in I Corinthians, says of the Israelites in the desert, "Now all these things happened to them in a figure"?[4] And what would be the relationship between figure and what Levinas calls "ethics"? For Levinas, as we have seen, ethics denotes not a set of moral precepts but a responsibility—at its most originary—that arises in the encounter with the face of the other. When the other is encountered *as* a face, the infinite alterity of the other is revealed. Yet the face escapes the very phenomenology of Levinas's descriptions. And

3. The terms are in quotation marks because "Greek" and "Christian" (and eventually "Hebrew") are not primarily historical; they refer to a conceptuality and the possibility of a language.

4. I Corinthians 10:11. The phrase "in a figure *[typikos]*" is variously translated as "in a warning," "as an example." Its force is monitory as well as typological. See *The Anchor Bible: I Corinthians*, ed. William F. Orr and James Arthur Walther (New York: Doubleday and Company, 1976). On the privileged status of this passage within medieval biblical interpretation, on the way in which it has been used to authorize the figural interpretation of the Hebrew Bible as a whole, see Henri de Lubac, *Exégèse médiévale: Les quatre sens de l'écriture*, vol. 2, pt. 2 (Paris: Aubier, 1964), 60–84.

it is largely in accordance with this antiphenomenological emphasis that Levinas asserts repeatedly that the face is by no means form and in no way figure.

Still, to ask about figure in relation to ethics is necessarily to ask about figure in relation to face. In "Persons or Figures" it is a question first of all not just of figure but of *figura*. Levinas's manifest concern in this text is with the figures of *figural* interpretation, namely, with those persons or events in the Hebrew Bible that are said to anticipate the New Testament proclamation. As Erich Auerbach has shown, there is considerable distance between *figura*, in the anticipatory, typological sense used by the Church fathers, and "figure," in the rhetorical sense largely developed by Quintillian.[5] And there would be an even greater distance to the technical sense of rhetorical figure that, in recent years, has been taken up and inflected by literary critics such as Gérard Genette and Paul de Man. For Auerbach, the different senses of *figura* would be distinct, yet related. They would emerge in the history of the word, as it moves from its earliest sense of plastic form, to (nonplastic) rhetorical figure, to its eventual patristic usage as prefigural type, a history that is itself, in its very movement from sensory to nonsensory sense, figural.[6] Thus the link between all these senses, and any future senses, of "figure" is *itself* prefigured and, in this way, necessarily presupposed by Levinas's discussion. It should be of no surprise, then, that it is precisely when Levinas faces the claims of *figural* interpretation that his discussion of the ethics of figural reading, or better, the ethics of figure, becomes most prominently and fully articulated.

LACKING FIGURE

The essay "Persons or Figures" was first published in 1950 in the French Jewish periodical *Evidences*. It was later reprinted in Levinas's 1963 collection, *Difficult Freedom*, which appeared two years after the publication of *Totality and Infinity*, and which was the first of his nonphilosophical or confessional works. (Levinas distinguishes between his confessional writings and his philosophical works, because the verses that function as bibli-

---

5. Erich Auerbach, "Figura," trans. Ralph Mannheim, in *Scenes from the Drama of European Literature* (Minneapolis: University of Minnesota Press, 1984).

6. Thus Auerbach gives "literally" a figural history of the word *figura*. On literal and figurative in Auerbach's discourse, see Timothy Bahti, "Auerbach's *Mimesis:* Figural Structure and Historical Narrative," in *After Strange Texts: The Role of Theory in the Study of Literature*, ed. Gregory S. Jay and David L. Miller (University: University of Alabama Press, 1985), 124–45.

cal and talmudic proof-texts within the former do not suffice as proof or justification of a phenomenological argument.)

The confessional writings are the place in Levinas's work where he makes explicit the reference to Judaism that is largely implicit in the philosophical works. Specifically these writings render explicit what Levinas calls "the hidden resources" of the Judaic tradition. These resources are hidden, if you will, because they have been for the most part covered up by the negative and privative determinations of the Judaic within the (Greco-)Christian conceptuality. Levinas's hermeneutic of Judaism entails a double interpretive movement: he takes a negative term for the Judaic (invariably the subordinated term within a dyadic hierarchy, as in the Pauline tropes of blindness/sight, servitude/freedom, letter/spirit), radicalizes a possibility inherent in it, and reinscribes it in order to bring out its positive force, even the alternative intelligibility that it harbors. For example, the observance of the law in traditional Judaism is not a yoke, a legalism, but an originary ethical orientation, a fundamental awareness of the other. In the terms of *Difficult Freedom*, it is freedom, albeit a weighty freedom made up of obligations. Ethics itself is this difficult freedom.[7] (Or, in the terms of the previous chapter, perhaps the nonfulfillment and the nonself-presence implied in Moses's itinerary indicate not an absence of plenitude or a lack of self but a turning away from self-reference, an originary going out to the other.)

In each of these cases, "Judaism"—the meaning of which we can no longer take for granted—provides Levinas with a privileged precedent for his own thinking of the ethical. Yet, at the very same time, there is no immediate access to Judaism. Once again, to approach the Judaic in its specificity *requires* the detour through the Christian conceptuality. That is why the essay "Persons or Figures"—the only place in Levinas's work where he comments explicitly on the procedures of Christian interpretation—only hints at how the Judaic would appear over and against the Christian conceptuality (and in the remarks that follow, I will not get to the Judaic either but will remain primarily within this detour).

The following statement from the opening essay of *Difficult Freedom* is typical of the double reading which characterizes Levinas's approach to Judaism. He writes:

---

7. "Dialogue with Emmanuel Levinas," trans. Richard Kearney, in FF, 27. Catherine Chalier makes explicit the meaning of Judaism in Levinas's work and the relation between Judaism and modern philosophy: *Levinas: L'utopie de l'humain* (Paris: Albin Michel, 1993); *Figures du féminin: Lecture d'Emmanuel Levinas* (Paris: La nuit surveillée, 1982); *Pour une morale au-delà du savoir: Kant et Levinas* (Paris: Albin Michel, 1998); *Judaisme et altérité* (Paris: Verdier, 1982).

> For a long time Jews have thought that all the situations in which humanity recognizes its religious direction find in ethical rapports their spiritual signification, that is, their meaning for adults. In consequence they have thought morality in a very vigorous manner . . . And yet a long acquaintance with Christianity in the West has been able to create, even among Jews who are sincerely attached to Judaism . . . a state of uneasiness. Morality, social action, the concern for justice—all this would be excellent. But it would be only morals! An earthly propaedeutic! Too abstract to fill an inner life. Too poor in figures of style to recount the story of a soul. (*DF*, 4)

In other words: Judaism thinks the ethical. But precisely *to* the extent that it thinks the ethical, it finds itself lacking. Its very concern for earthly justice, however commendable, leaves it earthbound, stuck in immanence. The point will be echoed in one of Levinas's talmudic readings, where the ritual life of Judaism is characterized as not just "abstract" but "flat," lacking the spiritual heights and depths that make up what Levinas refers to as the Christian "drama" of personal salvation and the rich inner life it allows.[8] Judaism, on the other hand, is so oriented toward the exterior and the outside, it seems to lack even the possibility of such interiority. By lacking that which Levinas calls *temptation*—denoting at once sin and trial—it lacks the very means by which Christian experience (or, for Levinas, any experience) organizes itself. Lacking the turns of Christian experience—the aversions, peripeties, and conversions that figure and prefigure its way toward personal salvation—it lacks even the turns of phrase that would recount them. It is, as Levinas says above, "too poor in figures of style to recount the story of a soul" (*DF*, 4). Thus unable to narrativize itself (and without, in any case, a story to tell), Judaism would find neither the forms of biography (saints' lives) nor autobiography (narratives of personal conversion) available to it. It is too "poor in figure" or lacking figure.

Of course, these lacks can and should be referred, once again, to the importance, within Judaism, of the second commandment, which prohibits the making of images, and which has had a decisive impact on the specific course of the Jewish imagination. As Geoffrey Hartman suggests, all the forms of expression of the Jewish imagination are marked by this anti-iconic tendency. This accounts not only for Judaism's "text-dependency" but also for its particular ambivalence about imagination. For example, the Talmud—its central achievement—is, in Hartman's words, at once "liberated" and "hemmed in" by its necessary relationship

---

8. Levinas, "The Temptation of Temptation," 33.

to text and to a tradition of commentary.⁹ Moreover, Judaism's orienta-tion toward the exterior—its being what Levinas calls "all ears and obedi-ence *[tout oreille et tout obeissance]*" (*DF,* 50), expressed in a single word, *shema*—and its turning away from the visible seem grounded specifically in the biblical account of Sinaitic revelation. In that experience, as it is retold in Deuteronomy: "The Lord spoke to you out of the fire; you heard the sound of words but perceived no figure *[temunah]*—nothing but a voice."¹⁰ Would this be why Judaism is lacking figure?

TOO MANY FIGURES

When it comes to the Christian interpretive imagination, it is a matter, if anything, of *too* many figures. The essay, "Persons or Figures," ap-pearing in a section of *Difficult Freedom* entitled "Polemics," engages a commentary on the Old Testament by the poet Paul Claudel. As a polem-ical target of Levinas's essay, Claudel's commentary represents not an authoritative tradition of Christian exegesis but an aesthetic response to the Old Testament on the part of a giant of French letters. Claudel had, as a young man, converted to Catholicism; later in life, he wrote several biblical commentaries, including the 1949 *Emmaüs.*

As a biblical commentary, *Emmaüs* can be classified as an imaginative or poetic retelling. Levinas calls it a "personal exegesis" (*DF,* 119). Suffice it to say that it abounds in figural readings, taking as its guiding principle the Pauline phrase, "now *all* these things happened to them in a figure": *omnia in figura.*¹¹ Claudel's figural reading discovers not just the Old Tes-tament types which prefigure and announce events and persons of the New Testament. It also finds in the Old Testament, in a gesture that cites and echoes similar exegeses by Paul, prefigurations of the (pre)figural relationship itself. Thus for Claudel, Joseph is "a prefiguration of the

9. Geoffrey H. Hartman, "On the Jewish Imagination," *Prooftexts* 5 (1985): 201–20. Observing the Talmud's "associative way of going from topic to topic," Hartman also com-ments that "it . . . lacks that hypotactic unity of form or field characteristic of learned treatises in the West," 209.

10. Deuteronomy 4:12. *The Torah* (Philadelphia: Jewish Publication Society, 1962). Cf. Exodus 20:4: "You are not to make yourself a hewn-image or any figure *[temunah]* that is in the heavens above, that is on the earth beneath, that is in the waters beneath the earth." *Now These are the Names,* trans. Everett Fox (New York: Schocken, 1986). *Temunah* is often translated as "likeness," "representation."

11. In this way, Claudel relies extensively on the exegeses of the ninth-century com-mentator, Raban Maur, whose hermeneutics are discussed by de Lubac in *Exégèse,* vol. 1, pt. 1, 156–65.

Savior"; Essau and Jacob are "the intertwined conflict between Law and Grace." The Israelites stand at the foot of Mount Sinai, but, Claudel addresses them, "later, on another mountain, there will be Someone who will speak to you in something other than thunder and there will be no need for a Moses to interpret him." For "the commandments from Sinai are no longer merely external to me, that is, on the tablets of stone on which I find them written; they are—in a new sense—in my heart, in my most inward sensibility, my most secret communication." Claudel even has (his) Moses assert, as he descends Mount Sinai with a veil over his face, "I am *only* a figure *[Je ne suis qu'un figure]*."[12]

When Auerbach describes *figura*, he emphasizes the interpretive invention it encourages, the way in which it foregrounds the *ability* of the interpreter to discover resemblances in the biblical text. (This is at least as important as any actual accord between the two testaments.) But is he also correct to insist on the diversity of its productions? The fact is that, in the hands of Claudel at least, the Old Testament—read figurally—is a monotonous document indeed. Levinas asks:

> If all the unsullied characters in the Old Testament announce the Messiah, and all the unworthy ones, his executioners, and all the women, his mother, does not the Book of Books—obsessed by a single theme and invariably repeating the same stereotypical gestures—lose its lifelike quality *[sa vie vivante]*? (*DF*, 121)

When does a *type* become a *stereo*type? Is there not a price to pay for the discovery of Old Testament types or, in Levinas's terms, a loss? The loss, as Levinas formulates it, would be to the "lifelike" quality of the Old Testament, its sense of being rooted in concrete everyday situations, "material interests, crimes, jealousy, hatred, murder, that even fraternity does not resolve" (*DF*, 101). Levinas's formulation further implies that what is lost is not just the lifelike quality of the Old Testament but life itself, "its living life *[sa vie vivante]*." Whereas Auerbach has emphasized the living quality of *figura*, Levinas maintains in effect that the Old Testament thus is killed off by figural interpretation, is perhaps rendered truly (and for the first time) a dead letter.

One may well object that as a *representation* of life, rather than life itself, the Old Testament never had any life to lose. But let us not take for granted that we know what Levinas means by "living." In this usage, "living" does not necessarily refer to an organic model of whole-

---

12. Paul Claudel, *Emmaüs*, in *Oeuvres complètes de Paul Claudel*, vol. 23 (Paris: Gallimard, 1964), 73–439; translation mine. The cited passages are found on pp. 154, 146, 191, 346, 246.

ness, or to the presence of the present. It will have to do with the face and the distinctive way in which the face signifies. "The face is a living presence; it is expression," in the phrase from *Totality and Infinity* (*TI*, 66).

But there are other losses that figural interpretation incurs when it reads the Bible as a procession of types, a repertory of figures. Levinas intertwines his polemic against figural interpretation with his polemic against the mythological and the sacred, a realm of involuntary participation where events are played out "in spite of the self," thereby absolving the self of responsibility to the other. He asks,

> [D]oes the spiritual dignity of these men come from their reference to a drama situated on a miraculous plane, in a mythological and sacred beyond, or rather from the meaning that this life—which is conscience—gives to itself? (*DF*, 121)

The central assertion here is that the Christian emphasis on the other-worldly is at the expense of the Bible's reference to *this* life, which, says Levinas above, "is conscience," that is, the space of the ethical. If the Christian religious imagination can be characterized by its movement from sensory to nonsensory sense both in its interpretive modes and in its understanding of the economy of personal salvation, Judaism, with its perpetual recourse to the interhuman, can be understood as a refusal of this movement. Elsewhere in *Difficult Freedom*, Levinas writes: "Moses and the prophets are not concerned with the immortality of the soul, but with the poor one, the widow, the orphan, and the stranger" (*DF*, 19–20). "[I]t is on the earth, among men, that the adventure of spirit unfolds . . . in responsibility—whence comes the conception of a creature who has the chance to save himself without falling into the egoism of salvation" (*DF*, 26). And finally: "History is not a perpetual test with a diploma of eternal life as its goal, but the very element in which the life of spirit moves" (*DF*, 100). In short, the reference to the interhuman, to *this* life, is precisely what is most specific to Judaism and to the Judaic reading of the Bible. It is this distinctively Judaic reference that is lost in figural interpretation.

For even when figural interpretation does represent the interhuman, a loss of historicity results. As Levinas puts it, "[T]he relationships which man holds with himself and with his neighbors appear frozen [*figés*], unalterable, eternal" (*DF*, 99). The problem seems to go even further than figural interpretation's manner of representing the interhuman, or, for that matter, even further than its manner of representing the self's preoccupation with personal salvation. It has to do with the possibility of representing these things at all. To represent the rapport between persons is to "freeze" it; it is to turn what ought to be an ethical relationship into a theatrical pageant, into what is referred to above as "a drama situated on a miraculous plane."[13] Similarly, to represent the self's relationship with itself as a dramatic journey on the way toward personal salvation is to fall into what Levinas calls "the egoism of salvation" (*DF*, 26). In short, to aestheticize and theatricalize these rapports is to cover up the ethical. The very complicity between Christianity and the aesthetic turns the Bible into "a world of figures instead of a world of faces" (*DF*, 140). It is in this way, according to Levinas, that the Christian reading of the Hebrew Bible *loses* face.

LOSING FACE

Levinas will, however, counter the figural claim, and specifically, its double casting of each and every Old Testament character as a figure within a Passion that is always already a passion play. He writes:

> The holy history is not the interpretation of a thesis play *[une pièce à thèse]*, even if it is a transcendent one, but the articulation, made by a human freedom, of a real life. Are we on stage or are we in the world? Is to obey God to receive from him a role, or a command? We distrust this theater, this petrification of our faces, this character that our person would embrace *[Nous nous méfions du théâtre, de la pétrification de nos visages, de la figure que notre personne épouse]*. We distrust the poetry that already scans and bewitches our gestures, and all that which, in our lucid life, plays *[se joue]* in spite of us. It is because of this that in the final analysis the Claudelian exegesis leads us totally astray. A man as a person, as an agent of history seems to him less real than a figure-man, a statue-man *[l'homme-figure, l'homme-statue]*. The freedom proper to conscious man is enveloped in a kind of sublime and sacramental fate in which instead of *being*, man *figures [au lieu d'être, l'homme figure]*. God the director effaces God the Creator. He commands actors rather than freedoms. (*DF*, 121–22)

Here, figural interpretation is not merely said to freeze the rapport *between* persons; it freezes the persons themselves. In Levinas's words, it turns them into "figure-men" or "statue-men"; it "petrifies" the face. The charge could not be more serious. For in Levinas's work, the encounter with the other's *face* is the irreducible experience of what is called "ethics." It is the central meditation of his work, the "figure," as it were, for the human, and for the interhuman order as a whole. "Face" denotes the

13. Levinas writes: "It is as if our ancestors were dressed up in exotic costumes and made to speak in accents that render them, finally, unrecognizable" (*DF*, 122).

other (person) insofar as the other breaks out of the phenomenon, looks back, and speaks. "Face" denotes the infinite alterity of the other who, in his or her very poverty and distress, commands ethical responsibility or response.

To speak, then, of the petrification of the face is to announce an event which, within the terms of Levinas's ethical thought, is one of the worst things that could happen. It would be a violence directed *at* the face, the essential characteristic of which is mobility: "The face is a living presence; it is expression. The life of expression consists in undoing the form in which the existent exposed as a theme, is thereby dissimulated. The face speaks *[le visage parle]*" (*TI*, 66). If the face, in Levinas's descriptions, is not reducible to a plastic image, surface, or mask, that is largely because the face is always on the move, divesting itself of its form, confronting the self with its expression, speaking a primordial speech. Hence, at issue here is a violence directed not just at a face or at particular faces; the petrification of the face would do violence to the very possibility of the ethical's arising. It would put a stop to the ethical at the level of its condition of possibility. This is a violence which (because it would occur on this originary level) could serve as an alibi for all violent action. This "image" of the petrified face, the frozen face, denotes at once the violence directed at the face of the other—the loss of the other's face—and also the loss of face on the part of the figural interpreter. Claudel's figural reading loses face in this double sense when the Old Testament is said to prefigure, and thus to charge itself with, deicide: "Cain represents a certain kind of prefiguration of the Jewish people, the assassin of God."[14] Such an anti-Judaic reading may be an occupational hazard of figural interpretation, especially in its patristic and late medieval form. But when such a reading is advanced in 1949, that is, "after Auschwitz," it is, says Levinas, discourteous of our troubles (*DF*, 122).

In Levinas's terms, the figural reading of the Old Testament covers up "freedom," that is, the heteronomous freedom in responsibility that a Judaic reading of the same testament could reveal. Moreover, in saying that figural interpretation petrifies the face, Levinas implicitly reverses the Pauline reading of Moses descending Mount Sinai, tablets of stone in hand, a veil over his face to conceal its fading splendor, a reading in which the threat inherent in a literal, Judaic relation to the law, written on stone, is the petrification of the interpreter himself.[15]

14. Claudel, *Emmaüs*, 107.
15. 2 Corinthians 3:12–16. On the importance of this scriptural passage for medieval

But Levinas's ethical objection to figural interpretation goes well beyond his general assertion that the force of a specifically Judaic reading of the Old Testament is covered up. And here it is necessary to attend to a whole other register of Levinas's discourse, to a doubleness which makes it at once an ethical critique of Christian imaginative modes and also an antitheatrical, antipoetic, antiliterary discourse. Here the discourse on the Judaic—already double insofar as the Judaic is visible only in its difference from Christianity—is in turn doubled and intertwined with the discourse on the literary. In short, Levinas's antifigural discourse is not only anti*pre*figural but, ultimately, is directed against the *figurative* or *rhetorical* dimension of language as well.

TURNING AWAY FROM ART

In objecting to the "theatricalization" of ethical rapports in figural interpretation, Levinas seems also to object to the possibility of theatrical representation itself. "We distrust this theater," he writes. The very fact of a person's assuming a character or taking on a role is said to threaten the ontological status of the real: "instead of being, man figures" (*DF*, 122). To take on a character (*une figure*) is to risk *becoming* a figure, and thereby to lose what is human, to be turned into a statue, to be turned into stone. To take up a character is said to render one incapable of distinguishing illusion from reality, "stage" from "world," a directorial command from a divine one. In short, it is not just the figures of figural interpretation that are said to cover up the ethical. It is as if figures themselves were unethical, as if anything that *plays* were ethically suspect.[16] Levinas says: "We distrust that which plays *[se joue]* in spite of us."

One way to approach this distrust would be to situate Levinas's discourse within what Jonas Barish has called the antitheatrical prejudice. The tradition goes back to Plato, and his negative judgment on mimesis as ontologically derivative and debased, as well as to the Church Fathers, where the theater is viewed as too pagan and idolatrous, that is, as attached to what is visible and sensible. Levinas's formulations most resemble the antisacremental and antiliturgical strain within Protestant

---

biblical hermeneutics, see John Freccero, "Medusa: The Letter and the Spirit," in *Dante: The Poetics of Conversion*, ed. and with an introd. Rachel Jacoff (Cambridge, MA: Harvard University Press, 1986).

16. Robert Bernasconi also has noted this, with reference to a talmudic reading in which Levinas denounces those who sit in cafés. "The Ethics of Conscience," in *Between Levinas and Derrida* (Bloomington: University of Indiana Press), forthcoming.

Christianity, in which, as Barish puts it, the theater that is in question claims to *be* an enactment of the central truths of religion, and "the very thing . . . that reveals [its] devotional purpose . . . is the thing that offends . . . most bitterly."[17]

To consider Levinas's Claudel reading within such a context indeed helps to account for the specific crossing of religious and aesthetic motives there. But the larger problem at issue concerns this ethical philosopher's relation to the aesthetic. "We distrust the poetry that scans and bewitches our gestures," he writes. This statement should be read with the numerous instances in *Difficult Freedom* and in *Totality and Infinity* where Levinas invokes an aesthetic category to make an ethical charge. To cite just a few examples, "Violence is also in *poetic delirium* and enthusiasm, when we offer our mouth to the muse who speaks through us, in the fear and trembling of the sacred which tears us away from ourselves" (*DF,* 7). Or, "The numinous or the sacred envelops and transports man beyond his powers and wishes . . . [It] annuls the rapport between persons by making them participate, albeit ecstatically, in a *drama* not brought about willingly by them" (*DF,* 14). And finally, "When I maintain an ethical relation I refuse to recognize the role I would play in a *drama* of which I would not be the author or whose outcome another would know before me. I refuse *to figure* in a *drama* of salvation or of damnation that would be enacted in spite of me" (*TI,* 79).[18] In these statements, the terms of the aesthetic—poetry, drama, figure—are conjoined with Levinas's polemic against the sacred, against *participation,* a descriptive concept developed by Lucien Lévy-Bruhl to account for the blurring of the boundaries between the seen and the unseen world within mythical mentality. For Levinas the aesthetic terms denote (and substitute for) a loss of agency, a self-dispossession: the muse speaks *through* us; poetic delirium tears us away *from* ourselves, the drama is enacted *in spite of* me. These statements—all examples of the way in which the aesthetic gets troped—are altogether consistent with the explicit theory of the aesthetic Levinas proposes in the 1948 text "Reality and Its Shadow," to which I turn briefly now. Here too, the themes of petrification, immobilization, and freezing are prominent.

Art consists in substituting for the object its image, argues Levinas; it is an obscuring or a shadow of reality. Whereas "a concept is the object grasped, the intelligible object," and thus a "living" relationship with that

17. Jonas Barish, *The Antitheatrical Prejudice* (Berkeley: University of California Press, 1981), 79, to which my discussion of the tradition of antitheatricalism is indebted.

18. Cf. Levinas's reference to Claudel's singular poetic licence (*DF,* 119); and the opening and closing pages of "No Identity."

object, "the image *neutralizes* this real relationship" (RO, 3). Every image is in the last analysis plastic (and this includes the nonplastic arts of music and literature): every artwork is in the end a statue, an immobile instant, a stoppage of time and, ultimately, an idol. Levinas writes: "[T]he artist has given the statue a lifeless life, a derisory life, which is not master over itself, a caricature of life" (RO, 9). The interval, the between-time of art is "the petrification of the instant at the heart of duration." This makes the work of art something "inhuman" and "monstrous" (RO, 11).

The aesthetic state of mind is described by Levinas as participation, magic, captivation, incantation, play, and the "passage from oneself to anonymity" (RO, 4). The effect of the work of art on its audience is a loss of initiative, a passivity, a disengagement, an evasion of responsibility. Hence for Levinas the task of criticism becomes all-important: it serves to reintegrate the *in*human work into the *human* world, to detach it from its irresponsibility. As Levinas puts it, criticism puts the immobile statue into movement and makes it speak (RO, 12–13). I will provide a more detailed account of this essay in subsequent chapters, where I will endeavor to think through its relation to Levinas's other writings from the forties, especially around the notion of the *il y a*. But what does come into view even for a brief look is the severity of the denunciation of art, the presence of the now familiar oppositions—human/nonhuman, living/dead, mobile/immobile, play/ethical seriousness—and, finally, the specific argument that art brings about a passivity, a loss of initiative, and a loss of agency, the very agency from which ethics might spring. Here one must note that in the later works, which are *less* anthropological in their formulations, these very terms—loss of agency, passivity, loss of initiative—are positively inflected, are given, precisely, an ethical force. This double valence, this ambiguity surrounding key terms of Levinas's early discourse on art is, then, one of several issues that will be attended to.[19]

But what does emerge from Levinas's confrontation with poetry, drama, art, and figure is the way in which his position fits into a tradition of philosophical thinking about poetry, of philosophy's encounter with poetry, in which poetry, as Gerald L. Bruns puts it, is associated with things getting out of control.[20] Poetry is in tension with the philosophical

19. In an excellent article, Jean-Luc Lannoy notes the double valence of key terms. "D'une ambiguité," in *Études Phénomenologiques* 6 (1990), 11–44.

20. Gerald L. Bruns, *Hermeneutics: Ancient and Modern* (New Haven, CT: Yale University Press, 1992). Bruns also comments that while Levinas's insight sounds negative, and in a plain sense it is, he still gets at something essential. Heidegger too distinguishes between the nonhuman—animal, vegetable, mineral—and the inhuman, the not yet or no

project of wanting to get things right, to keep things straight, in tension with the self-control that characterizes philosophy's propositional style. Bruns identifies two paradigmatic ways in which philosophy deals with poetry: the Platonic strategy of exclusion, and the Aristotelian logic of exclusion *by* inclusion, namely, by the appropriation and domestication of poetry in a poetics.[21] Perhaps Levinas does not seem a philosopher who would be wedded to the propositional style: he has too many quirks, both conceptual and stylistic. But there is no question that he is a philosopher who is at pains to exclude the aesthetic. Perhaps, as Jean-François Lyotard remarks, he has put his wager so much on the *non*denotative discourse of the just and the unjust—an ethical discourse that we have frequently described as performative as opposed to constative—that he is compelled to exclude the *other non*denotative discourse, namely, rhetoric, the discursive arts of the writer and the orator "which draw on an 'aesthetic' value" and toward which "Levinas evinces the greatest suspicion" (LL, 124).

In closing this chapter then, and in necessarily abbreviated form, some questions. First, we have said that Levinas turns away from trope or figure when he articulates his (ethical) critique of figural interpretation, theatrical mimesis, and rhetorical figure. But in turning *away* from figure does he not also *turn?* Is there such a thing as a nonfigural position from which to speak? Second, we have noted Levinas's gesture of first subsuming all rhetoric under the category of persuasion, then rejecting it as ruse and violence. What if rhetoric were not conceived solely as intersubjective persuasion but also as trope, that is, as Paul de Man describes it, as having a cognitive dimension?[22] (Might this more complex view of rhetorical language be brought together with Levinas's own thinking about ethical language?) And, finally, what if all art, literature, and poetry were *not* mimesis? The terms of Levinas's ethical critique of mimesis (loss of the real world, loss of the person) are continuous with and proper to the very concept (mimesis) that he is purportedly criticizing. They rely on the same series of binary oppositions—stage/world, dramatic play/real life, character/person, and, the essay's central opposition, with the provocative either/or that its title reinforces, figure and person. But if mimesis were no longer *the* privileged trope for artistic making but simply one

---

longer human, the monstrous. He too associates poetry with the monstrous, and this is not altogether negative. See Bruns, *Heidegger's Estrangements* (New Haven, CT: Yale University Press, 1989).

21. Bruns, *Hermeneutics*, chap. 12.

22. See Paul de Man, *Allegories of Reading: Figural Language in Rousseau, Nietzsche, Rilke, and Proust* (New Haven, CT: Yale University Press, 1979).

trope among others, then it would be, as de Man suggests, like parono-
masis or punning, where language imitates sound on an *intra*linguistic
level, merely an example of language's choosing to imitate a nonverbal
entity with which it does not necessarily have anything in common.[23] In
short, if figure, rhetoric, mimesis, the literary were not what Levinas takes
them to be, then it might be necessary not to turn *away* from figure, as
Levinas does, but to face the figure otherwise, as language's ownmost
figurative potential, as that which is most distinctive to language, that is,
to face language *as* ethical possibility.

The resources for such a confrontation would be found—indeed, have
already been found—in Levinas's work itself, which describes the ethical
relation to the other as a kind of language, as responsibility, that is, as
language-response to the other who faces and who, "in turn," speaks.
"The face . . . *faces in* language" (*CPP,* xxx). And as Levinas himself has
surely taught us, ethics is something that "happens" in language. This is
what makes even the face, in the last analysis, a facing figure.

23. de Man, *The Resistance to Theory,* 10.

[4] *VISAGE, FIGURE*

SPEECH AND MURDER IN *TOTALITY AND INFINITY*

JUST SPEAKING

What would it mean to face "the ethics of ethics"? That is to say, to confront the very opening of the question of ethics—the grounds of both its possibility and impossibility—prior to the production and elaboration of all moral rules or precepts? According to Levinas, the face of the other is the very site and privileged figure for such an opening. In the face-to-face encounter, responsibility in its most original form of response, or language-response, arises. This chapter will consider the specificity of this language-response as Levinas describes it, the originary speech or "conversation" with the other. It will follow Levinas's description up to the point where all conversation ceases, namely, in the paradigmatic situation of murder that Levinas analyzes in *Totality and Infinity* (1961), "Freedom and Command" (1953), and in other early texts. In the course of this discussion, the Levinasian account of violence, as well as the relationship of violence to "face" and "speech," will be closely examined.

This chapter will also take up the question of the textual status of the face. Can there be a figure for the ethical? a figure for the face? The very question is problematic, in that rhetoric, as a science of figures, would be derivative upon Levinas's more originary description. Could the opening of the question of the ethical be marked with a certain figurality? And supposing that one can speak about an alterity that is rhetorical or textual, can the alterity of the other and textual alterity be even addressed in one breath? Here too, the question of ethics and the question of language come into their closest possible proximity.

Like the generosity which goes out *unto* the other without return or the aneconomical gift that demands consequently a radical ingratitude, "discourse" affirms the asymmetry and nonreversibility of the relation to the other. Discourse, in the particular interpellative sense that Levinas gives it,[1] is a direct and immediate relation to the other. It reaches the other without touching him. It maintains a relation of infinite distance, "without this distance destroying this relation and without this relation destroying this distance" (*TI*, 41). It is as if the discourse had the very movement of infinity in it.

In the *fact* of this speaking relationship to the face of the other can be found the entire significance of the ethical relation. This factical dimension of speaking is more important than any content of the discourse. The whole possibility of a *just* relation to the face is there. The term with which Levinas often characterizes this language relation is *droiture:* "straightforwardness," "uprightness," "rectitude," "justice." Not only is the language relation *to* the face characterized by a singular straightforwardness, but the language *of* the face is also said to possess an exceptional "sincerity" and "frankness": "the eyes break through the mask—the language of the eyes, impossible to dissemble *[indissimulable]*" (*TI*, 66). To the direct and straightforward rapport with the face, Levinas often opposes the indirection and obliqueness he associates with rhetoric. Rhetoric approaches the neighbor from (or with) an angle. Levinas's entire discourse on ethical language (and its distinction from nonethical language or rhetoric) is dominated by an opposition between the geometrical figures of facing and the angle.

Levinas's denigration of rhetoric, which he invariably conceives as persuasion, is essentially classical and Platonic. But even if Levinas assimilates *all* rhetoric to persuasion (to action between subjects, to an *inter*subjective level) and ignores the level of rhetoric that Paul de Man calls trope (a level which is cognitive and *intra*linguistic), it is not easy to assign a place to this fact, or to evaluate the consequences of Levinas's denigration of rhetoric and his privileging of ethical language. The "straightforwardness," the "sincerity" that is at issue, occurs not on the positivistic level of a denotative phrase universe but on the level of an originary language response to the other that *opens* ethics. There is an asymmetry

---

1. The interpellative sense Levinas gives "discourse" is at a distance from ordinary definitions. Compare Paul Ricoeur who, summarizing a tradition that goes back to Aristotle, defines discourse as "the intertwining of noun and verb," the conjunction of which "brings forth a predicative link." *Discourse and the Surplus of Meaning*, 1–2.

between what Levinas calls ethical language and rhetoric, just as there is an incommensurability between the originary discourse and the derivative science of figures. Even if this incommensurability turns out to be only apparent (if, say, a Levinasian view of ethical language and a de Manian view of rhetoric can be brought together), there may still be good reasons why figure is hostile to what Levinas calls "face."

To figure a face is to de-face it. Perhaps it is the legacy of *figura*, and the "plastic form" that is, for Erich Auerbach, its earliest meaning (even if, in the later, rhetorical usage, the sense of "figure" is nonplastic). Figure invariably implies a certain plasticity, but the face, in every description Levinas gives of it, is precisely that which is *not* reducible to a plastic image, to any phenomenal or visible figure. Levinas says in an interview: "I can certainly look at a face while defacing it *[je peux certes regarder le visage en le dévisageant]*, like any plastic form" (*IR*). But there is violence in reducing a face to an object or thing seen, "transforming faces into objective and plastic forms, into visible—but defaced—figures *[transformation des visages . . . en figures visibles, mais dévisagées]*" (*IR*).[2] To encounter the face *as* face is, as in the paradigmatically ethical transfer when my gaze turns into discourse, to face the other as interlocutor. Not only do I face the face in language, the face also faces *in* language: "the face speaks" (*TI*, 66).

SPEAKING FACE

Derrida has remarked in "Violence and Metaphysics" that it may be "tempting" to consider this discourse on the face a prosopopoeia (*VM*, 101). Surely this is because, in the most general sense, the giving of face or prosopopoeia is the governing figure of Levinas's discourse. More specifically, when Levinas gives the face *as* voice, as he repeatedly does, he in a sense de-faces it, gives it as *figure*. At times it is as if figuration performs the desired (ethical) break in phenomenality, the turn away from the optical. But while the ethicofigural transfer from gaze to voice seems tropological (and the figure would be synesthesia, a crossing of sensory attributes),[3] such a judgment would seem to presuppose a sequential narrative, which is in tension with the anteriority of the experienced that is

2. In this context to figure a face is lined up with the necessary violence in which the question of justice intervenes in ethics.

3. The figure is evident in the paradigmatic turn from vision to generosity and discourse. The verb which marks the transformation, *se muer*, "to turn, to moult, to metamorphose," implies a break, within the figural turn, in phenomenality.

described. The facing face does not become discourse; "[T]he manifestation of the face is *already* discourse" (*TI,* 66). The "already" belongs to an immemorial past that is accessible to no present.

The face occurs as a collision between world and that which exceeds world. To the extent that the face is out of world, it appears *in* the world as naked and destitute. Naked—that is, without clothing, covering, or mask—it signifies without attributes, outside any categories, not across its generality, but by itself, and this is the technical sense of Levinas's term expression *kath 'auto.* He says: "There is first the very uprightness of the face, its upright exposure, without defense *[la droiture même du visage, son exposition droite, sans défense].* The skin of the face is that which stays the most naked . . . the most destitute *[la plus nue . . . la plus dénuée]*" (*EI,* 86). The face's destitution is an essential destitution, its nakedness and its wretchedness a mark of its absence and exile from the world. In the nakedness of expression, the face signifies—before all semiosis—with an exceptional *droiture,* presenting itself in person, present to itself as a "coincidence of the expressed with him who expresses" (*TI,* 66).

Levinas insists often on the distinctive way in which facial expression signifies. Usually when we encounter things we do so within a system of relations, across a generality, or as categorized by disclosure (FC, 20). The signification of a being is relative to a *context* or in its relation to another thing (*EI,* 86). The face, however, is not disclosed; it is "divested of its categories, a being becoming naked, an unqualified substance breaking through its form" (FC, 20). While Levinas's discussion of the *kath 'auto* has a technical sense, takes in an entire philosophical heritage, and includes a polemic against Heidegger's emphasis on disclosure and dissimulation, there is a simple meaning as well. Unlike other signs, facial expressions signify only themselves. They do not refer to something else, to states of mind or feeling. Their autosignification is presemiotic and has no cognitive content:

> Expression does not consist in presenting to a contemplative consciousness a sign which that consciousness interprets by going back to what is signified. What is expressed is not just a thought which animates the other; it is also the other present in that thought. Expression renders present what is communicated and the one who is communicating *[le communiqué et le communiquant];* they are both in the expression. But that does not mean that expression gives us knowledge about the other. The expression does not speak about someone, is not information about a coexistence, does not invoke an attitude in addition to knowledge; expression invites one to speak to someone. The most direct attitude before a being *kath 'auto* is not the knowledge one can have about him but is precisely social commerce with him. (FC, 20–21)

Levinas would distinguish this self-coincidence (of addressor and message, as it were) from a Romantic (or proto-Romantic) view of facial expression as the exteriorization of an inward state. For example, Augustine formulates the self-coincidence of facial expression semiotically when, in the face of a friend, he finds "the signs which proceed from the heart . . . and are revealed in the face, the voice, the eyes." In describing a coincidence between the movement of the heart and facial expression, he proposes that the face's signs have a necessary rather than arbitrary relation to their meaning.[4]

Of course, Levinas would distinguish his view of facial expression from all semiotic accounts. He claims that if the face signified in the manner of other signs, it would be reducible to the referrals inherent in sign systems, namely, to a play of immanence. It would be an apparent contour, a surface, like "the face of a building." It would be a mask, which is for Levinas derivative upon face. In the 1963 essay "The Trace of the Other," Levinas distinguishes the face's signification from the order of disclosure, the symbolic, and the semiotic order: "A face . . . is not a form concealing, but thereby indicating, a ground, a phenomenon that hides, but thereby betrays a thing itself. Otherwise a face would be one with a mask—but a mask presupposes a face" (T, 355).

The question arises: Why does Levinas endow the face (whose facing happens in language) with a power of autosignification that is in language wildly impossible? The autosignification that is the limit condition of ethics and of "discourse" as ethics has nothing to do with language's everyday functioning. Perhaps one should expect a ground to be heterogeneous to that which it grounds. But why is the language that is proposed to condition language one that suffers neither deferral, dehiscence, or delay? To put the question in yet another but more restricted way: Can facial expressions be kept altogether apart from sign relations? In the semiotic version of the self-coincidence of facial expression suggested by Augustine, the face's signs reveal the movement of the heart and thus, in facial expression, the relationship between sign and meaning, usually conventional and arbitrary, is necessary. Such a view that sign and meaning coincide in the face is not atypical.[5] It can be argued, however, that

4. *Confessions* 4.8. In *On Christian Doctrine* 2.1–2, Augustine will describe facial expression as an example of a borderline case between the two types of signs, natural and conventional.

5. It is at the basis of physiognomy, the idea that the signs of facial expression reveal character. Edouard Dhorme summarizes the biblical view that "the affections of the soul . . . are painted on the face." He writes: "It is thus that the state of the soul of an individual appears on the face; it is by his face that one can know his passions, his emotions, his feelings

a facial expression can always *become* a conventional sign, that is, one in which there is discrepancy between sign and meaning. Paul de Man uses the example of "a smile that hides rage or hatred" in an examination of the double consequences of the arbitrary nature of the sign: "It is the distinctive privilege of language to be able to hide meaning behind a misleading sign . . . but it is the distinctive curse of all language, as soon as any kind of interpersonal relation is involved, that it is forced to act this way."[6] The discrepancy between sign and meaning liberates the subject, who is "privileged" to exploit and manipulate signs in a playful manner, to hide rage behind a smile (to privilege sign over meaning). But it also puts into question the subject, "who," in the case of an authentic smile (i.e., in a case where he would wish meaning to predominate over sign), is "forced" to use the same sign. For de Man, the impossibility of making sign and meaning coincide results in a world of "potentially inauthentic" social relationships.[7] But for Levinas and his philosophy of face, is this not to acknowledge that facial expressions necessarily employ semiotic conventions?

Of course, this is precisely what Levinas does *not* mean by face. The face in Levinas's descriptions cannot dissimulate; it is *prior* to rhetoric, mask, semiosis—to meaning itself. "The alternative between truth and lies, between sincerity and dissimulation, is the privilege of him who abides in the relation of absolute frankness *[absolue franchise]*" (*TI,* 66). For Levinas, to decode a face in the manner of other signs would be to reduce it violently, to turn it—horribly—into a mask, that is, not just a surface but something petrified and immobile.[8] To *figure* a face would

---

and even his wishes. His entire being is imprinted on his face and is expressed by it. If the soul or the heart characterizes his being in itself, the face characterizes it for others." *L'emploi métaphorique des noms de parties du corps en hébreu et en akkadien* (Paris: Librairie orientaliste Paul Geuthner, 1963), 51, 59.

6. Paul de Man, "Criticism and Crisis," in *Blindness and Insight: Essays in the Rhetoric of Contemporary Criticism,* 2d ed. rev. (Minneapolis: University of Minnesota Press, 1983), 11. The essay was first published in 1967.

7. De Man's assertion that "there is no a priori privileged position of sign over meaning or meaning over sign" and his emphasis on "inauthenticity" as a consequence may be compared to Umberto Eco's discussion of the close relationship between signification and lying. Eco writes: "Semiotics is concerned with everything that can be taken as a sign . . . Thus semiotics is in principle the discipline studying everything which can be used in order to lie." *A Theory of Semiotics* (Bloomington: Indiana University Press, 1976), 7.

8. For this reason, Erving Goffman's analyses and decoding of "face-work," while immensely suggestive for a (social) idiom of face, would be derivative upon the Levinasian conception.

have to be accounted a similar violence (and there is surprising agreement on this point between de Man and Levinas). If the face is presemiotic, it is certainly prior to figure as well.

One may well reflect on the necessity by which Levinas nonetheless seeks to privilege meaning over sign, on *this* side of meaning, on a level that precedes meaning, or the necessity by which Levinas reconstitutes metaphysical oppositions such as direct/indirect, expression/sign (aligned with facing/angle, justice/violence) *pre*semiotically, asymmetrically, situating the first term of the opposition on a quasi-transcendental level. There is a certain phonocentrism in Levinas's description of the self-coincidence of expression, which renders it complicit with what Derrida has called the metaphysics of presence. Such turns of phrase as "expression renders present what is communicated and the one who is communicating" (FC, 21) or, elsewhere in his work, the assertions that expression means "being behind the sign," or that "he who manifests himself comes, according to Plato's expression, to his own assistance" (*TI*, 66), all seem part of a privileging of oral discourse as "plenitude" (*TI*, 96), as a presence to oneself (VM, 101–2). As Blanchot remarks, it is at just these moments that the Levinasian "conversation" or *entretien* "becomes a tranquil humanistic speaking again" (*IC*, 56). This is largely a result of the privileging of oral discourse in Levinas. (For Levinas rarely uses the word "man." Recall that the *visage* is defined as the way in which the other presents himself, exceeding the idea of the other in me. The *visage* is man in his infinite alterity, man *insofar as* he is infinitely other. *Visage* is not a description added on to the conception of "man"; it is prior to it.) But that the Levinasian *entretien* would revert to a humanistic conversation is also due to a fault of the language ("our" language), which is weighted toward the hermeneutical and the dialectical.

In *The Infinite Conversation*, Blanchot elaborates on the radicality of the Levinasian *entretien*, which "is held between *[se tient entre]* two points which do not constitute a system, a cosmos, a totality" (*TI*, 96). Of this nontotalizing conversation in which the *entre* designates an interval held up over a void, an abyss, Blanchot writes: "[W]hat is present in this presence of speech as soon as it affirms itself, is precisely what never lets itself be seen or attained: something is there that is beyond the reach of the one who says it as much as of the one who hears it. It is between us, it holds itself between *[se tient entre]* and the *entretien* is approach on the basis of this between, an irreducible distance" (*IC*, 212). Joseph Libertson comments: "The French *entretenir*, unlike the English 'converse' has an intransitive resonance which suggests the pure impersonality of a subsistence 'between,' 'supported' by two instances, a pure abiding, which is absent from the sense of exchange and activity in the word 'conversation'" (*PRX*, 277). Speech with the other is "the other of closure . . . which is irreducible to the empirical or dialectical opposition of two subjects" (*PRX*, 277). Conversation not to be confused with the image of two constituted poles between which the speech appears (even if this confusion is to some extent unavoidable) (*IC*, 73), an image that "responds to the crude scheme of two powers" (*SL*, 199). Moreover, Libertson comments, this speech "does not stand between; it stands outside" (*PRX*, 279).

This founding conversation preserves the absolute asymmetry between discussants. The other, described alternately by Levinas as the Most-High and the weak one, seems at times the overlord, and at times the utterly helpless and destitute. Hence despite the formal symmetry of the phrase "face-to-face," despite the con-frontation it invariably suggests, Blanchot comments, "I never face the one who faces me. My manner of facing the one who faces me is not an equal confrontation of presences" (*IC*, 62). This is why Levinas speaks at the close of *Totality and Infinity* of "the curvature of intersubjective space which inflects distance into elevation" (*TI*, 291).

Speech with the other does not familiarize; it is "the access to man in his strangeness" (*IC*, 62). To preserve this strangeness, the speech must be characterized by nonreciprocity and noncomprehension. But how to speak *to* the other without comprehension (a form of "repatriation")? Would this not occasion the grossest misunderstanding?[9] Foundational and empty, contentless (or at least, precontent), it is "speech without comprehension [*entente*] to which I must nonetheless respond" (*IC*, 65), writes Blanchot. Such a speech (like the law that is done before understanding and even before hearing) is, in an important sense, impossible. *Parler sans pouvoir* is what Blanchot calls it, that is, to speak without power, to speak without being able (to speak), to speak without ability. Speech with the face as speech with the outside (although Levinas generally uses the term *exteriority*), for *Autrui* is "always coming from the outside" (*IC*, 56). Speech with the outside, it is speech with the "stranger, the destitute, the proletarian" (*TI*, 75), or, in the biblical locution that Levinas frequently invokes, "the stranger, the widow, the orphan." The

9. This question has been posed by both Lyotard and Derrida: If ethical discourse would be not a referential or denotative speech, which merely constates the ethical relation, but one which accomplishes and performs it, how to speak about Levinas's discourse without rendering its performative dimension constative, assimilating it to the denotative language of the same? See Lyotard, LL; and Derrida, ATM.

other is "always, in relation to me, without country, stranger to all possession, dispossessed and without dwelling, he who is as if 'by definition'
the proletarian . . ." (*IC*, 56).

SPEAKING MURDER

> The being that expresses itself, that faces me, says *no* to me by his very expression. (FC, 21)

> [The other] opposes to me not a greater force . . . but precisely the infinity of his
> transcendence. This infinity, stronger than murder, already resists us in his face, is his
> face, is the primordial expression, is the first word: "[T]hou shalt not kill." (*TI*, 199)

> The face, it is inviolable; these eyes absolutely without protection, the most naked part
> of the human body, offer, nevertheless, an absolute resistance to possession, an absolute
> resistance in which the temptation of murder is inscribed: the temptation of an absolute
> negation. The other is the sole being that one can be tempted to kill. This temptation
> of murder and this impossibility of murder constitute the very vision of the face. To
> see a face is already to hear: "Thou shalt not kill." (*DF*, 8)

It is only in Levinas's analysis of murder that the face's speaking is given
a particular content, albeit negative. Levinas asserts that the expression
"says no," that the "primordial expression," "the first word" is an order,
"[T]hou shalt not kill," that "to see a face is already to hear: '[T]hou shalt
not kill.' " How to understand this primordial expression? As an utterance
it is imperative and interlocutionary. To call it a prohibition may be to
take too much for granted. (What is a prohibition if it can occur on such
a primordial level?) Jean-François Lyotard likens the Levinasian description of the primordial utterance to the biblical diction in which God
commands, "Listen!" or "Hear O Israel." This is a prescription that in
effect tells its addressee, "Get yourself into a situation where you are
ready to hear a prescription." This prescription arises from the very *fact*
of the other's speaking to me. That is why as paradigm, "[T]hou shalt
not kill" has something misleading about it. Most of the time in Levinas's
descriptions the other's command is not a categorical prescription but a
more general "prescription that there be prescriptions" (*JG*, 22). In other
words, most of the time there is something deliberately empty and general about the other's speaking command. There is, however, a more
general (noncategorical) sense of the primordial "Thou shalt not kill" in
Levinas's work: it brings about a cessation of power and possibility in
the I who is thus addressed. As Lyotard reads it, the prescription "You
shall not kill" turns the I into a *you*, into the recipient of a command
(*DI*, 111).

"Thou shalt not kill," or its shortened form, "No," is the only utterance that Levinas, in his earlier work, proposes for the primordial lexicon. This choice suggests the enigmatic relation between murder and primordial speech. It suggests the way in which the (im)possibility of murder inhabits the language relation to the other at its origin. Blanchot writes:

> Such would be the speech that measures the relation of man face-to-face with man, when there is no choice but to speak or to kill. A speech as grave, perhaps, as the death of which it is the detour. The speech/murder alternative is not the tranquil exclusion of one by the other, as if it were a matter of choosing once and for all between good speech and bad death . . . in this situation, either to speak or to kill, speech does not consist in speaking, but first of all in maintaining the movement of the *either/or*; it is what founds the alternative. (*IC*, 62)

The speech with the face occurs on the level at which killing is avoided. With this primordial speech, an alternative presents itself: either to welcome infinity or to reject it, to speak or to kill. The sense of killing must be enlarged here beyond its literal meaning to a more general sense. The warrant for this will be found in the very continuity between Levinas's account of murder and his account of all instances of transcendental violence. The speech/murder alternative, however, does not belong to a subject who could choose or initiate an action. The ethical speaking without *pouvoir* takes its life from a certain experience of impossibility. It is a matter of not a humanistic speech that keeps the peace but a *grave* speech—in both senses of the term—a speech in which there circulates the violence that belongs to the very nature of possibility.

Just as the speech with the other is precisely not part of a dialogue in the usual sense, so too the other's primordial expression is not an utterance in the usual sense where the sender and the receiver are already constituted entities. Expression "speaks" on the level of face, that is, on the level of distress, nudity, and exposure to violence. In Levinas's descriptions, the face wears a double aspect. It is at once absolutely defenseless and also that which "opposes my power over it, my violence . . . in an absolute way" (FC, 21). The face is delivered up to my powers and, at the same time, refuses them.

These powers are, at the limit, murderous. Vision is a violence; it would possess the other; it is even "by essence murderous" (*TI*, 47). The habitual economy is shot through with violence and the drive for possession. According to the account Levinas gives in his writings from the 1950s there is violence within the habitual economy "whenever one acts as though one were alone" (FC, 18; *DF*, 6). This extends to satisfaction of a need, knowledge of an object. "Knowledge seizes an object; it possesses it" (*DF*, 8). What departs from the order of violence is the fact of facing and the discourse that ensues. "What characterizes a violent act is the fact that one does *not* face" (FC, 19).

But in the violence specific to vision there is a temptation of murder ("this temptation of murder . . . constitutes the very vision of the face" [*DF*, 8]). The temptation would seem to arise in the face's phenomenal-ization, in the sensuous moment of expression (*ex-primere*, to press out), that is, to the precise extent that the face can be contained by an adequating vision. But ultimately, the manner in which the temptation arises is more complicated. It is due to an ambiguity within expression itself, namely, the fact that the face lodges itself in form and also goes beyond the form. Not just its presenting itself in sensible form but also its divesting itself of its form, its nakedness, exposes it to murder. The temptation is inscribed then, not just in the face's phenomenality but in its beyond-phenomenality. Hence the face's expression invites murder. Yet, Levinas stresses, it also prohibits it. In its very defenselessness, it absolutely resists the murderous intent: "This temptation of murder and this impossibility of murder constitute the very vision of the face" (*DF*, 8).

There are several registers of this impossibility that we will let resonate in the following discussion of Levinas's analysis of murder. The first and the plainest sense is that murder is, morally, abhorrent: "The authority of the prohibition is maintained in the bad conscience of the accom-plished evil—malignancy of evil" (*EI*, 87). But the central emphasis that Levinas gives this impossibility is this: murder is doomed in advance to a certain failure. He writes: "Murder exercises a power over what escapes power. It is still a power, for the face expresses itself in the sensible, but already impotency, because the face rends the sensible" (*TI*, 198). Murder wants to kill the other, who is (by definition) beyond the sensible. Yet in murdering the other, it arrives only at the sensible. In this way, murder always misses its mark. No doubt it effects an annihilation of the other in his being. But it thereby misses the genuine alterity of the other, namely, that which in him goes beyond the sensible (and that which in him is beyond being).

It is here that we might begin to think the relation of murder and speech in yet another way. Does not murder aim at speech itself, at that language possibility (or language-trace) of the other that is his alterity? Does it not necessarily aim at the "discourse" by which the other comes from behind his appearance, namely, at a speaking face?

There is not the space here to pursue these complex questions. Suffice it to remark that in the other's language-trace, in the infinity that the other speaks, lies the impossibility of murder and the indestructibility of the other.[10]

One of the difficulties of Levinas's analysis comes from his assertion that it is in the face's absolute resistance to possession that the temptation of murder is inscribed. How is it that the resistance itself is the temptation? What is the nature of this resistance? As Levinas explains it, the face is "total resistance without being a force" (FC, 19). In murder, however, "one identifies the absolute character of the other with his force" (FC, 19). In other words, one mistakes the other's resistance *for* a force. The mistake comes from not facing, from indirection, from the angle: "Violence consists in ignoring this opposition . . . and catching sight of an angle whereby the *no* inscribed on a face by the very fact that it is a face becomes a hostile or submissive force. Violence is a way of acting on every being and every freedom by approaching it from an indirect angle" (FC, 19). Blanchot explains this colossal "mistake" as a violent misreading—as it were—of infinity: murder takes the infinity by which *Autrui* presents himself as if it were a property of *Autrui* and wishes to reject it absolutely. Thereby it misses *Autrui;* "it changes him into absence, but does not touch him" (IC, 61). Thus the one who murders is caught in a substitutive structure; he is like a man who must aim at his target (infinity) over and over again and always miss it. (That is why he cannot kill his victim enough times.) The infinite alterity of the speaking face is "incommensurate with a power exercised"; there is a "disproportion between infinity and my powers" (TI, 198). And it is in this sense that while murder is a *real* possibility, it is what Levinas calls an "*ethical impossibility.*"

"The face defies not just the weakness of my powers but my power of power [*mon pouvoir de pouvoir*]" (TI, 198). The other opposes to me "not a greater force" (TI, 199) but "the resistance of that which has no resistance—ethical resistance" (TI, 199) or "intelligible resistance," as Levinas calls it in "Freedom and Command."[11] Derrida calls this a "strange, unthinkable notion of unreal resistance" (VM, 104), thus implying its heterogeneity to philosophical intelligibility itself. The face's opposition is one that "no finite power can restrict" (VM, 104). The ethical

10. Blanchot's reflections on the indestructible, in a section of *IC* devoted to Robert Antelme's *L'espèce humaine* (130–35), are indispensable for such a direction of thought.

11. "If the impossibility of killing were a real impossibility, if the alterity of the other were only the resistance of a force, his alterity would be no more exterior to me than that

impossibility of murder means precisely, and here is, again, its enlarged sense: the face's expression, "which prohibits me with the original language of its defenseless eyes,"[12] brings about a cessation of my murderous *pouvoir* at the level on which any particular power could originate. Levinas has described it as an intentionality in reverse (*TI,* 84). But here is also the positive significance of the impossibility of murder. In "Freedom and Command," Levinas explains that the "no" that the face opposes to me is "not the *no* of a hostile force or threat . . . it is the possibility of encountering a being through an interdiction" (FC, 21). Again, not a force in the world, interdiction is unlike repression. It has an ethical positivity; it signals an ethical relationship. The interruption of the "imperialism of the same" (*TI,* 39) is also welcome, gift and the originary response of responsibility.

As in earlier textual instances in Levinas's work, this interruption is marked by an ethicofigural turn of speech, a quasi-synesthetic turn from my vision to the other's voice, or from the sense of seeing to that of hearing: "[T]o see a face is already *to hear* 'Thou shalt not kill.' " But is this a matter of hearing, with its connotation of self-coincidence, at all? The face's primordial expression is a *citation,* that is, it is characterized not by phenomenality but by the structure of the mark, with the constitutive absence that implies. Moreover, the "voice" delivers a commandment from an immemorial past, accessible to no present: "To see a face is *already* to hear [*voir un visage, c'est déjà entendre*]: '[T]hou shalt not kill' " (*DF,* 8). This "already" ruptures self-coincidence. Thus when Levinas gives the face as voice here, again he gives the face *as* (nonphenomenal, nonplastic, ethical) *figure.* He gives the face as a figure for, one might add, the originary donation of the law, in all the literality of its imposition. But that the face *(visage)* could be a figure *(figure)* was always possible within the semantic destination of the word.

Similarly, within the semantic field and also before the semantic field, face and mask can converge. Even an ethical reading of face yields this possibility. The murderer who takes violent aim at the face of the other does not truly *face* the other. He thus loses not only the face of the other

of nature which resists my energies, but which I come to account for by reason; it would be no more exterior than the world of perception which, in the final analysis, is constituted by me. The ethical impossibility of killing is a resistance made to me, but a resistance which is not violent, an intelligible resistance" (FC, 21–22).

12. Levinas, "Transcendence and Height," trans. Simon Critchley with Tina Chanter and Nicholas Walker, in BPW, 12. "Transcendance et hauteur," in *Bulletin de la Société Française de Philosophie* 56 (1962).

but also his own face, that is, he is ashamed, and, as it were, forfeits his own alterity. "When Cain saw that the Lord did not accept his sacrifice, he became inflamed and his face fell *[wa-niphlo panav]*" (Gen. 4:5). There is something overdetermined about the biblical diction here, beyond any physiognomy. Cain's face falls, denoting displeasure, anger, a feeling of rejection. He loses face proleptically, for he is about to try to make himself master of that which exceeds him absolutely, the other, Abel. (In Blanchot's reading, "the incomprehensible inequality of the divine favor" is, precisely, the other's transcendence [*IC*, 61].) Cain loses face, or is out of face, in part because that face was never anything but a showing, a mask, a violent angle on the other, like the ruse of a rhetoric. A great deal is at stake in Levinas's work in being able to keep separate face, the locus of the revelation of alterity, and mask, the covering or cloak for face. But if one *can* lose face (within a rigorously ethical understanding and in accordance with an ethical diction), cannot face be given? Is there not a dimension of face that is rhetorical in yet another sense (in the sense not of persuasion but of trope)? If one *can* lose face, then it is always possible that the face can be a mask. Always possible and hence a necessary possibility[13]: mask is structured as a necessary possibility of face. Despite the asymmetry between face and mask, like that between facing/angle, ethical language/rhetoric, justice/violence, expression/sign, trace/sign, the consequences of this necessary possibility would be a certain intercontamination of the governing oppositions of Levinas's discourse. Then there would be, again, a rhetorical dimension, a figurality, of face, of the very face that commands ethical response. This means that the face is to some extent a face-mask or a figure-face.[14] It also means that there can be "face" in figure. But is not "figuration" itself transformed by such a usage? What is figure, if there can be face in it?

It remains to consider the theological dimension of Levinas's description. After all, the primordial expression is a *biblical* citation, one of God's commandments, the sixth commandment, even if it is revealed not by God but, in Levinas's rewriting, in the face of the other man. Does its presence imply that Levinas's ethics are dependent on the revealed morality of positive religion? In brief, it does not, for Levinas's definition

13. Jacques Derrida, "Signature Event Context," trans. Samuel Weber and Jeffrey Mehlman, *Glyph* 1 (1977).

14. For a careful and rigorous discussion of what is at stake in the production of the rhetorical figure that gives face, especially in the writings of de Man, see Cynthia Chase, *Decomposing Figures: Rhetorical Readings in the Romantic Tradition* (Baltimore: Johns Hopkins University Press, 1986), 82–112.

of religion is as removed from the ordinary sense of the term as is his definition of ethics: "[W]e propose to call religion the bond that is established between the same and the other without constituting a totality" (TI, 40). Yet Levinas does, nonetheless, cite one of the ten commandments, which are at the center of the revealed morality of the Judeo-Christian tradition. Here it is necessary to observe that Levinas is concerned not with a unitary Judeo-Christian tradition but rather with the Judaic, and particularly the rabbinic, tradition as a "source" or a resource for his ethics. Moreover, Levinas distances the Judaic from the interpretation it has received within the unitary Judeo-Christian tradition. Judaism, as Levinas recovers it, is a reinscribed, post-Heideggerian Judaism that is equivalent neither to the determinations it has received within the dominant "Greco-Christian" conceptuality nor to Judaism as a historical or positive religion, although it necessarily takes off from there.

One may still wish to ask, What is the specific religious meaning of the commandment "Thou shalt not kill"? Is it not significant that within historical Judaism the concept of murder is enlarged, according to one commentator, to include even "*the omission* of any act by which a fellow-man could be saved in peril, distress, or despair"?[15] Such a reference may help to illuminate the spirit of Levinas's murder analysis and the way in which interdiction produces the very positivity of obligation, generosity, gift, and discourse. But Levinas's phenomenological descriptions of the relation to the other already make the "religious" (in his sense) meaning of the commandment quite explicit. Its "religious" meaning is the imperative of response or responsibility that arises in the encounter with the other who faces in language.

AND CAIN SAID TO ABEL

What did Cain say to Abel immediately before he murdered him? In Genesis 4:8, there is a lacuna in the text (preserved in the Masoretic tradition), where the verse is incomplete: "And Cain said to Abel his brother . . . " "The Hebrew *vayommer* means not 'told' or 'spoke to' but 'said unto,' and the words said ought to follow."[16] The text of Genesis 4, verses 3–8, in Everett Fox's translation, reads,

15. *Pentateuch and Haftorahs*, ed. J. H. Hertz (London: Soncino Press, 1978), 299. In *Correlations in Rosenzweig and Levinas*, Robert Gibbs calls Levinas's "a religion without sacrality" (Princeton, NJ: Princeton University Press, 1992), 266.

16. Harry M. Orlinsky, ed., *Notes on the New Translation of the Torah* (Philadelphia: Jewish Publication Society, 1969), 68.

It was, after the passing of days that Kayin brought, from the fruit of the soil, a gift to YHWH, and as for Hevel, he too brought—from the firstborn of his flock, from their fat parts. YHWH had regard for Hevel and his gift, for Kayin and his gift he had no regard. Kayin became exceedingly enraged and his face fell. YHWH said to Kayin: Why are you so enraged? Why has your face fallen? Is it not thus: If you intend good, bear-it-aloft, but if you do not intend good, at the entrance is sin, a crouching-demon, toward you his lust—but you can rule over him. Kayin said to Hevel his brother . . . But then it was, when they were out in the field, that Kayin rose up against Hevel his brother and he killed him.[17]

In numerous versions of the Bible (such as the Samaritan, Greek, Syriac, Old Latin, and Vulgate), and consequently, in most translations, the missing phrase is supplied: "let us go outside." This metonymic response seeks to provide a bridge to the place of the action that follows. The midrashic response to this lacuna in *Genesis Rabbah* 22: 16 is freely embellishing. It interpolates an extended discussion between Cain and Abel. This response, like that of Philo, assumes that the brothers had a *quarrel*. Philo even writes: "The plain is a figure of contentiousness."[18] And although the midrash explains alternately that the two quarreled about material possessions, religious ideology, and sexual jealousy, the fact of the quarrel seems more important than its content.[19]

Within contemporary interpretations of the episode as a whole, André Neher remarks Cain's silence in response to God's question, "Why has your face fallen?"[20] This silence is not entirely unreasonable, given the notorious obscurity, indeed, the near-unintelligibility of the admonitory verse that follows, "If you intend good, bear-it-aloft."[21] But, writes Neher, "in place of God, he chose his brother as the recipient

17. *In the Beginning: A New English Rendition of the Book of Genesis*, trans. with Commentary and Notes by Everett Fox (New York: Schocken, 1983).

18. *Philo*, vol. 2, English trans. F. H. Colson (Cambridge, MA: Harvard University Press, 1929), 205.

19. See the discussion by Nehama Leibowitz in *Studies in Bereshith*, trans. Aryeh Newman (Jerusalem: World Zionist Organization, 1972), 38–45.

20. As Claus Westermann notes, "J" understands Cain's reaction to the rejection of his gift as "psychosomatic." "He became inflamed . . . his face fell." *Genesis 1–11: A Commentary*, trans. John J. Scullion (Minneapolis: Augsburg Publishing House, 1984), 297. Everett Fox reminds us that "the text is punctuated . . . by changing connotations of the word 'face.' " *In the Beginning*, 19.

21. Commentators agree that the Hebrew of this verse is obscure and its textual difficulties irresolvable. Umberto Cassuto reports that "in ancient times the Rabbis counted it among the indeterminate verses because of the doubt in regard to the syntactic relationship

of his answer: And 'Cain said unto Abel his brother . . .'"[22] And thus, as Elie Wiesel remarks, he turned his quarrel against God against his brother instead.[23] What did Cain say to Abel here? For Neher, the initial "rupture in communication" between Cain and God underscores the failure of dialogue that is central to the episode as a whole: "Abel does not speak, whereas Cain speaks all the time" ("incessantly," Wiesel notes). Thus "dialogue was swallowed up in silence and death." Neher concludes: "It is as if the obliteration of the dialogue were the cause of murder."[24] The "dialogue" of which Neher speaks, based on an ideal of symmetry and an understanding of language as communication, is derivative upon the Blanchotian "speech or death," the asymmetrical *parole* that founds the possibility of "dialogue" in such a sense. Yet Neher's comment gives pause: it is as if the textual gap or lacuna in its materiality were the very cause of the murder that the episode recounts.

What did Cain say to Abel? Perhaps, as Neher suggests, he simply repeated God's words to him "in all their fearful ambiguity." These words were not only obscure but, Wiesel comments, "cruel": "Repudiated by God, Cain sank into a black depression. Whereupon God, with a cruelty as startling as it was unprovoked asked why he looked so crestfallen, why he was so depressed. As though He did not know, as though He was not the cause!"[25] Perhaps, Wiesel continues, Cain wanted to unburden himself to Abel, who did not listen.

And Cain said to Abel, "Let us go outside." Why did he direct him toward the outside? "Outside, where there were no witnesses," says one commentator.[26] Blanchot writes "as if he knew that the outside is the place of Abel, but also as if he wished to lead him back to that pov-

---

of the word *se'eth* ['to lift, carry']." One interpretive suggestion (based on the passage "then you will lift up your face without blemish" [Job 11:15]) "would imply an antithesis here to *the falling of the countenance* mentioned in the previous verses; but just the vital word *face* is wanting!" *A Commentary on the Book of Genesis, vol.* 1, trans. Israel Abrahams (Jerusalem: Magnes Press, 1961), 208–9.

22. André Neher, *The Exile of the Word: From the Silence of the Bible to the Silence of Auschwitz,* trans. David Maisel (Philadelphia: Jewish Publication Society, 1981), 97–98. See also the related discussion by Neher in *L'existence juive: Solitude et affrontements* (Paris: Seuil, 1962), 34–46.

23. Elie Wiesel, *Messengers of God: Biblical Portraits and Legends,* trans. Marion Wiesel (New York: Pocket Books, 1977), 54.

24. Neher, *Exile of the Word,* 95.

25. Wiesel, *Messengers of God,* 58.

26. Westermann, *Genesis 1–11,* 302.

erty, to that weakness of the outside where every defense falls away" (*IC*, 61).[27]

27. Although the reading of Genesis *4* that I have proposed (via Blanchot, Neher, Wiesel, and others) is more or less "Levinasian," this is not to say that Levinas would necessarily endorse this particular reading of the biblical chapter. Indeed, at one of the annual Colloquia of French Jewish Intellectuals, at which André Neher presented a version of his Cain and Abel reading, Levinas registered his disagreement. Neher's reading emphasizes both the impossibility of dialogue that leads to violence and also the "arbitrariness" and the "inadvertency" of God's dealings with man. The arbitrariness is in accepting Abel's sacrifice and not accepting Cain's, for although one can argue (as many midrashim do) that Cain's sacrifice was less well intentioned than Abel's (fruits of *the ground* versus *first* of the flock), Neher says that "the last nuance of the text asks us to admit that the sacrifices were equivalent." Moreover, Neher continues: "God only intervenes when it is too late . . . God intervenes like someone who will have seen nothing at the moment when the [murder] comes to pass." This "heedlessness" and "inadvertency" on the part of God invites us to think God's distance from man. But Cain senses that God is also close, facing him and speaking to him. Hence, Neher proposes "the poignant need for Cain to speak and at the same time to say: I do not understand; If I could lay my complaint before you I would be able to understand, but I am not able to, you grip me, as it were, by the throat, you are suffocating me."

Tellingly, Levinas took the other side of the debate and objected to what he termed "these Kierkegaardian paradoxes" concerning the distance and nearness of God. Levinas reasserted God's preference for Abel's sacrifice over Cain's, following the midrashim which "insist on the quality of the Gift." See André Neher, "Caïn et Abel," and the "Débats" that follow, in *La conscience juive: Données et débats* (Paris: P.U.F., 1963), 34–53.

PART II

LEVINAS AND THE AESTHETIC

[5] AESTHETIC TOTALITY AND ETHICAL INFINITY

POETRY AND THE ETHICAL

Throughout this book, ethics, in Levinas's conception, has been described as a radical putting into question of the self in the presence of the face of the other. The guiding question in this chapter is: Does the work of art give access to the ethical, as Levinas understands it? In the remarks that follow, the ways in which Levinas *in his work* has answered this question will be closely examined. But this is also a question that in a sense we put *to* Levinas and his work, attending not just to the constative level of his statements about art but to their performative dimension as well. That is to say, we will at the same time *read*—in a literary or rhetorical sense—his constative statements about the literary work of art.

The answer that Levinas most often provides to this question—Does the work of art give access to the ethical?—is a resounding *no*. His harsh assessment of the work of art is evident throughout his writings. But Levinas cannot be said to hold a stable view on the matter. Again, Levinas's assertions about the work of art in his earlier writings—from the forties and fifties—are mostly negative, while in key texts from the sixties and the seventies (specifically those on Blanchot, Laporte, Celan, Agnon) a more positive appreciation emerges. But rather than conceiving of this divided perspective as a transformation of his view, rather than thinking this tension in the temporal terms of a before and after, I prefer to approach this tension as one operative *within* each of his texts about art. I will begin with the view of art in the 1961 *Totality and Infinity*—the work that represents Levinas's mature ethical philosophy—and will then consider the way in which similar preoccupations emerge in a cluster of his texts from the late forties: "The Other in Proust" (1947), "Reality and Its Shadow" (1948), and "The Transcendence of Words" (1949).

According to a central emphasis of *Totality and Infinity*, the *non*totalizing relation to the face of the other, the relation (without relation) that is capable of preserving absolute separation, distance and the radical asymmetry between parties, may be produced in two ways, in generosity and in "discourse." Levinas understands discourse not as any kind of communication but as interlocution, as interpellation, in which ethics in its most originary sense—the ethicity of ethics—comes to the fore. In Levinas's descriptions, the face of the other signifies as *expression*—namely, as a speaking that surmounts and exceeds the other's plastic manifestation and that calls me to responsibility, even commanding me, "Thou shalt not kill." Levinas calls the link between expression and responsibility "the ethical condition or essence of language" (*TI*, 200).

This ethical language is repeatedly characterized as having an exceptional *droiture*, that is, straightforwardness, uprightness, justice; he also calls it "sincerity," "frankness." In privileging such an ethical language, Levinas quite explicitly (as I have demonstrated in previous chapters) excludes rhetoric—as a form of language that is devious, that is not straight, that does not face—and with it, implicitly, any language that is figured or troped; he denounces rhetoric as violent and unjust. The ethical language relation is to be found only in a vocative or imperative discourse, face-to-face. It is not then surprising that Levinas excludes from his conception of the ethical language relation to the other all forms of poetic speaking.

The first hint of this is given in the opening section of *Totality and Infinity* (1.A.2), in a discussion of the economy of the Same—that is, the concrete egoistic exchanges that characterize the self's very being in the world. The I, in its fundamental mode of identification, "recovers itself through all that happens to it" (*TI*, 36), and this includes all the extremes of self-loss and self-alienation in which the I is other to itself. Levinas writes:

> The I that repels the self, lived as repugnance, the I riveted to itself, lived as ennui, are modes of self-consciousness and rest on the unrendable identity of the I and the self. The alterity of the I that takes itself for another may strike the imagination of the poet precisely because it is but the play of the Same: the negation of the I by the self is precisely one of the modes of identification of the I. [*Le moi qui repousse le soi, vécu comme répugnance, le moi rivé à soi, vécu comme ennui—sont des modes de la conscience de soi et reposent sur l'indéchirable identité de moi et de soi. L'altérité du je, qui se prend pour un autre, peut*

*frapper l'imagination du poète, précisément parce qu'elle n'est que le jeu du Même:
la négation du moi par le soi—est précisément l'un des modes d'identification du moi.]*
(*TI*, 37)

Levinas's covert allusion to Rimbaud's "Je est un autre" serves to exemplify the relation to a spurious or finite alterity that characterizes the I in identification. He will contrast it to transcendence, the relationship with the infinitely other. But Levinas does not, in this exemplary gesture which includes using the literary text *as* an example, merely use Rimbaud's text as an example of a spurious alterity of an I that takes itself for another; he renders Rimbaud a figure for the poet in general, whose "imagination" is incapable of recognizing ethical transcendence. ("The alterity of the I that takes itself for another may strike the imagination of the poet precisely because it is but the play of the Same.")

Levinas's exclusion of the work of art from the possibility of ethicity is again apparent in *Totality and Infinity*'s discussion of works—including artistic productions—and expression. Having asked in effect if the other's *works* can attest to the other, he says that with the work

> [a] separation opens up between the producer and the product. At a given moment the producer no longer follows up, remains in retreat *[reste en retrait]*. His transcendence stops mid-way. In contrast with the transcendence of expression, in which the being that expresses himself *personally attends* the work of expression, production attests the author of the work in his *absence*, as a plastic form. (*TI*, 227)

In the work, the other's transcendence is somehow blocked, stopped, turned into immanence.[1] The producer is no longer present; the *décalage* or lag in self-presence turns the producer's presentation into a trace structure (he is *en retrait*). Levinas further contrasts the transcendence of expression and the failed or blocked transcendence of the work in terms of the opposition between presence and absence, between the author's "attending personally" his expression and the author's absence from his work.[2] There is indeed a certain phonocentrism, a complicity

1. By the time of "The Trace of the Other" (1963) and "Meaning and Sense" (1964), there will be at least *two* conceptions of the work, one which returns to same and the other which goes out to the other.

2. Cf. *TI*: Unlike facial *expression*, where a being "attends to his own manifestation," in the work a being "is simply signified in it by a sign in a system of signs, that is, as a being who is manifested precisely as *absent* from his manifestation" (*TI*, 178). A similar dyadic hierarchy of speech and writing, conceived as the difference between presence and absence, is evident in the 1949 Leiris essay, where Levinas opposes "the living word, which is destined to be heard *[le mot vivant, destinée à l'audition]*" to written words, which he characterizes as "disfigured words, 'frozen words,' in which language becomes document and vestige *[Paroles défigurées, 'paroles gelées' ou le langage se mue déjà en documents et en vestiges]*" (*TW*,

with the metaphysics of presence that emerges here and elsewhere in Levinas's ethical discourse. Suffice it to state that if the work, in Levinas's view, *cannot* present or signify the other that is precisely *because* it signifies; it signifies with the referrals inherent in sign systems and the constitutive absence that implies. The necessary indirection of a work's mode of signification falls short of the directness of the discourse of the face.

One last aspect of Levinas's gesture of exclusion of poetry in *Totality and Infinity* concerns the way in which poetry is troped. It often appears within a chain of terms that are negatively charged—*intoxication, ritual, the sacred, magic, witchcraft, incantation, play, participation*—a terminological cluster that is familiar enough from Levinas's earlier writings, where the work of art is something of a preoccupation. The Levinas of *Totality and Infinity* is more restrained in his polemic against poetry, less concerned with it. Nonetheless, the following passage from that work (section III.B.3) concisely lays out the set of terms with which Levinas, in all the writings up to and through *Totality and Infinity*, has always understood the aesthetic.

> The ethical relation, the face-to-face, also cuts across every relation one could call mystical, where events other than that of the presentation of the original being come to overwhelm or sublimate the pure sincerity of this presentation, where intoxicating equivocations come to enrich the primordial univocity of expression, where discourse becomes incantation, as prayer becomes rite and liturgy, where the interlocutors find themselves playing a role in a drama that has begun outside of them. Here resides the rational character of the ethical relation and of language. No fear, no trembling could alter the straightforwardness of this relationship, which preserves the discontinuity of relationship, resists fusion . . . To poetic activity—where influences arise unbeknown to us out of this nonetheless conscious activity, to envelop and beguile it as a rhythm, and where action is borne along by the very work it has given rise to . . .—is opposed the language that at each instant dispels the charm of rhythm and prevents the initiative from becoming a role. Discourse is rupture and commencement, breaking of rhythm which enraptures and transports the interlocutors—prose. (*TI, 201–2*)

What is referred to here as *the mystical* represents a threat to the basic principles of the ethical. Levinas had previously described discourse as the relation to the face of the other which respects and preserves separation and distance. The discourse with the face is one of straightforwardness and an original sincerity, a sincerity that precedes the opposi-

---

148–49). Again, by the time of "The Trace of the Other" (1963), it is precisely this vestigial, or trace structure, of language that will be privileged for the signification of alterity.

tion between veracity and deceit (*TI,* 202). The face's distinctive mode
of signification was described as expression, a way in which the face undoes the ambiguity or equivocation of its manifestation by speaking, by
an autosignification and an autoattendance that decisively calls upon me,
obligating me, opening the dimension of the ethical. But the mystical
relation would prevent the ethical from even arising, "overwhelming"
sincerity and straightforwardness, introducing "equivocation" into the
"primordial univocity," "transporting" the interlocutors of ethical discourse, turning discourse into "incantation," turning "prayer" (which is
ultimately, as will be shown, the essence of ethical discourse) into sacred
rite and liturgy, turning what is rational into a "fear and trembling," and
turning the respectful discontinuity into "fusion." All of this is how
Levinas always describes the false transcendence of *participation,* defined
in *Totality and Infinity* as a being's "submergence in the being toward
which it goes, which holds the transcendent being in its meshes, as to
do it violence" (*TI,* 48). One of the peculiarities of Levinas's discourse
on the aesthetic is his consistent tendency to think poetry together with
participation (and I will return to this point). Note simply here that at
the passage's end Levinas links the term *poetry* onto the set of oppositions
that have governed its logic thus far. He opposes poetic activity to ethical
discourse, in the process asserting that (1) poetic activity possesses or
dispossesses the subject: hence the work carries away not only its producer but also its audience; and (2) the manner in which poetry "charms,"
"enraptures and transports" its audience is *rhythm.*

The full significance of these assertions will be determined only when
they have been brought into relation with the earlier texts by Levinas,
which theorize the work of art, to which I turn now. Note simply that
the term *poetry* in *Totality and Infinity* denotes not a genre of art but the
work of art in general. The distinction that Levinas proposes between
poetic activity and prose, "the language that dispels the charm of rhythm"
and that lines up with the oppositions equivocation/sincerity, sacred
ritual/prayer, fusion/discontinuity, should be understood as a genre distinction on the hither side of genre distinctions. Neither poetry nor prose
represents for Levinas a genre of art but originary experiences, for the
prose in question is nothing other than the sobriety, the gravity of ethical
language.

In "The Other in Proust," the first of his essays devoted to the interpretation of a literary work, in the inaugural issue of *Deucalion,* founded
by Jean Wahl and published in 1947, Levinas formulates the difference
between the philosopher and the poet in this way. While the theory of

the philosopher refers unequivocally *(sans équivoque)* to its object, that of the poet

> harbors an ambiguity *[une ambiguïté]*, for it is concerned not to express but to create the object. Like images or symbols, reasoning is called on to produce a certain rhythm in which the reality that is sought will appear by magic. The truths or errors articulated are of no value in themselves. They are spells and incantations. (OP, 161)

The contrast is not merely (as one might expect) between the philosopher's denotative language and the poet's metaphorical language, between a language of communication and a language that suspends the communicative function, between a presumably single versus a multiple meaning. It concerns the way in which their theoretical statements relate to their objects, the difference between the philosopher's "expressive" relationship to the object and the poet's "creative" one. Levinas's operative distinction recalls another operative distinction formulated by Jean-Paul Sartre the same year in *Les Temps Modernes*. In a widely read essay, "What Is Literature?" Sartre had opposed the poetic attitude to prose in terms of their relations to language and the world: "Poets are men who refuse to utilize language."[3] While the prose writer conceives of language as a tool and discloses the world with the intention of changing it (thus exemplifying what Sartre termed *littérature engagée*), the poet "considers words as things not as signs"[4] and withdraws language from its instrumentality. The poet, who treats the aesthetic object as if it were a natural object, thus succumbs to what Sartre in 1945 had called "the temptation of irresponsibility known to all writers of middle-class origin."[5] Sartre's distinction between poetry and prose, like Levinas's, goes beyond the question of genre. Levinas casts the philosopher as the prose writer. The poet (and here Levinas's "poet" is Proust, whom Sartre rejected as irresponsible) is he who by magic, spells, and incantations "produces a certain rhythm." The centrality of the term *rhythm* to Levinas's aesthetic theory, as well as the way in which a terminology of the supernatural invariably arises in all of his writings on art, will soon become clear. Levinas began his essay by calling Proust "the magician of inexpressible rhythms" (OP, 161).

The essay's central argument is that in Proust's world there is an indeterminacy, in which "one course of action does not preclude other possi-

3. Jean-Paul Sartre, *"What Is Literature?" and Other Essays*, intro. Steven Ungar (Cambridge, MA: Harvard University Press, 1988), 29.

4. Ibid., 29.

5. Sartre, "Introducing *Les Temps Modernes*," 249.

bilities," in which "acts are shadowed by unpredictable 'counter-acts' and things by 'counter-things.'" This eventuates in, and these are Levinas's terms, "a compossibility of contradictory elements"—in which "everything is vertiginously possible"[6]—and thus, "a nullification of every choice," an "amorality." It is as if "magic begins . . . when ethics is finished" (OP, 162). But—the question arises—ethics in what sense? The essay's references to choice and amorality imply a subject who would choose or initiate a particular ethical action. In other words, they belong to a traditional conception of ethics that is derivative upon the way in which the ethical is thought in Levinas's mature work. They belong to *an* ethics rather than to the ethicity of ethics, to reinscribed ethics. This was certainly the case with Levinas's objection to figural, and ultimately, figur*ed* discourse, as that which produces a loss of "the freedom proper to conscious man" (*DF,* 122). The passage about poetry and the mystical from *Totality and Infinity* also made reference to a loss of initiative, indeed, a loss of subjecthood, as if Levinas, when faced with poetry, to some extent reverts to a vocabulary belonging to a conception of ethics that he himself has rejected.

But perhaps the magic of the Proustian art does *not* spell the end of ethics. Levinas goes on to say, of Proust's portrayal of the inner life: "Everything takes place as if the self were constantly doubled by another self, with a friendship that cannot be equalled *[dans une inégalable amitié]* . . . The mystery in Proust is the mystery of the other *[le mystère de l'autre]*" (OP, 163). And also: "It is not the inner event that counts but the way in which the self seizes it and is overwhelmed by it, as though it were encountered in another *[comme s'il le rencontrait chez un autre]*. It is . . . the dialogue in the self with the other *[le dialogue en soi avec l'autre]*" (OP, 163). These statements are not without a certain "ambiguity," because the inner life as it will be described in Levinas's work of ten years later is invariably closed off to the other,[7] and the term *mystery* will also, by that time, lose all its prestige.[8] But Levinas seems to be arguing that there *may be* an ethical dimension in Proust's work, an

---

6. "The very structures of appearances . . . are both what they are and the infinity of what they exclude" (OP, 162).

7. The difficulty here lies in the extent to which the inner life's relation to the other *[l'autre]* resembles the relation to the kind of *finite* alterity that the self encounters as a detour on the way to itself, that Levinas will later call "identification," and that is described in the Proust essay as a structure in which "everything that encounters me exists as coming *from* me" (OP, 164).

8. In "Heidegger, Gagarin, and Us" (1961), Levinas writes: "The mystery of things is the source of all cruelty with respect to men" (*DF,* 232).

encounter with the other. Textual support for this is found in the two occurrences of the term *l'autre*, and the reference to a fundamental "strangeness" of the inner life and its "insatiable curiosity about the *alterity of the other [l'alterité d'autrui]*." Indeed, Levinas starts by implying that Proust's work may be ethical and builds up to saying that Proust's work is totally ethical, that it marks out "a direct relation with that which gives itself in refusing itself, with the other as other *[avec autrui en tant qu'autrui]*, with the mystery" (OP, 164). (And here Levinas uses the alterity-word, *autrui*, in lower case.) Levinas ends up calling Proust "a poet *of* the social," even though he stops short of calling him a poet of the ethical.

But Levinas's ambivalence about the question of art is preserved in the essay's last sentence, in the hesitation of its punctuation.

> Proust's most profound teaching—if poetry can contain teachings—consists in situating reality in a relation with something which forever remains other, with the other as absence and mystery *[avec ce qui à jamais demeure autre, avec autrui comme absence et mystère]*, in rediscovering this relation in the very intimacy of the "I," and in inaugurating a dialectic that breaks definitively with Parmenides. (OP, 165)

The hesitation is important, the qualifier is enormous. For it is not at all clear that poetry—Proust's or anyone else's—*can* contain teaching. Teaching is an ethical relation, a paradigm of the ethical relation in *Totality and Infinity* (TI, 204)—and *this* teaching that Proust's work is said to accomplish involves no less than an (impossible) break with Parmenides, philosopher of the unity of being which suppresses the beyond, namely, a break with the governing conceptuality of philosophy in the West. Levinas says that Proust teaches the ethical—if poetry *can* teach—but we know that he knows that it cannot, or we know that he has grave doubts about this possibility, because magic and ethics are incompatible, or in the terms of *Totality and Infinity*, poetic rapture interferes with the straightforwardness of ethical discourse. In short, in the Proust essay, Levinas seems to want to have it both ways. Poetry does and does not give access to the ethical. By the time of the publication of "Reality and Its Shadow" the following year, Levinas's ambivalence toward the work of art would seem to have become an outright dismissal.

THEORIZING THE WORK OF ART

"Reality and Its Shadow," the only place in Levinas's work where he theorizes the work of art explicitly and in a sustained way, was published

in 1948 in *Les Temps Modernes*, the journal founded by and indissociable
from Sartre. Levinas's essay is severe in its denunciation of the work of
art and the work of criticism as well. Its tone with regard to *littérature
engagée* is polemical enough to have necessitated an editorial preface that
states that perhaps Levinas has not examined Sartre's theory fully
enough.[9] There is something aberrant about both the tonality and its
theoretical stance—namely, that art is a kind of irresponsibility, that it
is a type of death, an idolatry—which can't be explained away simply by
saying that it's an early piece, that Levinas's attention will later shift away
from aesthetics, and so on. The essay was published in the same year
as two of Levinas's important phenomenological analyses, *Existence and
Existents* and *Time and the Other*, and it has continuities with these and
other writings from the same time period. Despite its divergences from
what will become Levinas's mature ethical philosophy, it has continuities
with all of Levinas's future discussions of art. The essay is part of a tradition as well. John Llewelyn usefully situates Levinas's assertions that art
is "disengaged," without "utility," "outside 'being in the world,'" in relation to the thinking of the aesthetic in Kant and Heidegger.[10] Another
indispensable point of reference would be Plato's criticism of mimesis
and rejection of poetry in the *Republic* and elsewhere.[11]

Levinas begins by describing criticism as "parasitic" upon the work of
art, that is, as having a secondariness. He says that while criticism "may
seem suspect and pointless"—and he hereby introduces this judgment
under the guise that it be avoided (a rhetorical pattern often found in his
discourse on art)—it can be "justified," even—as he asserts at the essay's
end—"rehabilitated." A rehabilitated or what he calls a "philosophical
criticism" would represent "the intervention of the understanding neces-

9. This preface was probably authored by Merleau-Ponty, surmises Jean-Luc Lannoy
("D'une ambiguïté," 14), no doubt on the basis of the dates of MP's editorship of *Les Temps
Modernes*. Salomon Malka comes to the same conclusion in *Lire Levinas* (Paris: Cerf,
1984), 32.

10. Llewelyn, *The Middle Voice of Ecological Conscience*, 89–113. See also Llewelyn's subsequent study, *Emmanuel Levinas: The Genealogy of Ethics* (London: Routledge, 1995).

11. This classical theme might have already been detected in Levinas's doubts about
whether poetry can teach. Levinas's criticism of art in RO should be considered with his
denunciation of rhetoric in FC, *TI*, and elsewhere. For these and other Platonic motifs in
Levinas's discourse on the aesthetic, see Thomas Wiemer, *Die Passion des Sagens* (Freiburg/
Munich: Karl Alber, 1988), 315–46. In her 1974 study, *Emmanuel Levinas: The Problem of
Ethical Metaphysics*, Edith Wyschogrod remarks on not only this Platonic bias but also on
"the tone of unrelieved austerity" that Levinas's devaluing of art gives to his philosophy
(The Hague: Nijhoff, 1974), 73–74.

sary for integrating the *inhumanity* and the *inversion* of art into human life" (RO, 2).[12]

What is it about art that for Levinas makes such an intervention necessary? Art, as he conceives it, substitutes for the object its *image* and in the process "neutralizes" the "living" and "real" relationship with that object (RO, 3). Specific to the image is that it relates to its object by resemblance, a resemblance which is "not the result of a comparison between an image and the original but the very movement that engenders the image" (RO, 6). He asserts:

> Reality would not be only what it is, what it is disclosed to be in truth, but would be also its double, its shadow, its image . . . Thus a person bears on his face *[sur sa face]* alongside of its being with which he coincides, its own caricature, its picturesqueness. (RO, 6)

Levinas thinks the work of art as outside, or on the hither side, of truth and disclosure. Edith Wyschogrod characterizes sensation, within Levinas's theory of art, as a noncognitive relation of sensing and sensed (*EFP*, 137). Indeed, Levinas asserts that "non-truth is not an obscure residue of being but is its sensible character itself" (RO, 7). But there is something about the analogy that Levinas proposes—reality is to image as face (*face*, not yet *visage*) is to caricature—that, especially from the vantage point of *Totality and Infinity*, gives pause. The face, as Levinas will define it, is never reducible to its plastic image: it gives itself as form *and* also exceeds the form. *To miss* the way in which the face also exceeds its form, to have an image of the face, *to image* a face, is to turn it into a caricature, frozen, petrified, a mask. The whole possibility, indeed, the very temptation, of violence is inscribed in the face's presentation as form or image: "The contours of its form in expression imprisons this openness (which breaks up form) in a caricature. The face is at the limit of holiness and caricature" (*TI*, 198). In short, the analogy suggests that no aesthetic approach to the face could also be ethical. There is no *ethical* image of the face; there is no ethical image. And the substitution of an *image* for an object is what Levinas calls "the most elementary procedure of art" (RO, 3).

---

12. At the essay's end, Levinas specifies the approach to the work of art that a rehabilitated criticism would take: "Criticism already detaches it from its irresponsibility by envisaging its technique. It treats the artist as a man at work . . . inquire[s] after the influences he undergoes." He thereby seems in effect to endorse an *extrinsic* criticism, concerned with the relation of the work of art to features such as its author's biography, history, and social context.

Levinas ultimately sees this substitutive procedure as illegitimate, as amounting to idolatry: "[E]vil powers are conjured by filling the world with idols which have mouths but do not speak."[13] And in this substitution there is an utter evasion, an abdication of responsibility, indeed an elision of the ethical dimension of experience: "We find an appeasement *[un apaisement]* when, beyond the invitations to comprehend and act, we throw ourselves into the *rhythm* of a reality which solicits only its admission into a book or painting. Myth takes the place of mystery" (RO, 12).

How exactly does art take us away from the grave and difficult freedom which is responsibility to the other? The answer is to be found in the *musicality* of the image and in this key category of *rhythm*, which is the mode of the image: "The image," writes Levinas, "is musical. Its passivity is directly visible in magic, song, music, and poetry" (RO, 3).[14] Levinas wishes to detach the terms *rhythm* and *music* "from the arts of sound" in order to "draw them out into a general aesthetic category . . . To insist on the musicality of every image is to see in an image its detachment from an object" (RO, 4). Music is also the paradigm for all the arts in Levinas's theory, Llewelyn observes, because *rhythm* explains "*why* art has the magic power to bemuse us and to absorb our interest."[15] In Levinas's definition, rhythm "designates not so much an inner law of the poetic order as the way the poetic order affects us, closed wholes whose elements call for one another like the syllables of a verse, but do so only insofar as they impose themselves on us, disengaging themselves from reality" (RO, 4). That is, for Levinas, rhythm is not primarily an intrinsic feature of the work of art; it is pragmatically concerned with the work's relation to its audience, with the effect of the work on its audience.

That effect could not be more negative. In rhythm, the elements of the poetic order are said to "call for one another . . . insofar as they impose themselves on us." Levinas continues:

13. "Their idols are silver and gold, the work of men's hands. They have mouths but do not speak; eyes but do not see. They have ears, but do not hear; noses, but do not smell. They have hands, but do not feel; feet, but do not walk; and they do not make a sound in their throat. Those who make them are like them; so are all who trust in them" (Ps. 115: 4–8). Like the Bible's discourse against idolatry, Levinas's description of art is polemical and one-sided.

14. "The image marks a hold over us, rather than our initiative, a fundamental passivity . . . An image is musical. Its passivity is directly visible in magic, song, music, and poetry. The exceptional structure of aesthetic existence invokes this singular term magic" (RO, 3). Levinas's later reference to magic in the same essay—"the magic of poets like Gogol, Dickens, Chekhov, Molière, Cervantes and above all, Shakespeare"—is similarly double-edged.

15. Llewelyn, *Middle Voice*, 98.

But they impose themselves on us without our assuming them. Or rather, our consenting to them is inverted into a participation . . . Rhythm represents a unique situation where we cannot speak of consent, assumption, initiative or freedom, because the subject is caught up and carried away by it. The subject is part of its own representation. It is so not even despite itself for in rhythm there is no longer a oneself, but rather a sort of passage from oneself to anonymity. This is the captivation or incantation of poetry and music . . . The particular automatic character of a walk or a dance to music is a mode of being where . . . consciousness, paralyzed in its freedom, plays, totally absorbed in the playing . . . the subject . . . is exterior to itself. (RO, 4)

This passage makes reference to the now familiar themes—the loss of initiative, loss of selfhood, the subject's being carried away by the work—and some new emphases, the subject's exteriority to itself, anonymity, automatism, play. Levinas's aversion to play is often evident—just one example is found in the passage in *Totality and Infinity* where the poet's imagination is caught by and caught up in the *play* of the Same. It is one of the most negatively charged terms in his work. This becomes all the more striking when we realize that play is a centrally significant category of aesthetic experience, and for Hans-Georg Gadamer it is the clue to the ontology of the work of art. But the category that seems most destructive to the possibility of ethicity and toward which Levinas aims his greatest polemic is *participation*. He states above that in the mode of absorption characteristic of the aesthetic state of mind, "consent is inverted into a participation," or, as he also says, there is a "reversal of power into *participation*" (RO, 4).

The term comes from the ethnologist Lucien Lévy-Bruhl (1857–1939) who describes primitive mentality's mystic belief in unseen, supernatural forces, its emotional and affective relation to collective representations, which are perceived as having a transitive influence—through "transference, contact, projection, contamination, defilement, possession."[16] This belief structure functions concretely in magic and religious practices and "accounts for the place of dreams, omens, divination, sacrifices, incantations, ritual ceremonies and magic." Lévy-Bruhl calls the law or logic governing these connections *participation*, a way of thinking indifferent to the law of contradiction, "which finds no difficulty in imagining the identity of the one and the many, the individual and the species, of entities however unlike they may be."[17] For example, Lévy-Bruhl writes concerning wizards who are believed to turn into crocodiles: "Be-

16. Lucien Lévy-Bruhl, *How Natives Think*, trans. Lilian A. Clare (London: George Allen and Unwin, 1926 [1910]), 99.
17. Ibid., 135–36.

tween the wizard and the crocodile the relation is such that the wizard becomes the crocodile, without, however, being actually fused with him. Considered from the standpoint of the law of contradiction, it must be either one of two things: either the wizard and the crocodile make but one, or they are two distinct entities. But prelogical mentality is able to adapt itself to two distinct affirmations at once."[18] In short, the conceptual structures which characterize participation are utterly heterogenous to our own way of thinking, and constitute, for the evolutionist Lévy-Bruhl, an earlier prelogical stage of modern mentality.

A contemporary of Durkheim and on the margins of the *Année Sociologique* group, Lévy-Bruhl was a strong influence on the generation of Levinas's teachers. Two of Levinas's most important teachers at Strasbourg, Charles Blondel and Maurice Halbwachs, were themselves students of Lévy-Bruhl, and Blondel wrote a book about him. Lévy-Bruhl taught the history of modern philosophy at the Sorbonne. In 1917 he succeeded Theodore Ribot as editor of the *Revue Philosophique*. At the same time his interest turned increasingly to ethnology, where his emphasis, according to Émile Bréhier, was on structure rather than genesis.[19] Levinas's 1957 essay on Lévy-Bruhl, "Lévy-Bruhl and Contemporary Philosophy," written almost twenty years after Lévy-Bruhl's death, discusses the ways in which Lévy-Bruhl's ideas about primitive mentality have marked and influenced the orientation of contemporary philosophy, specifically the work of Husserl, Bergson, Otto, and, in particular, Heidegger's philosophy of existence. Levinas writes that in Heidegger "the existence of a being (of Dasein) does not happen as the tranquil subsistence of a substance, but as hold and possession, as a field of forces in which human existence is held, or is engaged, or in Lévy-Bruhl's terms, participates" (LB, 56–57). The originality of Lévy-Bruhl's thought, according to Levinas, is that it gives us to think the intentionality of affective states: "[E]motion, which according to classical psychology, closes us up within ourselves, here acquires a certain transcendence" (LB, 58). The fetish-objects of primitive mentality are like the "tools" in the Heideggerian analysis of world, not first things and then usable but usable things whose significance is a practical conjuncture. Hence, ultimately, Lévy-Bruhl's thought "puts into question the privilege of theoretical thinking" (LB, 65), the legislative function of reason, the unity of spirit and the subject (LB, 54). But, if Lévy-Bruhl's analyses "have helped to

18. Lévy-Bruhl, *Primitive Mentality*, trans. Lilian A. Clare (Boston: Beacon Press, 1923 [1910]), 55.

19. Émile Bréhier, "Originalité de Lévy-Bruhl," *Revue Philosophique* 199 (1949), 385.

forge" central concepts of modern thought, they—and this is Levinas's sole expressed reservation which will in time accumulate into the force of a polemic—have come also "to flatter a nostalgia for outmoded and retrograde forms," in particular a renewal of mythology and a kind of elevation of myth and a tolerance for "the cruelties which myth perpetuates in morality" (LB, 67).

Lévy-Bruhl's ideas also have influenced Levinas's descriptions (although Levinas does not mention this in his essay on him). For example, in *Existence and Existents*, participation is named in conjunction with the *il y a*. In *Difficult Freedom*, primitive mentality's law of participation is to some extent assimilated, anachronistically, to the Canaanite and "pagan" religions of the Ancient Near East from which Hebraic monotheism separated itself (although here the target of Levinas's polemic is also the contemporary religious revival represented by Louis Lavelle, Simone Weil, and Rudolf Otto). But the most prominent and most important usage is in *Totality and Infinity* where ethics is consistently thought of as "a break from participation." "A separated being maintains itself in existence all by itself, without participating in the Being from which it is separated" (*TI*, 58). As Adriaan Peperzak observes, according to Levinas, even the philosophy of the same "has had the merit of protesting against participation" (a reference to the mythical monism from which Greek philosophy first separated itself). But, he continues, "the error of this philosophy was to identify the separate existence with the existence of an egological I, integrating all beings as subordinate moments of the same."[20] In other words, there is a sense in which ethics can be thought as a break *from* the break from participation. For Levinas it is in ethical relations that philosophy is decisively "purified of everything with which an imagination . . . victim of participation charges our concepts . . . Everything that cannot be reduced to an interhuman relation represents not the superior form but the forever primitive form of religion" (*TI*, 79). And, of course, we have already analyzed the passage in *Totality and Infinity* where poetry is thought together with participation, *where poetry is described as and aligned with everything that ethics must struggle against.*

Hence, despite the diverse historical range of the term *participation* for Levinas, it is possible to state what the term does not mean in his work.

20. Adriaan Peperzak, *To the Other* (West Lafayette, IN: Purdue University Press, 1993), 49. The quotation is from Levinas's 1957 "Philosophy and the Idea of Infinity." Cf. *TI*, 48: "And to have substituted for the magical communion of species and the confusion of distinct orders a spiritual relation in which beings remain at their post but communicate among themselves will have been the imperishable merit of the 'admirable Greek people' and the very institution of philosophy."

"It is completely different from the Platonic participation in a genus" (*EE*, 60). Nor does it refer to the idea in Christian theology that the being of the creation partakes in the being of the Creator. Levinas describes the passage from Durkheim to Lévy-Bruhl thus: "The impersonality of the sacred in primitive religions, which for Durkheim is the 'still' impersonal God from which will issue one day the God of advanced religions, on the contrary describes a world where nothing prepares for the apparition of God. Rather than to a God, the notion of the *there is* leads us to the absence of God, the absence of any being" (*EE*, 61). Finally, when Levinas wishes to state the contribution of the conceptual figure of participation, it is most often by analogy to the Heideggerian analysis of affectivity: "To the primitive the world is never simply given, it is like an anonymous sphere which greatly resembles the anguishing anonymity of an existence not yet assumed by a subject" (LB, 64). Insofar as the Heideggerian descriptions of affectivity resemble *participation*, especially in their heterogeneity to the theoretical, the term also serves polemically in Levinas's discourse to denote a philosophical climate from which he wishes to depart.

In closing this chapter, some brief questions: How does Levinas come to see aesthetic experience in this way? An answer to this question would have to go by way of certain passages from Levinas's 1949 essay on Leiris, "The Transcendence of Words," which describes ethics as a kind of waking up from aesthetic existence, with its primacy on vision and "the visual experience to which Western civilization ultimately reduces all spiritual life" (TW, 147). In other words, it has to do with the way in which Levinas conceives of the relation or the divide between aesthetics and ethics. He also writes: "The use of the word wrenches experience out of its aesthetic self-sufficiency . . . To speak is to interrupt my existence as a subject and a master . . . The subject who speaks does not purely and simply situate himself at the heart of his own spectacle, as an artist does . . . but in relation to the Other . . . By proffering a word, the subject who poses himself is exposed and, in a sense, prays *[Par la parole proférée, le sujet qui se pose s'expose et, en quelque manière, prie]*" (TW, 148–49). In these passages Levinas associates the aesthetic with what he will call in the later work "the totality," as well as with a reversion to participation. But are we sure we can keep participation and ethics apart? We have already pointed to the puzzle in which the dissolution of the subject—condemned in the case of participation—is also positively valorized by Levinas's ethics, in which there is a formal or structural similarity between something that is ethical and its opposite. There is such a similarity between the subject's exteriority to itself in the mode of aesthetic absorption, and the exteriority of the face of the other which speaks infinity, and which commands me. Are we to think this as a bad versus a good exteriority? A false versus a true transcendence? Can we be sure that the two do not communicate with each other, interpenetrate and contaminate each other, according to what Derrida calls a "necessary general contamination"[21] in order to be thought of as two distinct and irreducible poles of experience? That would be to say that there is also the possibility of thinking the ethicity of poetry, or of thinking the ethical and aesthetics together, of thinking *in a literary text*, as Levinas himself also does in the Leiris essay, the transcendence of the other in "the proffered word," the word of the other that *teaches* us. And if this interlocutionary orientation, this pure vocativity of speech that is a quasi-prayer (or, if you will, a literary prayer, a *literary* ethical discourse) and that is the essence of ethical language, can be thought together with aesthetics, perhaps this will be an aesthetics, as Levinas also asserts in "Reality and Its Shadow," based on neither perception nor cognition. But that would be another story.

21. Jacques Derrida, "Some Statements and Truisms about Neologisms, Newisms, Postisms, Parasitisms, and Other Small Seismisms," trans. Anne Tomiche, in *The States of "Theory": History, Art and Critical Discourse*, ed. David Carroll (New York: Columbia University Press, 1990), 78.

[6] ART, PHILOSOPHY, AND THE *IL Y A*

ALLUSIONS AND ABRIDGEMENTS

Levinas's predominant strategy with regard to literature in the earlier works, especially in those he produced in the decade following the war, *Existence and Existents* (1947) and *Time and the Other* (1948) is allusion. (The strategy of citation will be more pronounced in the 1961 *Totality and Infinity* and in the works subsequent to it.)[1] As a strategy, allusion—a sometimes covert, noncitational reference to a shared literary or textual heritage—may not be well suited to preserve the alterity of the text at hand. For an ethical philosopher who wishes his thought to go (like Abraham) unto the other without return, as opposed to the circular and recuperative itinerary of Odysseus (T, 191), the fact of allusion threatens to effect a return to a shared literary or textual tradition, heritage, horizon, as I have argued elsewhere.[2] The consequent risk may be formulated in this way: when Levinas "says" Abraham, he "does" Odysseus.

The postwar works bear witness to Levinas's extensive readings in the traditions of Russian, French, English, and German literature. Their sheer volume is noteworthy; they include references to Gogol,

---

1. Within a discussion of intertextuality as "the effective presence of one text in another," Gérard Genette distinguishes between "its most explicit and literal form," namely, citation (with or without quotation marks) and allusion, "an enunciation of which the full comprehension supposes the perception of a rapport between it and another to which one of its inflections necessarily refers back." *Palimpsestes* (Paris: Seuil, 1982), 8.

2. Jill Robbins, *Prodigal Son/Elder Brother: Interpretation and Alterity in Augustine, Petrarch, Kafka, Levinas* (Chicago: University of Chicago Press, 1991), 107–11.

Goncharov, Lermontov, Dostoevsky, Shakespeare, Poe, Defoe, Racine, Molière, Gautier, Baudelaire, Huysmans, Maupassant, Proust, Valéry, Rimbaud, Giraudoux, and Blanchot. The most important intertexts for Levinas are Blanchot, Dostoevsky, and Shakespeare. In the following pages I will begin by considering the intertwining of the general topic of "literature" with Levinas's presentation of the *il y a* in the postwar works, *Existence and Existents* and *Time and the Other*. I will examine Levinas's practice of alluding as well as his specific "use" of Shakespeare and Blanchot. Within my discussion, I will have frequent recourse to Georges Bataille's review essay (the first review that Levinas ever received),[3] "From Existentialism to the Primacy of Economy," published in the 1947 *Critique*. Bataille's insights about Levinas's writing will prove decisive, especially insofar as they draw attention to the relationship between the philosophical and literary there, as well as to the "trouble" that the literary produces within Levinas's philosophical text.

As Levinas presents it in *Existence and Existents*, the *il y a* is a nocturnal space, a space of horror, "the event of being that returns at the heart of all negation" (*EE*, 61), "a return of presence in absence" (*EE*, 65). It is not the anguish before the nothing and the possibility of death that Heidegger described; it is a horror before being, the impossibility of death, the irremissibility of existence (*EE*, 63). In *Existence and Existents*, the description of the *il y a* is juxtaposed with the description of art as exoticism. The terms of the discussion of exoticism resemble closely and are continuous with those of the theoretical discussion of art in the 1948 essay, "Reality and Its Shadow": "The elementary function of art consists in furnishing an image of the object in the place of the object itself" (*EE*, 52). This effects a "neutralization" and an "extraction of the thing from the perspective of the world" (*EE*, 52). The suspension of the use-function of the thing in art reveals, "behind the luminosity of forms, materiality as the fact of the 'there is'" (*EE*, 57).

Within the context of *Existence and Existents*, the *il y a* should be understood in pendant to Levinas's description of hypostasis, namely, the way in which the existent contracts or takes up a position with regard to his existence: "[T]he *il y a* is the place where the hypostasis is produced" (*TA*, 50). The *il y a* effects not just a loss of world, "the disappearance of all objects," but also the "extinction of the subject" and of the very distinction between subject and object (*EE*, 67). It is "the rupture with the cate-

---

3. See the bibliography by Roger Burggraeve, *Emmanuel Levinas: Une bibliographie primaire et secondaire* (1929–89) (Leuven: Peeters, 1990).

gory of the substantive" (*EE*, 67).[4] Both the *il y a* and the aesthetic event may be understood, as B. Forthomme usefully suggests, as an antihypostasis.[5]

Hence the juxtaposition of Levinas's discussion of art as exoticism and of the *il y a* is by no means accidental. They are conceptually linked. But beyond this convergence, there is, in both *Existence and Existents* and *Time and the Other*, an utter intrication of art and the *il y a*. This intrication is irreducible, I will show, because of the seeming necessity for Levinas to employ numerous literary examples and illustrations in his presentation of the *il y a* and because Levinas's very access to the *il y a* is via an aesthetic category, the imagination. He writes, in *Existence and Existents* and *Time and the Other*, respectively:

> Let us imagine all beings, things and persons, reverting to nothingness. One cannot put this return to nothingness outside of all events. But what of this nothingness itself? Something would happen, if only night and the silence of nothingness. The indeterminateness of this "something is happening" is not the indeterminateness of a subject and does not refer to a substantive. Like the third person pronoun in the impersonal form of a verb, it designates not the uncertainly known author of the action, but the characteristic of this action itself which somehow has no author. This impersonal, anonymous, yet inextinguishable "consummation" of being, which murmurs in the depths of nothingness itself, we shall designate by the term *there is*. *[Imaginons le retour au néant de tous les êtres: choses et personnes. Il est impossible de placer ce retour au néant en dehors de tout événement. Mais ce néant lui-même? Quelque chose se passe, fût-ce la nuit et le silence du néant. L'indétermination de ce "quelque chose se passe," n'est pas l'indétermination du sujet, ne se réfère pas à un substantif. Elle désigne comme le pronom de la troisième personne dans la forme impersonnelle du verbe, non point un auteur mal connu de l'action, mais le caractère de cette action elle-même qui, en quelque matière, n'a pas d'auteur, qui est anonyme. Cette "consommation" impersonnelle, anonyme, mais inextinguible de l'être, celle qui murmure au fond du néant lui-même, nous la fixons par le terme d'*il y a.]* (*EE*, 57)

> Let us imagine all things, beings and persons, returning to nothingness. What remains after this imaginary destruction of everything is not something, but the fact that *there is*. The absence of everything returns as a presence, as the place where the bottom has dropped out of everything, an atmospheric density, a plenitude of the void or the murmur of silence. There is, after this destruction of things and beings, the impersonal "field of forces" of existing.

---

4. With the *il y a*, Levinas seeks to put into question the Aristotelian substantialist view, according to Bernard Forthomme, *Une philosophie de la transcendance* (Paris: Vrin, 1979), 82.

5. Ibid., 60, 65.

There is something that is neither subject nor substantive. The fact of existing imposes itself where there is no longer anything. And it is anonymous: there is neither anyone nor anything that takes this existence upon itself. It is impersonal like "it is raining" or "it is hot." Existing returns no matter with what negation one dismisses it. There is, as the irremissibility of pure existing. *[Imaginons le retour au néant de toutes choses, êtres et personnes. Allons-nous rencontrer le pur néant? Il reste après cette destruction imaginaire de toutes choses, non pas quelque chose, mais le fait qu'*il y a. *L'absence de toutes choses, retourne comme une présence: comme le lieu où tout a sombré, comme une densité d'atmosphère, comme une plénitude du vide ou comme le murmure du silence. Il y a, après cette destruction des choses et des êtres, le "champ de forces" de l'exister, impersonnel. Quelque chose qui n'est ni sujet, ni substantif. Le fait de l'exister qui s'impose, quand il n'y a plus rien. Et c'est anonyme: il n'y a personne ni rien qui prenne cette existence sur lui. C'est impersonnel comme "il pleut" ou "il fait chaud." Exister qui retourne quelle que soit la négation par laquelle on l'écarte. Il y a comme l'irrémissibilité de l'exister pur.]* (TA, 46–47)

In each case of his presentation of the *il y a*, Levinas uses the identical wording, "imaginons." In both instances, the imagination gives access to the *il y a*. Would this be because, as Bataille suggests, in "the murmur of silence" of the *il y a* there is something heterogeneous to discursive knowledge (EPE, 167)? Bataille observes that the *il y a* is arrived at only indirectly, through "the channel of its formal effects" (EPE, 171): in art, especially in modern art, in the surrealism to which Levinas makes explicit reference, and in sociology, in what the ethnologist Lévy-Bruhl described as participation. In mystical participation, Levinas writes, "the identity of the terms is lost. They are divested of what constituted their very substantivity . . . The private existence of each term . . . loses this private character and returns to an undifferentiated background . . . We recognize here the *there is*" (EE, 60–61).

Apart from the aesthetic category of the imagination and the experience of participation, the only other approach to the *il y a* that Levinas will suggest is the example of insomnia.[6]

> The insecurity does not come from the things of the day world which the night conceals; it is due just to the fact that nothing approaches, nothing comes, nothing threatens; this silence, this tranquility, this void of sensations constitutes a mute, absolutely indeterminate menace . . . One can also speak of different forms of night that occur right in the daytime. Illuminated objects

6. Note that in *Time and the Other* insomnia is introduced by Levinas as precisely *not* an imagined experience (TA, 48). Paul Davies points out that insomnia, at the limit, is not an example either; at stake is an insomniac philosophy. See Davies's "On Resorting to an Ethical Language," in EFP.

can appear to us as though in twilight shapes . . . Such is . . . the case with
the "fantastic," "hallucinatory" reality in poets like Rimbaud, even when they
name the most familiar things and the most accustomed beings . . . Certain
passages of Huysmans or Zola, the calm and smiling horror of de Maupassant's
tales do not only give, as is sometimes thought, a representation "faithful to"
or exceeding reality, but penetrate behind the form which light reveals into
that materiality which, far from corresponding to the philosophical materialism of the authors, constitutes the dark background of existence. It makes
things appear to us in a night, like the monotonous presence that bears down
on us in insomnia. *[L'insécurité ne vient pas des choses du monde diurne que la
nuit recèle, elle tient précisément au fait que rien n'approche, que rien ne vient, que
rien ne menace: ce silence, cette tranquillité, ce néant de sensations constituent une
sourde menace indéterminée . . . Aussi peut-on parler de nuits en plein jour. Les objets
éclairés peuvent nous apparaître comme à travers leurs crépuscules . . . (Telle) la
réalité "fantastique," "hallucinante" chez des poètes comme Rimbaud, même quand
ils nomment les choses les plus familières, les êtres les plus habituels . . . Certains
passages de Huysmans, de Zola, la calme et souriante horreur de tel conte de Maupassant,
ne donnent pas seulement, comme on le pense parfois, une peinture "fidèle" ou excessive
de la réalité, mais pénètrent—derrière la forme que la lumière révèle—dans cette maté-
rialité qui, loin de correspondre au matérialisme philosophique des auteurs, constitue le
fond obscur de l'existence. Il nous font apparaître les choses à travers une nuit, comme
une monotone présence qui nous étouffe dans l'insomnie.]* (EE, 96–98)

The decisive importance of the category of the imagination for the approach to the *il y a* may also account for the seeming necessity for Levinas
to make recourse to so many literary examples in the course of his presentation: Hoffman, Rimbaud, Huysmans, Zola, Maupassant, Racine, and
especially Shakespeare. Many readers will no doubt find something imaginative, even "literary" or poetic, about Levinas's presentation of the *il
y a*. I would like to resist this aestheticizing view of Levinas as a beautiful
stylist. While this "literary" aspect of Levinas's writing is pronounced in
his works from the late forties, it is not something that goes away in
subsequent works. I suggest, moreover, that we cannot take for granted
that we know what we mean by "literary." My aim is to interrogate critically what one calls "style" in a philosophical work. Derrida, asking about
"how Levinas writes his works," attends to a certain syntax or linking that
permits Levinas both to say the "otherwise than being" and to preserve
its ontological insecurity. But such an understanding of "style" is at a
considerable remove from the belles-lettristic conception that often can
be said to underlie Levinas's readers' appreciation of his prose and, for
that matter, Levinas's own celebration of the masterpiece or of "the beautiful" in poetry.

Closely interwoven into Levinas's writing on the *il y a* is a reading of

Shakespeare. There Levinas invests the aesthetic (and already philosophical) genre of tragedy with the revelation of the *il y a*. It is in Shakespearean tragedy, in the limit-situations of murder and of dying, that Levinas finds the inability to escape from being, from anonymous existence, the nocturnal horror of the return of presence in negation, the return of phantasms, shadows, and ghosts. He writes:

> In *Macbeth*, the apparition of Banquo's ghost is also a decisive experience of the "no exit" from existence, its phantom return through the fissures through which one has driven it. "The times have been, that when the Brains were out, the man would dye, and there an end; But now they rise again . . . and push us from our stools. This is more strange than such a murther is." "And it is over with" is impossible. The horror does not come from the danger. "What man dare, I dare . . . Approach thou like the rugged Russian Bear . . . Take any shape but that, and my firm Nerves shall never tremble . . . Hence horrible Shadow, unreal mockery hence . . ." It is the shadow of being that horrifies Macbeth; the profile of being that takes form in nothingness [*l'être se profilant dans le néant*]. (*EE*, 62)

Here Levinas hints at an extended reading of *Macbeth* in terms of the *il y a*. Levinas's reading of Shakespeare—whom Levinas privileges not just for his own philosophy but for philosophy as such—is an "existentialist" one.[7] Post-Heideggerian and to some extent contra Heidegger, it is at every point concerned with the impossibility of death, the impossibility of the suicide that would attempt to master nothingness: "[B]eing is evil not because it is finite but without limits" (*TA*, 29).[8]

Levinas's most telling use of a literary example can be seen, within a discussion of the irremissibility of existence, in the following footnote to Blanchot:

> Maurice Blanchot's *Thomas the Obscure* opens with the description of the *there is* . . . (cf. in particular ch. II, pp. 13–16). The presence of absence, the night, the dissolution of the subject in the night, the horror of being, the return of being to the heart of every negative movement, the reality of irreality, are admirably stated there [*y sont admirablement dits*]. (*EE*, 63)

Levinas refers to the opening pages of Blanchot's *recit* as a "description" of the *il y a*, as a place where the presence of absence, the night, the dissolution of the subject, the horror of being are "stated" or "said" (*sont*

---

7. Levinas says, "It sometimes seems to me that the whole of philosophy is only a meditation on Shakespeare" (*TA*, 72). He also states, "There is existentialism further back than Kierkegaard and Pascal, in Shakespeare and Socrates" (*SH*, 47).

8. In conceiving of evil not as a privation of being but as an excess of being, Levinas seems implicitly to contest the scholastic view.

dits). He does so, Joseph Libertson remarks, "without equivocation or even the hint of contrast" between his and Blanchot's articulation of the *il y a* (PRX, 206). Bataille makes this contrast explicit when he writes: "Levinas says of some pages of *Thomas the Obscure* that they are the description of the *there is.* But this is not exact. Levinas describes and Blanchot cries—as it were—the *there is. [Levinas décrit et Maurice Blanchot crie en quelque sorte l'il y a.]*" (EPE, 168).

BATAILLE ON DESCRIPTION AND CRY

Not only does the difference between description and cry organize Bataille's essay. It brings into view philosophy's problematic relation with the *il y a* and, at the same time, what was referred to earlier in these pages as a double bind that emerges every time Levinas introduces a literary allusion or citation.

Before considering what is at stake in the difference between description and cry, it must first be said that, like Blanchot and Levinas, Bataille also develops independently the thought of the *il y a*, in texts such as *Inner Experience.* As Libertson puts it: in each of their writings from the 1940s, the *il y a* is "a common denominator . . . the positing of a differential in being which is not negation, and a notation of the enormous consequences produced by this 'weakness' of the negative" (PRX, 208). Libertson points out that the writings which present the *il y a* are "thematically disparate." While the *il y a* is associated with something called "poetry" in all three cases, there are important differences. For Levinas it is associated with horror and suffocation; for Bataille with ecstasy, joy, and celebration, and for Blanchot, as we have seen, it has, at the very least, a *literary* specificity.

Hence, on the one hand, when Bataille says that Levinas describes *(décrit)* and Blanchot cries *(crie)* the *il y a*, he puts his finger on what we have called Levinas's overly denotative treatment of literary allusions. Levinas un-cries (or de-cries) what Blanchot cries as the *il y a*. Levinas constates what Blanchot performs in the cry. As Bataille says: "Levinas defines as an object, *by a formal generalization* (in other words, by discourse) that which in the *literary* text of Blanchot is *purely the cry of existence*" (EPE, 169). Here Bataille attends precisely to the difference between the modes of *philosophical* and *literary* writing. He attends to the specificity of the literary, to that which, in a literary text, may be unassimilable to a philosophical argument, even to Levinas's "philosophical" argument.

As if to emphasize the difference between a philosophical "constating" and a literary "performing" of the *il y a*, Bataille *cites* Blanchot's 1942 *Thomas*, where Levinas had given only an abridged (and constative) reference to it in a footnote. Whereas Levinas, in his own presentation of the *il y a* in *Existence and Existents*, had not only constated the *il y a* where Blanchot had performed it in *Thomas*, but had constated Blanchot's very performing of the *il y a*, thereby rendering it "hollow and void," Bataille gives the Blanchot text to perform the *il y a*:

> The night seemed to him far more somber, more terrible than any other night, as though it had truly issued from a wound of thought which no longer thought itself, of thought taken ironically as object by something other than thought. It was night itself. Images which constituted its obscurity inundated him, and his body, transformed into a demoniacal spirit, tried to imagine them. He saw nothing, and, far from being distressed, he made this absence of vision the culmination of his sight. Useless for seeing, his eye took on extraordinary proportions, developed beyond measure, and, stretching out on the horizon, let the night penetrate its center in order to create for itself an iris. Throughout this void, it was the look and the object of the look which mingled together. Not only did this eye which saw nothing apprehend something, it apprehended the cause of its vision. It saw as an object that which prevented it from seeing.[9] *[La nuit lui parut bientôt plus sombre, plus terrible que n'importe quelle autre nuit, comme si elle était réelement sortie d'une blessure de la pensée qui ne se pensait plus, de la pensée prise ironiquement comme objet par autre chose que la pensée. C'était la nuit même. Des images qui faisaient son obscurité l'inondaient et le corps transformé en un esprit démoniaque cherchait à se les représenter. Il ne voyait rien et, loin d'être accablé, il faisait de cette absence de vision le point culminant de son regard. Son oeil inutile pour voir, prenait des proportions extraordinaires, se développait d'une manière démesurée et, s'étendant sur l'horizon, laissait la nuit pénétrer en son centre pour se créer un iris. Par ce vide c'était donc le regard et l'objet du regard qui se mêlaient. Non seulement cet oeil qui ne voyait rien appréhendait quelque chose, mais il appréhendait la cause de sa vision. Il voyait comme un objet, ce qui faisait qu'il ne voyait pas.] (Thomas the Obscure)*

Any paraphrase of this passage from Blanchot's 1942 récit (such as, the eye "saw" the condition of impossibility of its seeing) would seem to risk turning the cry into a description. In Libertson's own commentary, the passage "*describes* the impossibility of a reality without power in which the inability to see does not exhaust the reality of seeing . . . the *il y a* as urgency and monotony" (*PRX*, 207; emphasis mine). It is as if no commentator on Bataille, Blanchot, and Levinas, however alerted to the

---

9. Bataille cites the first, longer version of Blanchot's *Thomas l'obscur* (1941), not the new version published in 1950. For an English translation of the new version, see *Thomas the Obscure*, trans. Robert Lamberton (New York: David Lewis, 1973).

difference between description and cry, can escape the tension between them. Suffice it to say that this tension, this problem of maintaining the *il y a* in its performativity, can be found at every level of the presentation of the *il y a*. It can be shown that Bataille will do the same thing to Levinas that Levinas had done to Blanchot, when, in "From Existentialism to the Primacy of Economy," Bataille correlates his own understanding of the *il y a* with Levinas's.[10] Similarly, in "Literature and the Right to Death," Blanchot will say that Levinas's account "illuminates" what Blanchot himself means by the *il y a*.[11] Ultimately, each is unable to quote the other.

Again, for Bataille, the dissolution of world, the existent's dissolution into existence, the "murmur of silence" that Levinas presents as the *il y a* is heterogeneous to all discourse. Bataille writes: "[C]ommon and coherent discourse only appears to accede to this dissolution: it speaks about it and cannot accomplish it, in that what discourse enunciates is always a meaningful proposition" (EPE, 167). Perhaps this is why literature, a nonconstative mode of utterance, seems to "perform" the *il y a* more felicitously than does philosophy. That would be to say that what the *il y a* performs is not only its heterogeneity to "world," "subject," "meaning," and "discourse," but also the heterogeneity and unassimilability of literature to philosophy. The question arises: Can Levinas's readings of Blanchot be said to respect this heterogeneity? Do his readings of Blanchot's texts do justice to their interpretive demand?

For the most part, in his writings on Blanchot from the 1940s, Levinas is content merely to allude, as he does in *Time and the Other*. Anticipating the description of the identification of the I in the Same that he will later propose in *Totality and Infinity* ("the I riveted to itself, lived as ennui, the alterity of the I that takes itself for another *[le moi rivé à soi, vecu comme ennui, l'alterité du je qui se prend comme autre]*" (*TI*, 37), and using a similar wording, he writes:

10. "*Inner Experience* expresses entirely this situation which is that of the *there is* of Levinas, and to which the sentence in question in Blanchot gives an accomplished expression . . . Levinas's thinking . . . does not differ, it seems to me, from Blanchot's and from mine" (EPE, 168).

11. "In his book *Existence and Existents*, Emmanuel Levinas uses the term *il y a* "to illuminate" this anonymous and impersonal flow of being that precedes all being, being that is already present in the heart of disappearance, that in the depths of annihilation still returns to being, being as the fatality of being, nothingness as existence: when there is nothing, *there is* being. Maurice Blanchot, "Literature and the Right to Death," trans. Lydia Davis, in *The Gaze of Orpheus* (New York: Station Hill, 1981), 51. On these and other intertextual intrications between Levinas, Blanchot, and Bataille, see Libertson, *PRX*, 204–8.

> Identity is not an inoffensive relation with the self but an enchainment to the self *[un enchaînement à soi]* . . . The I is already riveted to itself *[le je est déjà rivé à soi]* . . . The return of the ego upon itself is precisely neither a serene reflection nor the result of a purely philosophical reflection. Its relationship with itself is, as in Blanchot's novel Aminadab *[comme dans le roman de Blanchot, Aminadab]*, the relationship with a double chained to the ego *[enchaîné à moi]*, a viscous, heavy, stupid double, but one the ego is with precisely because it is me. (*TA*, 56)

Here what links Levinas's discourse to Blanchot's 1942 text, *Aminadab*, what allows Levinas to use that text *to illustrate* a philosophical argument, is the telltale simile, *comme* (like), which introduces so many of Levinas's literary allusions.[12] The *comme* presumes that it is possible to compare, to find a resemblance between a philosophical description and a literary text, or between, in Bataille's terms, a description and a cry. It would seem to exemplify, especially in the literary allusions in the postwar works, Levinas's pronounced tendency to read thematically. Yet one must also observe that Levinas's comparison to Blanchot's récit "works": it "serves" to illustrate the structure of identity. Moreover, Levinas's abbreviated comments on *Aminadab* are as successful, as convincing, a reading of Blanchot's demanding and enigmatic narrative prose as any commentator has achieved. (This is even more the case with regard to Levinas's 1975 reading of Blanchot's *The Madness of the Day*.) Is this because of the extent to which the Blanchot text is *already* philosophical? Because its "denotative" level is already found at a level of considerable abstraction? But the question nonetheless remains: Do not Levinas's "philosophical" readings risk draining Blanchot's texts of their literary specificity, as Lyotard implies in "Levinas's Logic"? Do not his readings risk turning Blanchot's texts into philosophy, as when he constated Blanchot's performing of the *il y a?* This would be to say that when a literary text is found interesting or significant by Levinas for his ethical philosophy, Levinas's reading is *least* literary, or that when Levinas's reading "works" philosophically; it doesn't work, it betrays.

---

12. Cf. "The consciousness of a thinking subject . . . is precisely the breakup of the insomnia of the anonymous being, the possibility . . . to take refuge in oneself, so as to withdraw from being, to, *like* Penelope, have a night to oneself to undo the work that one keeps vigil over and supervises during the day *[avoir, comme Pénélope, une nuit à soi pour défaire l'ouvrage veillé et surveillé dans la journée]*" (*EE*, 65–66). "In weariness we want to escape existence itself, and not only one of its landscapes, in a longing for more beautiful skies. An evasion without an itinerary and without an end, it is not trying to come ashore somewhere. Like for Baudelaire's true travellers, it is a matter of parting for the sake of parting *[Comme pour les vrais voyageurs de Baudelaire, il s'agit de partir pour partir]*" (*EE*, 25).

This double bind, or a version of it, was formulated previously in this book as Levinas's saying of Abraham and doing of Odysseus. It was formulated as the problem of how to receive the ethical, suggested by Levinas himself in the 1963 "Trace" when he asserts ingratitude, that is, a non return to origin, as the necessary response to the radical generosity of the one-way movement (the very passage where the allusion to Abraham and Odysseus occurred). It was elaborated by Derrida and Lyotard, when they bring the problem of how to receive the ethical to bear on "the ethics of interpreting Emmanuel Levinas." In each of these cases the double bind takes in variously the relationship between the philosophical and the literary, the constative and the performative, and, in Bataille's terms, *description* and *cry*. In Bataille's essay, I will show, the distinction between description and cry is extended not just to the oppositions between the philosophical and the nonphilosophical but also to the oppositions between philosophy and existence, and discourse and ineffability. The stakes around the *il y a*—the cry of existence—increase accordingly.

JEAN WAHL'S EXISTENTIALISMS

Bataille's essay is, in fact, a review not just of Levinas's *Existence and Existents* but also of Jean Wahl's *A Short History of Existentialism* (1947) and two other works on the same topic. Bataille rightly dismisses the term *existentialism* as having virtually no value. He certainly does not wish to include himself within such a designation (EPE, 157). Nonetheless, "existentialism" is, in Bataille's essay, a rubric that can take in at once Levinas's discussion of existence and Jean Wahl's presentation of the work of Kierkegaard, Heidegger, Jaspers, Sartre, and others. Wahl himself, in *Short History*, is at pains to show that, while the problem of existence is important in the writing of these philosophers, one cannot even call it "existence philosophy" much less "existentialism." First of all, these are terms that Heidegger rejected.[13] Second, insofar as the object of this philosophy—lived or felt existence, namely, its affective and factical dimensions—is prior to knowledge, "existentialism" would be as Jaspers asserted the death of the so-called philosophy of existence. It would be, as Bataille puts it, "comparable to the ancient sacrificer who revealed the truth of a victim by killing him" (EPE, 160).

Jean Wahl's role in French philosophical life, and in Levinas's philosophical life in particular, should be acknowledged. Levinas's teacher,

---

13. See *SH*, 2, and the letter from Heidegger included at the close of Wahl's *ET*, 134.

mentor, and personal friend, Wahl is the author of numerous books, including *Le malheur de la conscience dans la philosophie de Hegel* (1929), *Études Kierkegaardiennes* (1937), and *Existence humaine et transcendance* (1944), *Poésie, pensée, perception* (1948), *Les philosophies de l'existence* (1954). The founder of the College Philosophique (the forum in which Levinas first delivered *Time and the Other* as a lecture course), the editor of the journal *Deucalion* (in which Levinas's presentation of the *il y a* first appeared), Wahl not only gave courses on Kierkegaard, Hegel, Husserl, Heidegger, and others, but he was an indefatigable organizer of international colloquia devoted to these thinkers.

Wahl's view of philosophy could be termed *inclusive*. Philosophy is something that is nourished by its contact with the arts, especially poetry and painting. As Levinas comments in the 1975 essay "Jean Wahl: Neither Having nor Being," for Wahl, philosophy is not only in philosophy; it is in existence, and it is in art (*JW*, 14). The "pluridisciplinarity" (*TA*, 34) of the College Philosophique makes this explicit, as well as Wahl's 1946 editor's Introduction to the first volume of *Deucalion:* "The upheavals in the milieu in which we find ourselves have been accompanied by profound modifications of thought . . . if philosophical concepts must be revised, that will come about through the very contact between philosophy and these other activities."[14] In his works, Wahl repeatedly asserts the "kinship" between poetry and philosophy, or between poetry and metaphysics (*PPP*, 26). Wahl tends to privilege not only poetic expression *within* philosophy, particularly as represented by Kierkegaard and Nietzsche. He proposes a new, hybrid category of poet-philosophers (*CME*, 9) who are said "to resolve the problem of philosophical research in poetic effusion" (*EPE*, 159). Hence in addition to the nonsystematic or "literary" philosophers like Kierkegaard and Nietzsche, Wahl frequently names poets, writers, and artists, such as Rimbaud, Nerval, Blake, Hölderlin, Dostoevsky, and Van Gogh.

Two aspects of Wahl's own philosophy which influenced Levinas can readily be identified. First, Wahl's description of transcendence, as a relation that absolves itself from the relation, "a quasi-ineffable junction between relation and nonrelation" (*ET*, 10) is brought to bear on *Totality and Infinity*'s account of transcendence, and Wahl's particular term, *transascendance*, is explicitly evoked there (*TI*, 35). Wahl always emphasizes the radical separation and distance proper to trans(as)cendence: "If the

---

14. Wahl, "Presentation," *Deucalion* 1 (1946): 10–11. See the superb discussion of Wahl by Paul Ricoeur in Jeanne Hersch, ed., *Jean Wahl et Gabriel Marcel* (Paris: Beauchesne, 1976).

movement of transcendence can be explained by transcendence as a term, then there is no transcendence properly speaking" (*ET*, 35). For Wahl, the term or limit is the very negation of this very movement. That is why "the greatest transcendence is perhaps the transcendence that transcends transcendence, that is to say, to fall again into immanence" (*ET*, 38). Second, for Wahl, the individual is transcended not just by the "up above *[en haut]*," and "beyond *[au delà]*" of trans-ascendence but also by the "down below *[en bas]*," which is expressed by Wahl's corresponding term *transdescendance* (*ET*, 45). ("*Je suis rendu à la terre . . . et à la sous-terre, aux racines,*" writes Rimbaud, quoted by Wahl [*PPP*, 250]. The other poet-philosophers that Wahl privileges—Nietzsche, Kierkegaard, Dostoevsky—are similarly fascinated by the demonic.) There is an equivocalness in the very idea of a transcendence "down below" that I will return to later. Suffice it to note that what Wahl calls "transdescendence" provides the terminological and the conceptual link between the aesthetic event and the *il y a* in Levinas's *Existence and Existents*. The term is explicitly used by Levinas to describe the ontology of the work of art in "Reality and Its Shadow" (RO, 8).

While these two marks of Wahl's influence on Levinas are certainly significant, I propose to put them in the context of a larger question of Wahl's presentation of "existentialism," and ultimately Wahl's position with regard to aesthetics. In the following pages I will show that Levinas's negative discourse on art is something of a reaction to Wahl's position. Similarly, Levinas's intertextual encounter with the "literary" philosopher Kierkegaard, and the somewhat dismissive reading he offers of him in two texts from the 1960s, is mediated by Wahl's particular interpretation of him.

That interpretation, especially in such works as *Études Kierkegaardiennes, Existence humaine et transcendance, Kierkegaard Vivant* (the proceedings of a 1964 Unesco conference on Kierkegaard that Wahl organized), and in Wahl's introduction to the French translation of *Crainte et tremblement* is always probing but sometimes too reverential for Levinas, who, in the essay devoted to him, will refer to Wahl's "appurtenance in the family of Kierkegaardian spirits" (JW, 16), an appurtenance Levinas apparently does not share. Levinas expresses a similar reserve vis-à-vis Lev Shestov's *Kierkegaard et la philosophie existentielle*, translated from the Russian in 1937, a book that Levinas read and reviewed.[15] Shestov's book

---

15. Levinas's review of Shestov's *Kierkegaard et la philosophie existentielle* appeared in *Revue des Études Juives* 2 (1937) 139–41. His reservations concern the very Christianized Bible that emerges from Shestov's interpretive emphasis on the unity between the two testaments.

places Kierkegaard (and Dostoevsky) in a line that goes back to biblical "existentialism," signaled by the book's subtitle, *vox clamantis in deserto*. This does not prevent Levinas from sharing in the broadest sense what Shestov calls Kierkegaard's opposition to speculative truth,[16] or what for Wahl would be Kierkegaard's "cry of suffocated existence" (EPE, 158), over and against the system that would reduce the individual subjectivity "to a paragraph" (*SH*, 4) to the "sum total of his acts and works."[17] Levinas himself will call this, in the preface to *Totality and Infinity*, "the Kierkegaardian protestation against the totality" (*TI*, 26).

Wahl describes Kierkegaard's philosophy as "a cry of a subjectivity toward that which goes beyond it" (*EK*, 256). *Fear and Trembling* is also, for Wahl, "a cry" (*EK*, 204) addressed to Regina, after he has broken his engagement to her. He hopes that it will effectuate her return to him, just as Isaac was returned to Abraham. Kierkegaard hopes to return, as did Abraham, to the finite, after renouncing it infinitely. But Regina does not heed Kierkegaard's cry; in a sense it is inaudible to her. Wahl calls *Fear and Trembling* "a fruitless attempt to say *yes* to the real" (*CT*, XXIII).

To say that this attempt failed is not to say that there is not success in it, that it did not succeed *in* failing. For Kierkegaard, Abraham achieves an absolute relation to the absolute, the price of which is the radical solitude and the incommunicability of his religious position. Abraham is silent because, in being willing to sacrifice his son, and with him the kind of generality that Kierkegaard (and Hegel) determine as "ethical," he puts himself outside the general, outside the realm where one can "say everything."[18] Kierkegaard's cry *is* Abraham's silence. Since in *Fear and Trembling* the demonic is also the realm of silence—and outside what Kierkegaard, after Hegel, calls the general—thus the demonic is in effect twinned with the divine (as Derrida will eventually argue in *The Gift of Death*). According to Wahl, Kierkegaard indicates precisely "this vast and somber region" between the good and the bad transcendence (*CT*, IX).

CRIES AND LACERATIONS (KIERKEGAARD)

If Kierkegaard's attempt in *Fear and Trembling* to say yes to the real, to achieve repetition fails and succeeds precisely by failing, for Wahl such

16. Levinas refers to this as "the wound from which Leon Shestov, stricken by the very necessity in which reasoned and reasoning reason triumph, bleeds throughout all his works" (*SMB*, 163–64).

17. Jean Wahl, *Philosophies of Existence*, trans. F. M. Lory (London: Routledge, 1968), 76.

18. Søren Kierkegaard, *Fear and Trembling*, trans. Hong and Hong (Princeton, NJ: Princeton University Press, 1983), 61.

a paradoxical success would illuminate a paradox inherent in all "existentialisms." Wahl asks: "[D]oes not the existentialist risk destroying the very existence that he wishes above all to preserve?" (*SH*, 33). There are several senses that Wahl would give to this necessity of self-destruction. First of all, Kierkegaard pushes thinking to its limit (*ET*, 24) by the intensity of his individual feeling *(intensité de ses sentiments individuelles)* (*ET*, 50), and because he drives individuality to its extreme tension or laceration. No one is as solitary, as miserable, as is "Kierkegaard." His is an "intense consummation of life *[un consommation si intense de la vie]*" (*EPE*, 161), a consummation of life "to the limit of death *[à la limite de mourir]*" (*EPE*, 161). Second, the generalizing and universalizing mode of philosophical discourse recuperates every contestation of it by or in the name of subjective existence. Kierkegaard's affirmation of subjectivity in its heterogeneity to the totality necessarily passes by way of the universal, gets sucked into the universal, destroys itself. Therein lies its very intelligibility. Kierkegaard's anti-Hegelianism is still Hegelianism. Finally, for the same reason, if the affirmation of existence in its heterogeneity to philosophy necessarily destroys itself, that is because, as Wahl puts it. "[T]he metaphysics of human reality is not simply a metaphysics about human reality; it is metaphysics necessarily coming to produce itself as reality" (*ET*, 51). That is to say that there *is* no *philosophy* of existence. In Wahl's view, there are lives—those of Kierkegaard, Rimbaud, Van Gogh, for example—which are *more* existential than the so-called philosophies of existence (*ET*, 41). As Bataille summarizes this contribution of "existentialism": "a pathetic existence *[un existence pathétique]*, forcefully expressed, would be substituted for the position of philosophical truth" (*EPE*, 159).

That is why, for Bataille, "the choice that Jean Wahl makes of Rimbaud and Van Gogh is significant; it is a matter of spirits so strained that they do not survive *[il s'agit d'esprits si tendus qu'ils ne survivent pas]*" (*EPE*, 163). Not only does Kierkegaard consume himself rapidly in his agitation and his despair. The poet Arthur Rimbaud, at the age of twenty, after writing his greatest work, *A Season in Hell* (a work that ends with a "farewell" to literature), stopped writing. "He amputated himself alive from poetry," in Mallarmé's formulation. As Marc Froment-Meurice has observed, he commits literary or spiritual suicide.[19] Rimbaud and Kierkegaard thus exemplify for Wahl the self-destructive paradox of all "existentialisms." Bataille formulates it as follows:

19. Marc Froment-Meurice, *Solitudes: From Rimbaud to Heidegger*, trans. Peter Walsh (Albany: State University of New York Press, 1995), 45; *Solitudes: de Rimbaud à Heidegger* (Paris: Éditions Galilée, 1989).

The experience of a profound subjectivity has always one condition: it destroys the one who has it . . . One separates *A Season in Hell* from the silence of Rimbaud; but one fails to discern the silence that is already in the cry, the cry still in the silence. Kierkegaard did not know, when dying (but death here counts little, it is the failure, the nonsatisfaction, the laceration) that he would ultimately give to his reader of a hundred years later, Hegel's achieved satisfaction (but linked, immanently, to its opposite). Nevertheless, the reader, in general, would not have a clear conscience about this. He would put the accent on the cry (on the protestation of the individual), not on the silence, even while a feeling of calm desolation already impregnates it. There are opposed possibilities which touch each other and are linked. *[On sépare* Une Saison en Enfer *du silence de Rimbaud: on perçoit mal, on ne discerne pas clairement dans le cri le silence déjà, dans le silence encore le cri . . . Kierkegaard (. . .) ne sut pas en mourant (mais la mort, ici compte peu, c'est l'échec, l'insatisfaction et le déchirement), qu'il donnerait à la limite, à son lecteur, cent ans plus tard, la satisfaction achevée (mais liée, immanente à son contraire) de Hegel.]* (EPE, 163–64)

In Bataille's dialectical reading, Rimbaud's paroxysmal cry of existence in *A Season in Hell* implies, even depends on, his subsequent silence. This is the silence *in* the cry and the cry *in* the silence. This insight is lacerating: while Kierkegaard thought he was protesting the Hegelian totality or crying out, he was silent. And the reader who is attracted to the cry of a subjectivity of a Rimbaud or a Kierkegaard thus has a bad conscience. The reader chooses to hear the protestation or the cry but not the silence, the death, that subtends it.

Furthermore, the individual's cry, his protestation, on the one hand, and his silence, his disappearance, on the other, should not be conceived as the difference between life and death, presence and absence. Both mark the limit of what is expressible, what Wahl and Bataille (differently) term the *ineffable*. Recall that for Bataille, the cry of the *il y a* is arrived at only indirectly, "through the channel of its formal effects" (EPE, 171). Rather than being opposed to each other, both cry and silence would be opposed to something called "discourse" or "philosophy." There is no doubt something inherently "self-destructive" here, as Wahl would understand it. The cry of a solitary subjectivity deprives the individual of the very solitude he or she would express when it is shared with others. Kierkegaard can only announce his secret to others by abolishing it.[20] If Kierkegaard's achievement is the reinscription of the pathetic or affective aspects of existence (and this is precisely what, according to Levinas, Hei-

---

20. Maurice Blanchot, "Le 'Journal' de Kierkegaard," *Faux pas* (Paris: Gallimard, 1943), 29.

degger retrieves in Kierkegaard),[21] those thoughts are necessarily destroyed once they are brought into philosophical intelligibility. Ultimately, that there is silence *in* the cry means that the subject is the disappearing condition of the experience of subjectivity.

This is a far cry from the "aesthetic solution" that Wahl proposes to the heterogeneity of the existential cry to philosophy. As Wahl would have it, there is a privileged kind of translatability of the existential cry into art, poetry, literature. For Wahl, the "poet-philosopher" creates a dialectic between ineffability and expression and thus gives voice to the ineffable. Poetry would be a superior form of this silence. Just as there are lives, according to Wahl, more existential than the philosophies of existence, so too poetry "says" the heterogeneity of existence to philosophy better than does philosophy. In Wahl's Romantic position, the poet-philosopher "reconciles" in a dialectical fashion the opposition between philosophy and poetry, philosophy and nonphilosophy. Such a view of poetic achievement, and the creative powers of a subject that it would celebrate, seems at odds with the grim paradox Wahl himself has articulated, namely, that the affirmation of subjective existence depends on the obliteration of the self. But in Bataille's reading, the nonarticulate, existential cry can no more be translated into a phrase or into a philosophical discourse than can the literary cry of the *il y a*. The (performative) cry cannot be translated into the (constative) discourse without its performative dimension's being neutralized. That is why, Bataille remarks drily, there is no literature of existentialism: "[A] literature illustrating a system just withdraws from it all the more" (EPE, 159).

In short, it is as if for Bataille there is something too dialectizable about Wahl's understanding of the ineffable. While Wahl would locate the problem of the relationship between philosophy and nonphilosophy, all too reassuringly, *within* philosophy, Bataille attends to how this relationship is *inscribed* within philosophy, as a certain outside. The ineffable, as Wahl understands it, doesn't really trouble anything, whereas for Bataille the ineffability has a more radical sense.

Bataille most decisively departs from Wahl's aesthetic solution to the problem of philosophy's relation to its other—nonphilosophy, existence, literature, "cry"—when he elaborates on Wahl's "paradox"—which, for Bataille, is not one—and radicalizes it:

---

21. He retrieves "those thoughts—which may be called 'pathetic'—which have been disseminated throughout the history of philosophy" (*SH,* 49).

But those who, on the condition that they disappear, express existence in intensity, are not destroyed by a necessity of which they are conscious. They themselves do not attain the universal, only the commentaries and the effects of their works and their life on others render their particularity universal. But an illusion is maintained: in the value accorded to their work, one does not know that the intensity of feeling that renders the work attractive also founds a universal, by the destruction of the author of whom it is the promise. *[Mais une illusion est maintenue: dans la valeur prêtée à l'oeuvre, on ne sait pas que l'intensité des sentiments qui rend l'oeuvre attirante, fonde aussi un universel, par la destruction de son auteur dont elle est la promesse.]* (EPE, 163)

Bataille calls attention to a structure that differs radically from Wahl's (logical) "paradox" of an awareness that the price of the affirmation of subjectivity is the destruction of that same subjectivity. It is the difference between what Blanchot calls "the consciousness of disappearing *[conscience de disparaître]* and conciousness disappearing *[conscience disparaissante]*" (SL, 97). Or as Levinas formulates this with regard to the ethical putting into question of the self by the other, it is the difference between a consciousness or awareness *of* being put into question *(une conscience de la mise en question)* and consciousness put (i.e., radically) into question *(la mise en question de la conscience)* (T, 353). In short, it is the difference between something that is available to consciousness and perception—the kind of cognition called aesthetic that Wahl would privilege, and that the very title of his book, *Poésie, pensée, perception,* in effect announces—and that which is not available to a consciousness or a subject, not accessible as a secure perception, in other words, not an aesthetic value at all.

This "value" of the work is, precisely, what Bataille calls "illusion." What "works" in these author's works, as well as everything that gets reified as poetic achievement, depends on the destruction of the author: it is, in fact, an affirmation of death. But this is a death that no author or subject can appropriate. Rather than speaking of death as the consequence, price, or effect of an intense and lacerated subjectivity, one would have to speak of subjectivity and the inner life as an effect of death or destruction, a subjectivity-effect. The *experience* of a profound subjectivity—insofar as it is available neither to a subject nor to the presence of the present—is not one. And certainly, within the works of Wahl's "poet-philosophers," any notion of poetic authority and its concomitant celebration of the creative powers of a subject is simply a death trap.

Bataille's critique of Wahl's aesthetic solution to the problem of philosophy's relationship to its other has certain resemblances to Levinas's, although Levinas's reasons for finding the aesthetic solution problematic will be quite different. In Levinas the critique will turn on the specific alterity of the ethical, which also is never recuperable for dialectics but is always held at a distance from what Bataille calls "poetry." Nonetheless, Bataille's emphasis on the radical consequences of the subject as the disappearing condition of subjectivity, which, I have proposed, has affinities with a signature move of both Blanchot and Levinas, points to further convergences. Bataille asserts, in a sentence that either Blanchot or Levinas might have written, that "what is at stake in the laceration of [human] life, can only be at stake in lacerating *[ce qui est en cause dans le déchirement de cette vie ne peut être en cause qu'en déchirant]*" (EPE, 164). At the limit, "existentialism" would be not a philosophy *of* heartrending cries and lacerations but a lacerating philosophy. Not a philosophy of rending but a philosophy of rending that also rends "itself."

LEVINAS READING KIERKEGAARD

In his 1963 essay on Kierkegaard, "Existence and Ethics," Levinas characterizes subjective existence in Kierkegaard as *une tension sur soi*, namely, as a tension, a becoming tense, or a being tensed up over the self. For Levinas the notion of subjective existence in Kierkegaard resists the Hegelian idealism in which "the tension over the self relaxes to become consciousness of self *[la tension sur soi se relâche pour devenir conscience de soi]* (NP, 68). But the Kierkegaardian philosophy of existence nonetheless shares with speculative philosophy this presupposition of "a subjectivity tensed up over itself *[subjectivité tendu sur elle-même]*, existence as a concern—even as a torment for itself—that a being takes with its own existence" (NP, 72). This is for Levinas "an egoism," even when it is sublime, as in "the thirst for salvation" (NP, 68). Egoism not in the psychological sense, but as a concrete structure of selfhood or ipseity, what Levinas describes as identification: "[T]he 'A is A' is 'the A anxious for A' or the 'A enjoying A' or the 'A tensed up over A' *[le 'A tendu sur A']*" (T, 345). This egoistic structure is primordial.

Levinas finds a forerunner to this philosophical notion of subjectivity in the Christian notion of existence, "an older tension of the human soul *[une tension plus ancienne de l'âme humaine]* . . . which is consumed with desires" (NP, 67). He comments that perhaps for this reason the human soul is "naturally Christian" (NP, 67). The central contrast of Levinas's essay is between this "tension over the self *[la tension sur soi]*," in both its ancient and modern form if you will, and a "new tension in the self *[une tension nouvelle dans le moi]*," which Levinas will describe as ethical

(*NP*, 73). The contrast is between the economy of salvation that structures the self within Christian existence, in its very continuity with the Kierkegaardian notion of subjective existence, and, simply put, subjectivity as responsibility, the radical putting into question of the self by the other.

This is why, as Derrida notes in "Violence and Metaphysics," "Levinas's protest against Hegelianism is foreign to Kierkegaard's protest" (*VM*, 111). As Levinas says in the preface to *Totality and Infinity:* "It is not I who oppose the system, as Kierkegaard thought; it is the other" (*TI*, 40). In other words, Levinas seeks an alternative *both* to Hegelian specular totality and to Kierkegaardian subjectivity. That Levinas's protest against Hegelianism is foreign to Kierkegaard's, however, does not mean that there is not complicity among the anti-Hegelians, as Levinas himself acknowledges. He writes: "Kierkegaard's philosophy has marked contemporary thought so deeply that the reservations and even the refusal that it elicits attest to its very influence" (*NP*, 71). Moreover, and more important, it is a matter of the "commonality" not just among the anti-Hegelians but between the Hegelians and the anti-Hegelians.[22] Levinas credits Kierkegaard's protest against Hegelianism with the return to Hegelian thought: "Neohegelianism assumes a kind of nobility from its reaction against the exacerbated subjectivism of existence. After one hundred years of Kierkegaardian protestations, one would like to get beyond that pathos *[on veut aller au-delà de ce pathétique]*" (*NP*, 71).

What would it mean to get beyond the Kierkegaardian pathos? There are places in Levinas's work, particularly in the "nonphilosophical" writings, where he strongly suggests that this would involve getting beyond Kierkegaard's specifically Christian idiom and retrieving a dimension of spiritual life that Levinas would term "Judaic." In the 1952 essay "Ethics and Spirit," later reprinted as the first chapter of *Difficult Freedom*, Levinas proposes such a hermeneutic itinerary when he contrasts the spiritual, moral, and social—even activist—renewal within contemporary Christianity to Judaism's long-standing preoccupation—emblematized by "prophetic morality"—with the ethical dimension of spiritual or religious life. Within Post-Emancipation Judaism, Levinas observes, the Jewish ritual life cannot but appear lacking. With its pharisaical attachment to the letter of the law, its attention to the most minute aspects of ritual observance, it is "too abstract to fill an inner life" (*DF*, 4). It lacks the affective power, the anguish of self-loss, and the exaltation of self-recovery, not to mention the storial character, of Christian existence. Levinas

22. See Derrida, VM, 99, 110–11.

proposes, however, that the specificity of Jewish ritual life be understood otherwise.

> One must desire the good with all one's heart, and, at the same time, desire it not only in a heartfelt way. At once to maintain and to break the naive springs of heart—perhaps Jewish ritual is but this. Passion distrusting its pathos and re-becoming conscience. *[Il faut désirer le bien de tout son coeur et à la fois, ne pas le désirer simplement dans l'élan naïf du coeur. A la fois maintenir et briser l'élan—le rite juif c'est peut-être que cela. La passion se méfiant de son pathos et redevenant conscience.]* (DF, 6)

This is consistent with the interpretation of Judaism that Levinas will later propose in the talmudic readings: the function of Jewish ritual life is to break up spontaneity, and therein lies its dimension that can be termed, in the specifically Levinasian sense, *ethical*: the putting into question of my spontaneity, of my joyous possession of the world by the presence of the other (*TI*, 75–76). The unceasing laws, obligations pertaining to the most variegated aspects of life, are in fact a ceaseless reminder of the self's obligation, the obligation to the neighbor, and to the most defenseless members of the community, in the biblical diction, "the stranger, the widow, the orphan."

Levinas's hermeneutic here exemplifies the procedure that I have termed in this book's preceding pages *reinscription*. Levinas takes a negative and privative determination of the Judaic within the dominant Christian conceptuality, reverses one of the dyadic hierarchies that organize it, and rereads it, radicalizing a possibility inherent in the subordinated term. It is not that Jewish ritual life lacks affect and spontaneity but that it constitutes in effect a critique of these modalities of religious life. What appears to be a deficiency is in fact an alternative intelligibility. The valued categories of the current religious revival within Christianity are simply incommensurable with Judaism. The passion that distrusts—or interrupts—its own pathos would be precisely the ethical contribution of a "reinscribed Judaism."

Levinas follows up this reinscription with a series of rhetorical questions and ironic—or antiphrastic—assertions.

> Will the renewal of Judaism take place under the sign of the Irrational, the Numinous, the Sacramental? . . . We need a Saint Theresa for ourselves! Can one still be Jewish without Kierkegaard? It's a good thing we have Hasidism and the Kabbalah. *[Est-il dès lors possible qu'un renouveau juif se fasse sous le signe de l'Irrationnel, du Numineux, du Sacramental? . . . Il nous faut une sainte Thérèse*

à nous! Peut-on encore être Juif sans Kierkegaard? Heureusement qu'il y eut le has-sidisme et qu'il y eut la cabbale!] (DF, 6)

While acknowledging in effect the compelling quality of Kierkegaard's retelling of Genesis 22 in *Fear and Trembling*, indeed, its inescapable contribution within the history of exegesis, Levinas's rhetorical question—Can one still be Jewish without Kierkegaard?—simply points out that while it is as if Kierkegaard supplied something that we thought, within the dominant conceptuality and the negative and privative inter-pretation of Judaism, that we were lacking, the Jewish exegetical tradition about the Akedah is already compelling. In fact, its distinctive intelligibil-ity has been covered up and its hidden resources need to be critically retrieved.

But, consequently, the Judaism that is recovered after such a herme-neutic no longer means what it did before reinscription. If the term Christian is not historicist in Levinas's discourse, the term Judaism would not be historicist either. For this reason—an important qualifier—get-ting beyond pathos would not, strictly speaking, be reducible to the dif-ference between the Judaic and the Christian. When Levinas writes: "Can one still be Jewish without Kierkegaard? It's a good thing we have Has-sidism and the Kabbalah" (DF, 6), his polemical target is precisely the commonality between a secular pathos—the kind of aestheticized econ-omy of personal salvation that is so seductive in a Kierkegaard and in a Dostoevsky—and a sacred pathos—whether that sacred pathos be the Christian experience of the numinous, the Pauline "fear and trembling" to which Kierkegaard refers, or the mystical joy and emotion that within Judaism is associated with Hasidism.[23] Tellingly, Levinas's epigraph to this section of *Difficult Freedom* is Rashi's comment on Leviticus 10:2: "Let them not enter the sanctuary drunk." In other words, at stake in the division between the pathetic and the nonpathetic is not simply an opposition between Christianity and Judaism because this division is al-ready internal to Judaism. Ultimately, any affective and mystical relation to the divine, a pathos that is either Christian or Jewish, would be classed by Levinas as participation.

Levinas intends his question—Can one still be Jewish without Kier-kegaard?—rhetorically and thus implies the answer, "Yes, of course." But if one were really to ask, instead of only pretending to ask—Can one still be Jewish without Kierkegaard?—the answer might well be "No." It is

---

23. This is not to exacerbate or renew the quarrel between Hasidism and *mitnagdim* within Eastern European Jewish life. There is an oversimplification inherent to this opposi-tion.

significant that the very section within *Difficult Freedom* where this question occurs is entitled "Beyond Pathos *[Au-delà du pathétique]*." If Levinas's hermeneutic, his critical retrieval of Judaism, is precisely a procedure of rereading and reinscription, it must necessarily go by way of the dominant conceptuality Levinas characterizes as "Greco-Christian" or "Christian," and its negative and privative interpretation of Judaism. It must necessarily go by way of the Kierkegaardian pathos. It must go by way of what he calls "that which flatters our taste for the pathetic, our sensibility nourished by Christianity and by Dostoevsky *[flatte notre gout du pathétique, notre sensibilité nourrie de Christianisme et du Dostoevsky]* (*DF*, 65). This is what he elsewhere calls "the temptation *of* temptation," the structure of philosophical as well as religious experience in the West. The impossibility (as well as the possibility) of being Jewish without Kierkegaard does not lessen the urgency and the need to go beyond pathos. But it does indicate what a formidable hermeneutical undertaking that is.

In his philosophical as well as his nonphilosophical writings, Levinas's ambivalence toward Kierkegaard—and particularly Kierkegaard's Romanticism—is considerable. This is no doubt aggravated by Jean Wahl's wholehearted and adulatory endorsement of this "literary philosopher." Levinas finds something "immodest" *(impudique)* in the subjectivity that Kierkegaard relentlessly affirms over and against the universal that would suppress it. He is too self-centered, even in his self-division. But Levinas's major criticism of Kierkegaard, articulated for the first time at the Unesco Conference and reprinted in the 1973 *Proper Names*, concerns the way in which Kierkegaard conceives the ethical as an adequation between the internal and the external. He writes: "Is the relationship to the other such an entry into the generality? This is what one must ask oneself against Kierkegaard, as against Hegel" (*NP,* 72). Not only is Kierkegaard's emphasis on Abraham's "teleological suspension of the ethical" too Hegelian, ultimately, Levinas implies, it is too Christianized. *Fear and Trembling*'s obsession with Abraham's getting Isaac *back* and its iconic repetition of the moment when Abraham takes the knife to slay his son is, I have argued elsewhere, typological in its interpretive impulse but also necessarily carries with it a reduction of the Hebrew Bible to a prefigural letter that kills.[24]

But when Levinas reads Kierkegaard's Abraham, it is as if he is not being Levinasian enough. Where we might expect Levinas to elaborate on the Abrahamic departure without return, that he in "The Trace of the Other" (published, like "Existence and Ethics," in 1963) associates

24. Robbins, *Prodigal Son/Elder Brother*, 71–79.

with the one-way movement of radical generosity, Levinas instead emphasizes Abraham's ability to hear God's revocation of the command to sacrifice his son, to hear the second occurrence of God's voice, "the voice that *returns him* to the ethical order" (*NP*, 74, 97). The question that Levinas does not ask in his reading of Kierkegaard and the Akedah and that Derrida unerringly homes in on is: What if the voice that commands the sacrifice and the voice that revokes it were one and the same voice within a story that dramatizes "the narrative ellipsis of obligation?"[25] Then, as Hent de Vries puts it, "the ethicity of ethics is not kept at a safe distance from its other" anymore than the "ilyatic" alterity is kept at a safe distance from ethical alterity. Rather, the *il y a* "forms and deforms the condition of possibility of every ethical intrigue."[26]

This interpretive emphasis recalls Wahl's insistence on the twinning of demonic and divine transcendence, on the "interchangeability of the beyond and the hither side," to which Levinas refers, in his essay on Wahl, as a "permanent temptation" to which Wahl always yields (JW, 21). In the 1937 lecture "Subjectivity and Transcendence," Wahl states his "indifference" to the difference between the good and the bad transcendence (JW, 28) as follows: "A being would be anguished because it does not know in the face of what it is, in the face of a beneficent transcendence or of a maleficent one, in the face of God or in the face of a demonic force, if the movement that he accomplishes is a movement of 'transascendence' or 'transdescendence'" (*ET*, 39). In the discussion that followed Wahl's lecture Gabriel Marcel objected to Wahl's formulation as "a terrible equivocation," arguing that it "denatures" the idea of the good (*ET*, 114), and here his view is very close to that of Levinas. Like Marcel, Levinas would preserve a hierarchy between good and evil, high and low. Levinas refers to transcendence as "the height beyond all ascension and descent" (JW, 29). Hence it would seem that Derrida's reading of Kierkegaard, while certainly ultraethical in one Levinasian sense, contains a risk that is distinctly un-Levinasian: either that in Wahl's words "one does not know" the difference between the two types of transcendence, or that the difference is not one.

While Levinas's reading counters the typological emphasis of Kierkegaard's reading of Abraham, he nonetheless dilutes its radicality. For it is not as if Levinas himself has not shown the resources of Kierkegaardian thought for his own thinking of the ethical. Even though Kierkegaard,

25. Jacques Derrida, *The Gift of Death*, trans. David Wills (Chicago: University of Chicago Press, 1995), 66.
26. Hent de Vries, "Adieu, àdieu, a-Dieu" in *EFP*, 214.

in conceiving the ethical as an adequation between internal and external, thinks the ethical in an impoverished and derivative way, even though Kierkegaard thinks the old tension over the self instead of the tension within the self, at the same time, Levinas asserts: "No one has unravelled with greater rigor than Kierkegaard the 'phenomenology' of crucified truth" (*NP*, 70). The "persecuted truth" with which Kierkegaard describes the very manifestation of the divine is cited in "Enigma and Phenomenon" to illustrate the other's distinctive mode of signification, the "manifestation without manifestation" that he calls enigma, or the "past that has never been present" he calls trace. In short, the ambivalence toward Kierkegaard suggested in Levinas's rhetorical question, "Can one still be Jewish without Kierkegaard?" characterizes his entire intertextual engagement—broken, if you will—with him.

Finally, it is necessary to ask again, this time in terms of what Levinas terms his *philosophical* writings, what the impossibility of getting beyond pathos would mean. Levinas primarily understands pathos as Kierkegaard's aestheticized economy of personal salvation in its continuity with a structure of relation of the self to its self that is a philosophical "egoism." But in the cries and the lacerations of a Kierkegaard, Rimbaud, or a Dostoevsky, is there no opening up unto the ethical? This was the gist of Poirié's question to Levinas in a 1986 interview, and Levinas's answer in effect was, no: suffering is always of the other, not of me. But he did qualify his remark as follows:

> Suffering is experienced as being closed up in the self par excellence; this superiorly passive passion *[ce pâtir supérieurement passif]* is like an impossibility of "getting out of one's self." At the same time, there is in this being closed up in the self of passion, the sigh or the cry which is already a search for alterity: I would even say, but one must be cautious here, it is the first prayer. *[Cependant il y a dans cet enfermement en soi du pâtir, le soupir ou le cri qui est déjà recherche d'altérité: je dis même, mais il faut prendre là beaucoup de précautions, la première prière.]* (*IR*)

These assertions rejoin Blanchot's meditations on the significance of the word chain *pas, passivité, patience, pâtir, passion*, in *The Writing of the Disaster*, and his reflections on *parler sans pouvoir*, in *The Infinite Conversation*. There Blanchot asserts that precisely insofar as the cry escapes what he and Levinas (after Heidegger) call "possibility" *[pouvoir]*, it constitutes a certain escape from pathos.

> Suffering is suffering when one can no longer suffer it, and when, because of this non-power *[non-pouvoir]*, one cannot cease suffering it . . . We must admit

that . . . this experience has a pathetic appearance, but on condition that one also give the word pathos its nonpathetic sense. It is a question not of that paroxysmic state where the self cries out and is torn apart, but rather of a suffering that is almost indifferent, not suffered but neutral (a phantom of suffering) insofar as the one who is exposed to it, precisely through this suffering, is deprived of the "I" that would make him suffer it. (*IC*, 44–45)

For Blanchot, suffering is not something that the "I" can do. This "nonpathetic sense of pathos" is perhaps the grid for what Levinas had called "the new tension in the self" (*NP*, 73) which is ethical. It is at a distance from the more traditional vocabulary Levinas had deployed in his 1952 formulation, "passion distrusting its pathos and rebecoming conscience" (*DF*, 6). For is it not precisely in *im*possibility that the ethical experiences that go beyond pathos become legible? The intrication of Blanchot's and Levinas's reflections on the cry suggests as much.

THE ALIBI OF METAPHYSICS

The first few lines of *Totality and Infinity* were always enigmatic: "'The true life is absent.' But we are in the world. Metaphysics arises and is maintained in this alibi" (*TI*, 33). Levinas means *metaphysics*, as he asserts in the subsequent sentence, "in the most general form it has assumed in the history of thought," namely, as a movement from a world that is familiar to us, the here, the "at home," to an elsewhere, an outside of oneself (*TI*, 33). He also means it in a manner that has affinities with Heidegger's reading of the history of metaphysics as ontotheology, and in a manner of contesting Heidegger that would not, as Levinas asserts in *Existence and Existents*, be pre-Heideggerian (*EE*, 19). Levinas means by metaphysics both the philosophical tradition and the reinscription of the tradition. It is not limited to "the most general form it has assumed in the history of thought." By the end of section 1.A.1, Levinas offers a renewed sense of metaphysics as "goodness, the desire of the absolutely other" (*TI*, 35). This gesture can and should be compared to that of section 1.A.4, entitled "Metaphysics Precedes Ontology," where Levinas contrasts theory, as a comprehension of being, which has *most often* been an ontology, and which reduces the other to the same, to what he calls "the critical essence of knowledge or theory," which is precisely ethics, a calling into question of the same by the other (*TI*, 43).

To call metaphysics, as Levinas determines it, an alibi, a being elsewhere when the crime in question is committed, is certainly to yoke together two terms which may be incommensurate: a frequent example of this is "imperialism of the same" (*TI*, 39).[1] Levinas has in mind a transcendental violence (or an ontological violence). But how can transcendental inquiry—an inquiry into the grounds of what is—be violent? Power is a relation between existents, an ontic relation, as Derrida reminds us in "Violence and Metaphysics" (VM, 137). How then can there be violence at the level of the difference between what is and the being of what is, at the level of the ontico-ontological difference? Perhaps we should rephrase the question: What is metaphysics, if it can be violent? What is violence, if it can occur on this originary level? This *other* oppression, remarks Derrida, is not *in* the world but rather "origin and alibi of all oppression *in* the world" (VM, 83). Philosophy's alibi for the suffering and distress of the other is in the being else-where of its questioning, when it effects the metaphysical movement, or when it simply goes about its business, doing phenomenology, and so on.[2] In any case, what is at stake in the alibi is the false innocence of philosophy. Derrida writes that "all the classical concepts are thus dragged toward the agora, are summoned to answer for themselves in an ethico-political language that they have not always wished for or that they believed not to speak . . . here lie the premises for a non-Marxist reading of philosophy as ideology" (VM, 97).

If we turn to the end of *Totality and Infinity*'s section 1.A. as a whole, we see that Levinas intends a middle ground or, better, a strategic hesitation between "the true life is absent" and "we are in the world," between idealism and materialism, between a philosophy of transcendence (like that denounced by Nietzsche as a world behind the world) and a philosophy of immanence.[3] He writes: "Between a philosophy of transcendence

1. Cf. "self-coincidence or happiness" (T, 350).

2. In his use of the term *alibi* (from *alius*, other, else, + *ubi*, where) Levinas certainly plays on its etymological sense. This may be compared to Roland Barthes's usage in *Mythologies* (1957): "The ubiquity of the signifier in myth exactly reproduces the physique of the alibi (which is, one realizes, a spatial term): in the alibi too, there is a place which is full and one which is empty, linked by a relation of negative identity ('I am not where you think I am; I am where you think I am not')" (trans. Richard Howard [New York: Hill and Wang, 1972], 123). For Barthes, "the turnstile revolving" of myth is its "perpetual alibi: it is enough that a signifier has two sides for it always to have an 'elsewhere' at its disposal." Similarly, for Levinas, metaphysics reproduces the physique of the alibi in the very décalage between the elsewhere of the true life and the here of the world (If you will: "I am not responsible for the here, because the true life is elsewhere; I am not responsible for the elsewhere, because I am here").

3. See Tina Chanter, "Neither Idealism nor Materialism: Levinas's Third Way," in *Postmodernism and the Holocaust*, ed. Alan Milchman and Alan Rosenberg (Amsterdam: Rodopi), 1998. See also Chanter's *The Ethics of Eros* (London: Routledge, 1995); and *In the Time of Death: Levinas and Heidegger*, forthcoming.

that situates elsewhere the true life to which man, *escaping* from here, would gain access in the privileged moments of liturgical, mystical elevation, or in dying—and a philosophy of immanence in which we would truly come into possession of being when every 'other' (cause for war), encompassed by the same, would vanish at the end of history—we propose to describe, within the unfolding of terrestrial existence . . . a relationship with the other that does not result in a divine *or* human totality, that is not the totalization of history, but the idea of infinity. Such a relationship is metaphysics itself" (*TI,* 52). In short, to say that the true life is absent, to seek flight from the here which is always lacking toward an elsewhere, is as totalizing as the objective history of the historiographers, which is only a history and a remembrance of the survivors (*TI,* 223).[4]

LEVINAS READING RIMBAUD

Totality and Infinity begins then with a citation, discreet, unattributed: . . . *la vraie vie est absente* ("the true life is absent"). Does it make a difference when we learn that the citation is from a poet, Arthur Rimbaud?[5] If to say in a poem that "the true life is absent" makes a difference, surely this could not be the kind of difference that the ethical makes. Levinas's attitude toward poetry and the aesthetic in *Totality and Infinity* can readily be seen as a prolongation of the negative and dismissive assessment he offered in the 1948 "Reality and Its Shadow." There poetry was linked with a cluster of negatively charged terms—*intoxication, the sacred, play, magic.* Its essence—and that of all the arts—was said to be rhythm, incantation, music. As in the ecstatic rites described by ethnographers (RO, 4), poetry, argues Levinas, renders the subject exterior to itself. The subject is part of its representation. At stake in what Lévy-Bruhl calls *participation,* a descriptive concept for mythical mentality's blurring of the seen and the unseen worlds, and of the logic of noncontradiction, is an affective relation to collective representations. For Levinas it constitutes "the *pathos* of the imaginary world of dreams" (RO, 4). Its consequences include the loss of subjecthood, a passage from oneself to anonymity (RO, 4), and,

---

4. Adriaan Peperzak notes that the opening lines of *Totality and Infinity* make reference to a determination of metaphysics in Plato (as ascension toward the true) and in Aristotle (as an orientation that is beyond, *meta,* the *physis*). He comments that in "the true life is absent," it is hard not to hear an echo of "the Greek and Christian traditions about *eudaimonia, vita beata,* perfection, self-realization, and so on," *To the Other,* 132. See also Peperzak's discussion in *Beyond* (Evanston, IL: Northwestern University Press, 1997), 164.

5. This is noted by the Dutch translator of *Totality and Infinity,* and by Peperzak.

ultimately, an abdication of responsibility. Indeed art, in the "petrification," the "immobilization," and the "freezing" action it effects with regard to face, can be said to put a stop to the ethical at the very level where responsibility could originate.

Throughout his description of poetry in "Reality and Its Shadow," and in *Totality and Infinity*, thirteen years later, Levinas's antiludic discourse is in evidence. While the mode of being of poetry and music as well as the way in which it captivates its audience (along with its artist) is in the earlier work described as one where "consciousness, paralyzed in its freedom, *plays*" (RO, 4), in *Totality and Infinity* there is a consistent effort to keep separate ethical discourse from all singing, dancing, and laughter. The sobriety, the gravity of ethical discourse, Levinas says, "freezes all laughter" (*TI*, 200).

Throughout *Totality and Infinity*, as in his earlier work, Levinas intertwines his discourse against art with his discourse against participation, especially ecstatic behavior like poetic rapture and possession, mystical and religious experiences of "fear and trembling," the numinous and the sacred. Moreover, to the transcendence and the autoattendance of the face's expression *kath 'auto*, he opposes works—including aesthetic productions—that are characterized by indirection and that block transcendence. Finally, in section 1.A.2, "The Breach of Totality," Levinas makes a disparaging reference to the poet as one who is incapable of ethical transcendence: "The alterity of the I which takes itself for another may strike the imagination of the poet precisely because it is the play of the same" (*TI*, 37). Here Levinas's *example* of the poet is again, in a covert allusion, Arthur Rimbaud. This allusion is significant, not just because it suggests a more sustained intertextual engagement with Rimbaud in *Totality and Infinity* that had first appeared, and not just because of what it tells us about Levinas as a reader, but because of what it tells us about the relationship between poetry and ethics.

This passage follows a quotation from Hegel describing self-consciousness, which Levinas had described as "express[ing] the universality of the same identifying itself in the alterity of objects thought, despite the opposition of self to self" (*TI*, 36).[6] He continues, and here is the fuller context of the allusion:

6. Robert Bernasconi discusses the significance of Levinas's subsequent citation of Hegel, and its significance in the *Phenomenology* where it describes "the dialectical passage of the consciousness of a thing to self-consciousness." "Hegel and Levinas: The Possibility of Forgiveness and Pardon," *Journal of the British Society of Phenomenology* 13, no. 3 (October 1982): 267–76.

The I, as other, is not an "Other" *[Le je, comme autre, n'est pas un "Autre"]* . . . The I that repels itself, lived as repugnance, the I riveted to itself, lived as ennui, are modes of self-consciousness and rest on the unrendable identity of the I and the self. The alterity of the I that takes itself for another *[l'altérité du je, qui se prend pour un autre]* may strike the imagination of the poet precisely because it is but the play of the same: the negation of the I by the self is precisely one of the modes of identification of the I. (*TI*, 37)

Levinas describes identification as a concrete structure in which the "I is identical in all its alterations," be they the extremes of alienation, self-loss, or self-nonidentity. For Levinas, this structure is always in relation to a finite or spurious alterity as opposed to the relation to the infinite alterity of *Autrui*. The poet, for whom Rimbaud stands as the figure, is said to be attracted to this very play of the same, as well as, invariably, to play itself. I might add that it is no accident that the passage occurs after the reference to Hegelian self-consciousness. Levinas distinguishes transcendence from negativity; he sees the I's relation to itself as finite instead of, as Hegel and Kierkegaard would, infinite.

Before speculating further on *why* Levinas uses Rimbaud in the way that he does—why he silently cites him (and here one should note that *Totality and Infinity* not only begins with a citation from a poet but also ends with one, again unattributed, this time from Baudelaire),[7] let us attempt to make Levinas's implicit interpretation of Rimbaud explicit, to ask *how* Levinas uses him. Rimbaud's *je est un autre* is the formulation of his poetic program. According to Edward Ahearn, it seems to describe "an enlargement of the self" to the point of self-transcendence.[8] Poetry

7. "Situated at the antipodes of the subject living in the infinite time of fecundity is the isolated and heroic being that the State produces by its virile virtues. Such a being confronts death out of pure courage and whatever be the cause for which he dies. He assumes finite time, the death-end or the death-transition, which do not arrest the continuation of a being without discontinuity. The heroic existence, the isolated soul, can gain its salvation in seeking an eternal life for itself, as though its subjectivity, returning to itself in a continuous time, could not be turned against it—as though in this continuous time identity itself would not be affirmed obsessively, as though in the identity that remains in the midst of the most extravagant avatars "tedium, fruit of the mournful incuriousity that takes on the proportions of immortality" did not triumph *[comme si, dans ce temps continu, l'identité elle-même ne s'affirmait pas comme une obsession, comme si dans l'identité qui demeure au sein des plus extravagants avatars, ne triomphait pas l'ennui, fruit de la morne incuriosité qui prend les proportions de l'immortalité']*" (*TI*, 307). The citation is from Baudelaire's second "Spleen," *Les fleurs du mal*.

8. My understanding of Rimbaud's poem is indebted to Edward J. Ahearn's *Rimbaud: Visions and Habitations* (Berkeley: University of California Press, 1983), 92; Yves Bonnefoy's *Rimbaud par lui-même* (Paris: Seuil, 1961); and Froment-Meurice, *Solitudes.*

here is conceived as visionary possession by the Muse, an essentially
Greek model. Rimbaud formulated this in the context of a disrespect-
ful letter to his teacher, Georges Izambard, in 1871, in one of the so-
called letters of the Seer *(lettres du voyant)*. (And it would be possible,
in the purview of another discussion, to explore the ethical significance
of this letter as an address, since the context of Rimbaud's formulation
is interlocutionary—as is all ethical discourse for Levinas. Moreover,
the certain ingratitude that Rimbaud evinces toward his teacher would
seem to fulfill the necessary criterion for asymmetry which Levinas says
that the gift of the ethical demands.) I cite from selected parts of the
letter:

CHARLEVILLE, 13 May 1871

Dear Sir,

All you see in your principle is subjective poetry . . . [which] will always be
horribly insipid. One day I hope I will see objective poetry. Now I am degrad-
ing myself as much as possible. Why? I want to be a poet and I am working
to make myself a seer. You will not understand this . . . It is a question of
reaching the unknown by the derangement of all the senses . . . I is another
[Je est un autre]. It's too bad for the wood which finds itself a violin . . . you
are no longer a teacher for me.

Warm greetings, Arthur Rimbaud[9]

It is evident enough why the ecstatic and mystical self-dispersal and the
poetics of monstrosity that Rimbaud articulates are not to Levinas's lik-
ing. The derangement of the senses, the debauchery, and the delirium
to which Rimbaud commits himself in the service of visionary poetry will
be reflected in *A Season in Hell*'s reference to a variety of experiences of
"trance, collective frenzy, dissociation, quasi-mystical dissolution," the
efforts to achieve "a rhythmic and musical state of being" by magic
and by techniques of dance and drum,[10] for example, in the section of
the poem entitled "Bad Blood" *(Mauvais Sang)* in the rapid often mono-
syllabic exclamations: "Cris, tambour, danse, danse, danse, danse!" or
"Faim, soif, cris, danse, danse, danse, danse!" This would certainly be in
Levinas's view an instance of aesthetic absorption as participation, always
opposed in his discourse to the ethical.

---

9. Arthur Rimbaud, *Complete Works, Selected Letters*, trans. Wallace Fowlie (Chicago:
University of Chicago Press, 1966), 302–4. All references to *Une saison en enfer* are to this
edition.

10. Ahearn, *Rimbaud*, 92, 139–40.

But this is not to say that Rimbaud's formulation indeed illustrates the spurious relation to alterity in the I's structure of identification, as Levinas had claimed when he refers to "the alterity of the I that takes itself for another." In fact, far from being any kind of celebration of the I's alterity to itself and the creative powers of a poetic self that such a structure would liberate, "je est un autre" seems, rather, to function as a self-obliteration, a renunciation of the self as author, what Ahearn calls "a poetic unselving,"[11] in which the poet is receptacle rather than an initiator, an instrument rather than an intention, in Rimbaud's phrase "like the wood which finds itself a violin." Moreover, in the context of his letter to the uncomprehending Izambard, Rimbaud's phrase "je est un autre" is very explicitly a reaction *against* what he calls subjective poetry, associated with the self-conscious aestheticizing mode of the Parnassians that Rimbaud had formerly revered.[12] In short, the precise context of the phrase "je est un autre" would even seem to forbid the kind of reading Levinas gives to it.

For it is telling that in his paraphrase/translation/ interpretation of the phrase, Levinas elides its anacoluthic change in grammatical construction—I *is* another, je *est* un autre. When he paraphrases it as "the alterity of the I that takes itself for another" (*TI,* 37) he renders it in effect as je *suis* mon autre, I am my own other, that is, as a determinate negation within the play of the same. Probably this would not matter to Levinas, who here lines up any form of alteration within the I, as well as the mood of boredom, with self-consciousness.[13] In Yves Bonnefoy's reading, Rimbaud hopes with his poetic program to arrive at what he calls "the true life," to rejoin in a communion of love the participation in divine being, to transcend himself.[14] Probably this would not matter to Levinas, being no doubt yet another instance of what Derrida calls the complicity between mystical communion and theoretical objectivity (VM, 87). Both experiences leave us alone with ourselves. In either case, what Levinas calls the ethical experience of face would be missing. Even the serious play of rejecting the same that Rimbaud seems to engage in would still be part of the play of the same. The forms of alteration within the I would not have the specific imperative of ethical alterity, an imperative that Levinas both constates and performs in his exhortative ethical prose.

But is it indeed Rimbaud who says "the true life is absent"? In *A Season*

11. Ibid., 163.

12. Bonnefoy, *Rimbaud,* 53.

13. Even though the mood of boredom can be said to bring into view something like existence as a whole, Levinas does not give it the radicality of finite transcendence here.

14. Bonnefoy, *Rimbaud,* 17.

in Hell, where the line occurs, it is not even said by the poetic or "autobiographical" persona or speaker of the poem, which begins, "Once, if I recall correctly, my life was a banquet . . . where all wines flowed *[Jadis, si je me souviens bien, ma vie était un festin . . . où tous les vins coulaient].*" It is said in the section titled "Delirium I: The Infernal Bridegroom," which recounts the failure of love and where there is a shift in speaker. The line (or the couplet) "The true life is absent. We are not in the world" is said by a ventriloquized Verlaine figure. Rimbaud, speaking through a "poetic" I, speaks through another, ventriloquized "I." In other words, Rimbaud's use of the line in *A Season in Hell* is characterized by several levels of disavowal and thus has no more of a link to a poetic creator or originator than does *je est un autre.* Levinas's use of the line at the beginning of *Totality and Infinity* turns out to be something like a double citation. (Since Levinas does not assign the citation to Rimbaud, we do not know that he does not recognize that Rimbaud's poetic persona is not speaking. He certainly uses the line to serve his argumentative purpose.)

Levinas reads the line in an aggressively literal way in order to overturn its supposed meaning. Where Rimbaud wrote (or ventriloquized), "The true life is absent. We are not in the world *[La vraie vie est absente. Nous ne sommes pas au monde],*" Levinas writes (or ventriloquizes), "'The true life is absent.' But we *are* in the world *['La vraie vie est absente.' Mais nous sommes au monde].*" He ventriloquizes the first phrase of the couplet and alters the second, by deleting "not" and by adding the adversative "but." His is the trope of contradiction. By reading the line thematically, as an *illustration* of the desire for transcendence, in order to dismiss it, he necessarily elides the more complex significance it may have in Rimbaud's poetic work.

Simply put, the states of plenitude to which *A Season in Hell* refers have all been lost by the poem's beginning (although it is hard to say exactly when or how many times this loss has occurred)—such as the childhood proximity to nature the poem recounts ("Didn't I once have a delightful youth, heroic and fabulous, to be written on sheets of gold *[N'eus-je pas une fois une jeunesse aimable, héroïque, fabuleuse, à écrire sur des feuilles d'or]*"), the charity by which the poet hopes "to find again the key to the ancient banquet *[rechercher la clef du festin ancien],*" the "true life" the speaker hopes to rejoin by his poetic program, the eternal happiness and purity that the speaker glimpses in the refrain "O seasons, O castles! *[O saisons, ô châteaux!].*" It is followed by the assertion: "All this is over. Today I know how to greet beauty *[Cela c'est passé. Je sais aujourd'hui saluer la beauté].*"

Most important to the evaluation of what "the true life is absent" means in Rimbaud's poem is that the poem itself dismisses and criticizes such a desire for transcendence.[15] The poem recounts not just the failure of love but several failures. In "Delirium II: The Alchemy of the Word," the speaker recounts the failure of his poetic program (which he had formulated in the letter to Izambard) and of his effort to arrive at "the true life." He debunks the illusions of poetic magic. Ultimately, the speaker not only denounces but renounces his poetic program. In the poem's final section entitled "Adieu" (Farewell), the speaker says: "I must bury my imagination and my memories! *[Je dois enterrer mon imagination et mes souvenirs!]*." After *A Season in Hell*, at the age of twenty, Rimbaud stopped writing.

The "mystery" of this renunciation increases, observes Maurice Blanchot, "when one discovers what Rimbaud asks of poetry: not to produce beautiful works or to answer to an aesthetic ideal but to help man go somewhere, to make of literature an experience that concerns the whole of life and the whole of being."[16] Rimbaud bids adieu to the very poetry that had offered him the sole means of self-transcendence. That is what Marc Froment-Meurice calls a quasi-suicide, at once literary and spiritual.[17] Blanchot comments that once writing is conceived of as the deployment of all human possibilities, to stop writing is "to renounce the very possibility that, once glimpsed and pursued, cannot be destroyed without a diminution in comparison with which suicide and madness seem nothing."[18] Bonnefoy recalls that for Rimbaud the aim of poetry had been "to transform lack into a resource, to turn the privation of love into 'a love to be reinvented,' 'to change life *[changer la vie]*.' "[19] When Rimbaud dismisses poetry as a future, he dismisses in effect the future of the future, he affirms the end, a "new hour" which is, in the words of "Adieu," "very severe," and in which "one must be absolutely modern."[20]

It is arguable that "the true life is absent," as, Froment-Meurice contends, "an impossible statement," like Mallarmé's "There is no present

15. Ahearn, *Rimbaud*, 139; and Bonnefoy, *Rimbaud*, 108.

16. Maurice Blanchot, "The Sleep of Rimbaud" in *The Work of Fire*, trans. Charlotte Mandell (Stanford: Stanford University Press, 1995). "Le sommeil de Rimbaud" in *La part du feu* (Paris: Gallimard, 1949). Blanchot's other key essay on Rimbaud is "The Final Work" ("L'oeuvre finale"), in *IC*.

17. Froment-Meurice, *Solitudes*, 45.

18. Blanchot, "The Sleep of Rimbaud," 155.

19. Bonnefoy, *Rimbaud*, chapters 1 and 2.

20. Maurice Blanchot, "The Final Work" ["L'oeuvre finale"], in *IC*; and "The Sleep of Rimbaud."

[Il n'y a pas de present]." Since the present by definition names all that is
. . . the present itself, if it is not (present), swallows up everything with
non-being. If the being of the present is not present (like an entity) but
is nothing, the statement is the very culmination of a certain nihilism . . .
For Mallarmé's "the present," we only need substitute Rimbaud's "the
true life."[21]

But to conclude our discussion of *how* Levinas reads Rimbaud, one
can argue that Levinas's reading/ventriloquism of Rimbaud in his silent
citation of "the true life is absent," like his alteration of the poetic line
"je est un autre," is an overturning. These poetic phrases, however, may
support not only more complex readings but readings that are precisely
the opposite of what Levinas takes them to mean. (This can be shown
with the quotation from Baudelaire that ends *Totality and Infinity* as well.)
It is not that Levinas's readings are impossible but that his ventriloquism
of Rimbaud in the one case, and his paraphrastic "betrayal" in the other,
bring him close to what Rimbaud may be trying to accomplish by his
own ventriloquizing of Verlaine in the first place. Indeed, Rimbaud's renunciation of or farewell to writing (something that takes place not just
after the poem but within the poem)[22] would seem to have, in very general
terms, an ethical dimension. This is certainly the force of Blanchot's reading of Rimbaud. That is, before any prescription, before it is possible to
determine something as ethical or nonethical, it would be situated at a
more originary level, at the level of the opening of the question of the
ethical. Can Levinas acknowledge this?

In a 1980 interview with Philippe Nemo, Levinas seems to do just
that. In answer to Nemo's question, How does one begin thinking? he
responds:

> It probably begins through traumatisms to which one does not even know
> how to give a verbal form: a separation, a violent scene, a sudden consciousness
> of the monotony of time. It is from the reading of books—not necessarily
> philosophical, that these initial shocks become questions and problems, giving
> one to think. The role of national literatures is here perhaps very important.
> Not just that one learns words from it, but in it one lives "the true life which
> is absent" but which is precisely no longer utopian. (*EI,* 21)

---

21. Froment-Meurice, *Solitudes*, 2–5, asks, "*Who* affirms 'the true life is absent.' The
poet? But affirming this non-presence, must not he himself be (present)? Or does he also
sign his non-presence, the equivalent of suicide?" Suffice it to say that at stake in Rimbaud's
phrase is no mere nihilism, but another nihilism that might have a relation both to the
experience of poetry and to what Levinas calls the *ethical.*

22. Norbert Bonenkamp observes this in "Exit and Save," in *A New History of French
Literature,* ed. Denis Hollier (Cambridge, MA: Harvard University Press, 1989), 758–61.

Extraordinary here is that Levinas accords literature, in the specific form of "the true life is absent," with the opening of the question of the ethical. In Levinas's phrase, in literature "one *lives* 'the true life which is absent' " (and note that even here Levinas changes it from an interlocutionary assertion to a descriptive phrase). It is as if Levinas, in the extraphilosophical medium of the interview, is more easily able to grant the question that emerges from his philosophical writings only under duress. Thus, if poetry is not what Levinas takes it to be, namely, something that is aesthetic, that is, something that is phenomenally available as a cognition, and something that seeks to revert to participation, then poetry may be not an abdication of responsibility but may draw close to what Levinas calls the ethical.

THE ALTERITY OF LITERATURE

I want to draw together these reflections and return to the question of *why* Levinas cites Rimbaud, why *Totality and Infinity* is bookended by citations from poets, by turning to an essay Levinas wrote in 1970 entitled "No Identity." This essay written in the distinctive idiom of the "later" Levinas, contains three references to Rimbaud. (It was first published in *L'Ephémère*, an avant-garde literary publication on whose editorial board both Celan and Leiris served, and reprinted in *l'humanisme de l'autre homme*.) There, as in other texts from the same time period, Levinas seems to offer, via Rimbaud, a much more positive assessment of poetry and the aesthetic than he had proposed in his 1948 article and in the 1961 *Totality and Infinity*.

Another interest of this essay is that it represents a relatively rare instance in which Levinas positions himself with regard to structuralism and post-structuralism. There is a note of crankiness that creeps in from time to time that is also apparent in the essays collected in *Proper Names*. For what again seem to be polemical reasons, Levinas often avoids the complex hermeneutical demand that texts by Nietzsche, Foucault, Derrida, and others present by reducing them to "slogans" or "the latest fashion," worn-out clichés. "No Identity" is specifically concerned with "the end of humanism" and "the death of man," "the death of God," topics he first introduces in a dismissive way in order to later rehabilitate them (NI, 141).[23] The following comments on this essay will necessarily be very brief and schematic.

23. Cf. Levinas's references to "a play" of "signifiers without signifieds" (*NP*, 4), and to "a language in dissemination." In interviews with François Poirié and with Florian Rötzer, Levinas dodges a question about poststructuralism and refers polemically to the

The essay's overall argument begins with an analysis of the critique of the subject in the human sciences; it goes on to discuss the "convergence" of the questioning of subjectivity by the sciences of man and by Heidegger's post-philosophical thought; it then proceeds to develop in effect what an *ethical* putting into question of the subject would mean. In the section devoted to the human sciences, Levinas evinces hesitation with regard to structuralism's totalizing emphasis on structure, formalism, and system: "[T]he psyche and its freedoms . . . would be but a detour taken by structures in order to link up into a system and show themselves in the light . . . The whole of the human is outside" (NI, 142). But he nonetheless finds something salutary in the human sciences' elimination of the constitutive subject. Important for our purposes is how he describes the distinctive contributions of the human sciences:

> The rediscoveries of self with self are missing. Inwardness seems to be not strictly inward. *I is another.* Has not identity itself been defeated? *[Les retrouvailles de soi et de soi se manquent. L'intériorité ne serait pas rigoureusement intérieure. Je est un autre. L'identité elle-même n'est-elle pas en échec?]* (NI, 143)

Rimbaud's phrase, still unattributed (not in quotation marks but in italics, and cited correctly this time) is used to illustrate the insights of the human sciences, to illustrate its emphasis on nonself-coincidence. It is associated somewhat ambivalently with a certain post-structuralism.

In the section on Heidegger, Levinas affirms: "The inward world is contested by Heidegger as by the sciences of man" (NI, 144). That is, Heidegger thought this too; he demonstrated that identity is a metaphysical construct. Levinas's criticism is couched in terms readily recognizable to those readers familiar with Levinas's often polemical reading of Heidegger: Heidegger ends up with "the enrootedness of man in being, of which he would be the messenger and the poet" (NI, 144). It becomes increasingly clear that the embarrassment that the essay is in fact called upon to resolve is Levinas's very proximity to the human sciences (the relationship to Heidegger is a separate question). Levinas's tone of vexation and defensiveness abates as the essay proceeds, when Levinas begins to accord the critique of identity and inwardness that had been offered by the human sciences and by Heidegger with precisely a positive ethical significance.

---

work of Lévi-Strauss (*IR*), a polemic which is also apparent in *Difficult Freedom*. Levinas has read and in NI refers to Blanchot's "Humanism and the Cry" (1967) where Blanchot summarizes Foucault's take on the human sciences as follows: "[I]t is not the subject which possesses knowledge, but the constituted field of knowledge which holds in it the subject" (*IC*, 250).

When he does so, in the section of the essay devoted to his own philosophy, he flags this new emphasis given to the critique of the subject with the adversative: "*But* it is time to raise some questions." The questions that follow are all rhetorical:

> Is not subjectivity able to refer . . . to a past that passes by every present? . . . In approaching another . . . "something" has overflowed my freely taken decisions . . . thus alienating my identity. Is it then certain that in the deportation or drifting of identity . . . the subject would not signify with all the dash of its youth? Is it certain that Rimbaud's formula "I is an other" only means alteration, alienation, betrayal of oneself, foreignness with regard to oneself and subjection to this foreigner? Is it certain that already the most humble experience of him who puts himself in another's place, that is, accuses himself for another's distress or pain, is not animated with the most eminent meaning of this "I is an other"? [*La subjectivité n'est-elle pas à même de se rapporter . . . à un passé qui passe tout présent? . . . Dans l'approche d'autrui . . . "quelque chose" a débordé mes décisions librement prises . . . aliénant ainsi mon identité. Est-il, dès lors, certain que, dans la déportation ou la dérive de l'identité, . . . le sujet ne signifiait pas de tout l'éclat de sa jeunesse? Est-il certain que la formule de Rimbaud: "Je est un autre," signifie seulement altération, aliénation, trahison de soi, étrangeté à soi et asservissement à cet étranger? Est-il certain que déjà l'expérience la plus humble, de celui qui se met à la place de l'autre—c'est-à-dire s'accuse du mal ou de la douleur de l'autre—n'est pas animée du sens le plus éminent selon lequel "je est un autre"?*]
> (NI, 145)

In the distinctive diction and conceptuality of the later work, Levinas refers to the trace structure, namely, to the mode of signification of the other, to responsibility for the other as something that is not the result of an initiative or a decision by a subject, and to youth—a technical term in this essay for what is before or otherwise than being—but also no doubt an allusion to the events of May 1968, and perhaps an anticipatory reference to Rimbaud's youth, to his poetry of youth. This time Rimbaud is named (and his phrase is again cited correctly, twice, each time in quotation marks).

In this passage, Levinas offers two meanings of "Je est un autre." The first, clarifying "No Identity's" earlier allusion, is alteration, alienation, betrayal of oneself, presumably the dialectical sense referred to and rejected in *Totality and Infinity*, namely, the poet who takes himself for another. The second meaning of the phrase that Levinas proposes is "its most eminent meaning." In a gesture similar to the reinscription of metaphysics in *Totality and Infinity*, Levinas goes from a most general to its most eminent sense. He tells us what he meant previously by "je est un autre" when he cites it later. "Is it certain that Rimbaud's formula only means [*signifie seulement*]?" Referring to Rimbaud's formulation of his poetic program as a "formula," Levinas tells us what it "only meant" earlier.

There is something astonishing about this reinscription. What was previously a relation to a finite or spurious alterity here denotes no less than ethical substitution, the operative concept for responsible subjectivity in *Otherwise than Being*. Here the phrase "je est un autre" has an ethical positivity; its meaning is ethical substitution. In fact, Levinas had offered a similar reinscription in the 1968 essay "Substitution," which is the germ of chapter 4 of *Otherwise than Being*: "*Je est un autre, sans l'aliénation rimbaldienne* (I is an other, without the Rimbaldien alienation)" (*OB*, 118). In short, nonself-coincidence becomes ethical. In "No Identity" Levinas writes: "Here is the impossible inwardness which is *in our day* disorienting and reorienting the sciences of man, an impossibility we learn of neither from metaphysics nor from the end of metaphysics. There is a divergency between the ego and the self, an impossible recurrence, an impossible identity" (NI, 149).

This *via eminentia* on which everything hinges deserves more attention that we can give in the space of this discussion.[24] It is what allows Levinas to find this second (ethical) meaning of Rimbaud's phrase as a suppressed possibility of the first (nonethical) meaning. For if the most eminent meaning of Rimbaud's phrase can be retrieved as a hidden possibility of its most general sense, *Totality and Infinity* is not simply an overturning of Rimbaud's poetry. It is a writing within as well as against him. In other words, if Levinas needs the resources of art to write his ethical philosophy, it is no longer certain that we can call poetry "poetry" in the sense that Levinas determines it, or in any aesthetic sense.

This *via eminentia* is also what makes it possible to conceive of the crossing of the projects of ethics and poststructuralism and deconstruction, which we could summarize as: (1) ethics, as subjectivity always already put into question by the other, is the very deconstruction of the self; (2) the deconstruction of the self by the other which borders it internally has, precisely, an ethical significance; and it points to the possible commerce or dialogue between (ethical) alterity and alteration in general. The alteration *within* the I can be ethical; it is not merely reducible to the dialectical experience of negativity.

Indeed, Derrida had asked in 1963: "How can there be the play *of* the

---

24. This is a term proposed by Stephen Smith in a fine article entitled "Reason as One for the Other: Moral and Theoretical Argument in the Philosophy of Emmanuel Levinas," *Journal for the British Society for Phenomenology* 12 (1981): 231–44.

same if alterity itself was not already *in* the same?" (vм, 126–27). More recently Derrida again pointed to the double bind of the non-relation between alteration and alterity: "To be sure, in order to respect the totally other of alterity, it would be necessary that alteration itself—which always presupposes contact, an intervention, a socio-political or psychological transformation—is not possible . . . There is a moment, however, when in my view one *must* reengage negotiation; it is a political or, let us say, historical concern. It is that if one holds this alterity without alteration in pure respect, one always risks lending a hand to immobilism, conservatism, etc., that is, to the very effacement of alterity itself" (4, 31). In short, because of the double bind that menaces even the most rigorous ethical propositions, who is to say that there is not alterity in speculative dialectics?

In closing, let us come back to the words of Levinas's reinscription of "Je est un autre." "Is it certain that Rimbaud's formula only means alienation, alteration, etc.? Is it certain that already the most humble experience of him who puts himself in another's place . . . is not animated with the most eminent meaning of this 'I is an other?' " (NI, 145). The interrogative phrase, "Is it certain?" occurs three times. If we take this question as it is intended, namely, rhetorically, the implied answer is "No." But if we take this as a question that really asks, instead of a question which only pretends to ask, the answer, while still being "No," might continue: what "je est un autre" "only means" was never certain in the first place. It is never—or almost never—certain, when it is a question of reading Rimbaud, not just because polysemy and ambiguity predominate in his work, but also because of the differential within Levinas's reading of him. The consequence of such uncertainty in my view is this: perhaps rather than reading Rimbaud's poetry as an illustration that serves in *Totality and Infinity*, all of *Totality and Infinity* can be read as a gloss on Rimbaud's *A Season in Hell*.

[8] EXCEPTIONS

THE FROZEN FACE

Given Levinas's understanding of ethics as an interruption of the self's habitual economy and its dominance by vision and representation, it should come as little surprise that in *Totality and Infinity* the face is most emphatically *not* a work of art. The face's expression is described in terms of what it is not: "Expression does not radiate a splendor that spreads unbeknown to the radiating being, which is perhaps the very definition of beauty" (*TI*, 200). If to encounter the face *as* a face is precisely to encounter that which de-plasticizes itself, it should be clear why an aesthetic approach to the face is condemned in *Totality and Infinity* and in the works preceding it. The plasticity of the image would do violence to the face and the image is the most basic feature of the work of art in Levinas's description. He states: "[T]he most elementary procedure of art consists in substituting for the object its image" (RO, 3). Moreover, Levinas asserts, *every* image is in the last analysis plastic (and this includes the nonplastic arts of music and literature). Every artwork is in the end a statue, an immobile instant, an idol (RO, 8–9): "[T]he artist has given the statue a lifeless life, a derisory life" which makes the work of art something "inhuman and monstrous" (RO, 9–11). While Levinas's polemical vehemence within his ontology of the work of art may give pause, his rejection of art seems to follow clearly enough from his understanding of the necessary plasticity of the image.

Levinas's account of the violence specific to the aesthetic gathers around one image—if it can be called an image[1]—of the freezing or the

1. Rather, it would be more like the image of an image.

petrification of the face. This is made explicit in his intertextual engagement with Paul Claudel and his poetic commentaries on the "Old Testament," discussed in Chapter 3. Levinas's four essays on Claudel—"Persons or Figures" (1950), "A Voice over Israel" (1951), "Poetry and the Impossible" (1969), and "Claudel and Israel" (1981)—express an aversion to Claudel's obsessively figural reading method with regard to the Hebrew Bible. It is as if to read the Old Testament as an announcement of events and persons of the New Testament is to return to the plasticity of *figura*'s origin ("plastic form"). One of the matters at issue here is the complicity between Christianity and the aesthetic, which covers up the ethical. To represent the rapport between persons not only freezes it, it takes violent angle on the face. In Levinas's words, "[I]t petrifies the face," producing an alibi for oppression on a transcendental level.

Levinas's reaction to Claudel's reading of the Bible is no doubt a response to the Holocaust. To write, as Claudel did, that in the figure of Cain, the Old Testament prefigures and thus charges itself with deicide may be the result of an overenthusiastic figural reading, but to write this, as Claudel did, in 1949, is indeed as Levinas puts it "discourteous" (*DF*, 122). So was the sacrificial and sacramental reading of the Holocaust that Claudel advanced in another biblical commentary in 1951, *L'Évangile d'Isaïe*. This text lines up Auschwitz with the cultic sacrificial offerings in Ancient Israel. At Auschwitz, Claudel argues, Israel, instead of sacrificing, *became* the sacrifice (a word Claudel uses interchangeably with "Holocaust"). It thus illuminated the meaning of Christ's expiatory death, which, as the firstborn of God, it had always shown the light of but could not see itself, blind as it was to the Christian proclamation. The Synagogue thus remains mysteriously faithful to its pre- *and* postfigural role as the elder brother of the Church, to its priority which is, says Claudel, "its capital." This reading is not just objectionable, it is, in Levinas's words, "hallucinatory" (*DF*, 128). Levinas's essay was later reprinted in a special issue of the *Cahiers Paul Claudel*, which sought to come to terms with Claudel's "evolving" perspective on the figure of Israel.[2]

It is indeed possible to argue that Levinas's rejection of art is to some extent a response to the Holocaust. But it is also necessary to observe that when Levinas *does* speak positively about art, as he does in the essays on Agnon, Celan, Blanchot, and Laporte, written in the 1960s and the 1970s and collected in *Proper Names* and *On Maurice Blanchot*, that art always has a relation to the Holocaust. Either it is art made by survivors

---

2. *La Figure d'Israël*, in *Cahiers Paul Claudel*, vol. 7 (Paris: Gallimard, 1968). The volume also included contributions by André Chouraqui, Claude Vigée, and Edmond Fleg.

or it is art that deals with the Holocaust in some way. This also can be shown with regard to Levinas's references in the 1980s to the Soviet writer Vassily Grossman and to the visual artists Jean Atlan and Sascha Sosno. (Even the two writers most often valorized by Levinas at various points in his career, Shakespeare and Dostoevsky, arguably are part of the canonical discussion about evil in Holocaust literary studies).[3]

My guiding question in the discussion that follows: Why, after renouncing art, does Levinas make some exceptions? To argue that Holocaust art is not really art, or is art at the limit of art, would be to beg the question of why Levinas makes the exceptions. But the apparent contradiction must be dealt with: because of the Holocaust, art is rejected as insufficient; because of the Holocaust, art is said to be ethical. Is this a contradiction? An instance of Jewish chauvinism? If this is not simply a contradiction, its significance may lie in the fact that Levinas's entire discourse about art is *traced*, as it were, by the Holocaust. But with regard to Levinas's literary and artistic exceptions, it will become clear that the art that makes the ethical difference can no longer be conceived as aesthetic.

NAMELESS

The key place where Levinas attributes a positive significance to art (apart from the essays collected in *On Maurice Blanchot*) is the 1976 collection *Proper Names*. The "proper names" to which the title refers are, as Levinas glosses them in the volume's preface, "the names of persons whose saying signifies a face" (*NP, 4*). The relation that Levinas holds with them is intertextual. *Proper Names* includes essays on literary figures (Agnon, Celan, Proust, Jabès, Laporte), literary philosophers (Kierkegaard, Wahl, Derrida, Delhomme), and religious philosophers (Buber, Lacroix, Père van Breda).

Some further comment about the organization of the volume is in order. The persons, the proper names alluded to in the title, are arranged alphabetically in the volume. Levinas even draws attention to this alphabetical order on the contents page of the French edition: "The studies gathered in this volume are arranged—with the exception of 'Nameless' *[Sans nom]* given at the end—in alphabetical order of the names to which they are consecrated." This alphabetical arrangement may be liturgical,

---

3. Thanks to Ben Friedlander for bringing this to my attention. On the relation between Ivan Karamazov's "all is permitted," theodicy, and the Holocaust, see Lawrence Langer, *The Holocaust and the Literary Imagination* (New Haven, CT: Yale University Press, 1975).

in the manner of Lamentations, whose verse, "No one to console her!" (Lam. 1:21) is even evoked in "Nameless" (*NP*, 120).[4] The Book of Lamentations records Israel's response to the fall of Jerusalem and the beginning of the Babylonian exile in 685 B.C.E. Alan Mintz shows that the nation is represented as an abandoned woman, who is spoken about in the third person until the middle of the first chapter, when a voice begins to speak in the first person. (The cry of pain gives way to a reflection on the limits of biblical structures of making sense of catastrophe. In the third chapter, a new, male speaker appears: "I am the man who has known affliction" [Lam. 3:1]).[5] Lamentations, composed as an acrostic, its five chapters shaped according to the Hebrew alphabet, is used in public mourning over the destruction of Jerusalem on the Ninth of Av.

What, in "Nameless," does Levinas mean by this lack of proper name? Like the book's preface (which opens with a reference to world wars, National Socialism, Stalinism, the camps, and the gas chambers), "Nameless" is "about" the Holocaust. (But perhaps to use the term *holocaust* is only to repeat the sacrificial and sacramental reading challenged in Claudel. The term *shoah*, the biblical word for catastrophe, like "Nameless," names the Nazi genocide otherwise.) Perhaps Levinas's reference to namelessness is commemorative, as is Claude Lanzmann's in his scriptural epigraph to the film *Shoah:* "I shall give them [the murdered] an everlasting name" (Isa. 56:5). But "Nameless" has an alternative title. The essay was originally published in an issue of the French Jewish periodical *Les Nouveaux Cahiers*, which included an excerpt from Jean-François Steiner's *Treblinka*, under the name "Honor without a Flag." In the context of Levinas's essay this phrase is a reference to Diaspora Judaism. According to Levinas, the "flag" of Israel flew only when the temple stood (*NP*, 122). The essay therefore speaks of "the fragility of our assimilation," and ends with an image of "a chilling wind" sweeping through "still decent or luxurious rooms, tearing down tapestries and pictures, putting out the lights, cracking the walls, reducing clothing to rags and bringing with it the screaming and howling of ruthless crowds." The scene depicted—and evoked in the safety of 1966—is, of course, the state of the Jews during the war (even though it sounds much like a pogrom). Levinas compares it implicitly to the fall of Jerusalem, the beginning of the Diaspora period, which came to an end with the founding of the State

4. What seems a citation is actually an allusion to Lamentations 1:21: "None to comfort me." Levinas's allusion conflates the third-person personification and the first-person speech within first chapter of Lamentations.

5. Alan Mintz, "The Rhetoric of Lamentations and the Representation of Catastrophe," *Prooftexts* 2, no. 1 (1982): 1–17.

of Israel in 1948. Upon the essay's 1976 republication in *Proper Names*, Levinas changed "Honor without a Flag" *("Honneur sans drapeau")* to "Nameless" *("Sans nom")*—in French the enigmatic "without" *(sans)* is still maintained.[6] By placing "Nameless" anomalously outside a scripturally established alphabetical form of mourning and lament, in the margins of his book, Levinas makes a (liturgically) counterliturgical gesture.

THE KNOTS OF AGNON

"Poetry and Resurrection"—Levinas's essay on the modern Hebrew writer S. Y. Agnon and arguably the strongest essay in *Proper Names*— was written in 1973, seven years after Agnon received the Nobel Prize for literature, and three years after Agnon's death. Levinas's intertextual engagement with Agnon is significant for several reasons. First, it marks Levinas's decisive encounter with Hebrew imaginative literature. The certain affinity, I will show, between Agnon's poetics and the ethico-hermeneutical procedures of rabbinic interpretation make him exemplary as an ultraethical writer for Levinas. ("To admit the action of literature on men, that is perhaps the ultimate wisdom of the West in which the people of the Bible will recognize itself" [*DF*, 53].) From the perspective of Levinas's Judaism, it is not surprising that he would find a hermeneutical approach to text common to both secular and sacred "literatures." Agnon, whose modern Hebrew literary language refers constantly to a wealth of classical Hebrew sources would seem to be, short of the Bible, as good as literature gets.

Agnon was born and raised in Polish Galicia in a town that often figures in his writing, Buczacz. He emigrated twice to Israel, first in 1908, and established himself among pioneers and writers of the Second Aliyah period.[7] He lived in Germany (in Homburg, near Frankfurt) for a dozen years in the interim, where he participated in Franz Rosenzweig's Judisches Lehrhaus in Frankfurt am Main.[8] Agnon's work is prolific and diverse, ranging from the genres of the folktale, the fable, scriptural exegesis, the anthology, all drawn from traditional Jewish sources, to the modernist tale or story, often in a surrealist idiom, and the modernist novel. Many of his works, including the novel, *A Guest for the Night*

6. "Honneur sans drapeau" disappears from the text of the essay proper, although it is retained in the table of contents as a subtitle.

7. Gershon Shaked, *Shmuel Yosef Agnon: A Revolutionary Traditionalist*, trans. Jeffrey M. Green (New York: New York University Press, 1989), 2.

8. Agnon knew Buber and Scholem. The latter recollects him in "S.Y. Agnon: The Last Hebrew Classic," *Jews and Judaism in Crisis* (New York: Schocken, 1976).

(1939), center on the vanished world of Eastern European Jewry, the stories of wonderworking rabbis and the religious piety of a world organized around the study of the classical texts of Judaism, populated by scribes, scholars, bookbinders, and book collectors. It has been pointed out, however, that the pious narrator of so many of Agnon's works is, precisely, a persona, created by an eminent modernist versed in secular as well as sacred literature.[9] Levinas registers an awareness of this in his essay's opening question: "Does Agnon belong to the world of the Jewish tradition to which the best known and most admired part of his work is devoted? Or does it, on the contrary, bear witness to the breakdown, the collapse, the end of that world?" (*NP*, 15).

A good deal of Agnon's work focuses on the destruction of Eastern European Jewry and on the possibility of a liturgical response to catastrophe within Jewish history, a mourning that situates it within the context of the pogroms and the Chielmnicki massacre (in 1648) and ceaselessly reaches back to the laments for the destruction of the two temples (in 685 B.C.E. and 70 C.E.). This characterizes the stories "Buczacz" and "The Sign," to which Levinas refers. Levinas read Agnon in Hebrew, and his essay demonstrates his familiarity with the range of Agnon's canon. Levinas also refers to the 1945 novel *Only Yesterday*, and he no doubt knew the stylistically similar stories from the thirties and forties, collected in *The Book of Deeds*. These center on the figure of the artisan or artist in the Israel of the Second Aliyah period—an alienated figure, argue Alan Mintz and Anne Golomb Hoffman, whose "creative" ambitions situate him ambivalently in relation to a tradition where the office of writer, or scribe, *sofer*, is concerned with the preservation and the transmission of the central sacred texts.[10] These works are also concerned with destruction or loss, but here that loss might be understood as a constitutive erosion within Jewish literary history.

Levinas explains the ceaseless (auto)reference[11] in Agnon to writing, inscription, to the materiality of books, paper, bindings, the collecting, preservation, and transmission of texts as an instance of what he elsewhere calls "the ontological reference to the book in Judaism," exemplified by the relation to scripture. "Agnon's language and the life it lets

9. See Arnold Band, *Nostalgia and Nightmare* (Berkeley: University of California Press, 1968); and Robert Alter, *Hebrew and Modernity* (Bloomington: Indiana University Press, 1994), 135.

10. Introduction to *A Book That Was Lost and Other Stories*, ed. Alan Mintz and Anne Golomb Hoffman (New York: Schocken, 1995).

11. Anne Golomb Hoffman, *Between Exile and Return: S. Y. Agnon and the Drama of Writing* (Albany: SUNY Press, 1991), chapters 2 and 3.

speak (whether in its wholeness *or* its disintegration) . . . all that is referred to books, loses itself there or issues from them. All this goes back to a past concerning which we are justified in wondering whether it could ever have been contained within a present" (*NP,* 8). Distinguishing Agnon's poetry from either a "craft" *(métier)* or a "work" *(travail),* Levinas invokes the terms *sonority, song,* and *sound* (*NP,* 8).

For Levinas, the birth of Hebrew as a modern (and spoken) language is a "resurrection," a "resuscitation." Its life would seem to be opposed to the death, the fixed immobility of signs which is said to characterize the ancient language of the scriptures.

> Here is a living, modern language, but one whose birth was a resurrection, a raising up from the depths of the scriptures, a life emerging from within the swell of letters where oral discussions and traditions become numb *[dans la houle arrêtée des lettres où s'engourdirent discussion et traditions orales].* Beneath the foam, threaded like lacework *[sous l'écume, ajourée comme une dentelle],* minuscule signs of commentaries upon commentaries. The dead language of the scriptures, in which each expression stands in its final, inviolable space. But is it a death—an immobility and nothing else? . . . A living language, a resuscitated language, whose words are summoned to signify, among the living, things of the present and things hoped for. But is this a life, beneath the persistent dream that these words convey, beneath the ineradicable memory of their semantic homeland in the texts? (*NP,* 8)

But Levinas's series of mock rhetorical questions ("But is it a death? . . . But is this a life?") serve to put into question the very values of the terms *life* and *death* that organize his argument. For insofar as within traditional Judaism scripture is always read in conjunction with its rabbinic interpretation, the seeming immobility and fixity of the square letters cannot be thought separately from the mobile orientation that characterizes the Saying of rabbinic interpretation. Rabbinic interpretation "enters into the static movement of the signs and goes toward the 'deep past' of the scriptural text, without ever rejoining it" (*NP,* 9). Here and elsewhere, Levinas's descriptions of rabbinic interpretation emphasize its perpetual, self-renewing mode of questioning that never comes to rest in a single interpretive answer. As Levinas specifies above, while interpretation in a sense makes possible the ethical meaning of scripture and while it "goes towards" this ethical meaning (its "deep past"), it does not coincide with it, for that would put an end to its potentially interminable questioning.

The achievement of Agnon's specifically literary language lies, for Levinas, in his way of letting the biblical word *resound* in the modern resuscitated Hebrew. Referring to Agnon's tendency to use biblical turns of phrase "with no quotation marks for the experienced reader" (*NP*, 9) (what Gershon Shaked describes as *pseudoquotation* and *pseudomidrash*),[12] Levinas asserts the "ambiguity" or the "enigma" of the Hebrew word. It signifies "both in the context of the passage in which it occurs, and in counterpoint, in the scriptural context oriented toward an unrepresentable past" (*NP*, 17). Levinas describes in effect an eminently midrashic procedure of reading one scriptural verse in relation to another verse (often its most distant scriptural neighbor). Moreover, Levinas describes this as being like "an echo anticipating the sound of a voice, a footprint preceding the step" (*NP*, 7). Lest we have any doubt about what such anachronistic figures mean, lest we have any doubt about that which gestures toward an immemorial past, a past so past that it can never come into the form of a present, Levinas states that "such is the enigmatic modality of a resuscitated language, beginning again with its own trace" (*NP*, 9). Agnon's writing, especially in its quasi-biblical or midrashic diction, has a trace-structure, that is, it has the distinctive form of signification in retreat, which is, in the idiom of Levinas's later work, precisely the way in which the other signifies. That is, it is ethical in precisely Levinas's sense.

"Is this a marvel of the imagination?" Levinas asks. But imagination, he recalls, "is the presence of images which represent the substratum of being" (*NP*, 12). Could the specificity of the Jewish imagination be in its ability to indicate an unrepresentable past? Let us look more closely at the genre of rabbinic interpretation that Levinas evokes in describing Agnon's diction. Midrash (from the root word *darash*, to study or search out) is a "searching" attitude toward the scriptural text, an extreme form of close reading that attends to every detail and diacritical mark there. Midrash looks for problems in and poses questions of the scriptural text, and in postbiblical and midrashic Hebrew such an interpretive problem or question may be referred to as a *kesher*, or knot. Midrash reads until it finds a knot, like a hard place, or node, a bump in the smooth text of reading. Moreover, if the midrash does not find a problem, sometimes it creates one. Posing a question may be a pretext for advancing a specific exegetical answer. The conversations between rabbinic interpreters, often over many generations, consist of the answers to these often unstated questions.

Agnon's "Knots upon Knots" (*"Kishre kesharim"*), a story Levinas does

12. Shaked, *A Revolutionary Traditionalist*, 29. See also Shaked's piece in *Midrash and Literature*, ed. Sanford Budick and Geoffrey Hartman (New Haven, CT: Yale University Press, 1985), 12.

not mention but almost certainly knew, dramatizes precisely such a midrashic procedure within rabbinic interpretation, in the figure of untying and tying knots. Knots are cruxes—hidden meanings, sometimes mystical meanings—that need to be untied. But in the terms of Agnon's story, untying a knot merely produces another knot; untying is inseparable from retying, and the unraveling is always a re-knotting. In Agnon's story the activity of untying is interrogated up to the point where it is shown to be impossible. Ultimately, the interpretive activities of untying as well as tying up are shown to be exposed to the risk of disintegration, of the desubstantiation of the very thread, cord, or rope of which they consist.

Like the other stories in the collection *The Book of Deeds* which portray everyday activities—such as mailing a letter, trying to get served in a restaurant, carrying a bundle of books—as hopeless undertakings, mysterious, intractable problems, "Knots upon Knots" revolves around a familiar and trivial enough Agnonian "deed." The narrator attends a "craftsman's convention," experiences anxiety after two disturbing intersubjective encounters, then has trouble carrying his bundle of books. The narrator's hands become "sluggish," "weakened." He reports, "My fingers became intertwined *as if* they had been tied with ropes":

> I . . . took package after package and tied them one to another. . . . The rope was old and knotted in knots upon knots, and on every knot that I unravelled I bruised my hands and tore my fingernails. And when I had finally unravelled all the knots, the rope fell apart. Its mate that I untied from a different package was no better. I unravelled it and it weakened. I knotted it and it disintegrated.[13]

Note that whether the narrator of Agnon's story unties or reties meanings, they come to naught, to nothing (an inauspicious sign for the reader of Agnon's story who would try to untie its meaning). But also significant, the story's central image, the "knots upon knots," is in turn knotted with the question of the other. The two disturbing intersubjective encounters render the narrator guilty, anxious, in the wrong. He himself is "all tied up in knots" as it were. Within the space of a larger discussion it would be possible to show that there is in "Knots upon Knots" an interlacing between the procedures of rabbinic interpretation and the ethical. Therein would lie what Levinas understands as its trace-structure.

Insofar as Agnon's quasimidrashic diction has the ability to indicate

---

13. S. Y. Agnon, "Knots upon Knots," in *A Book That Was Lost*, trans. Anne Golumb Hoffman, 123–27.

an unrepresentable past, it thereby, says Levinas, "breaks away from a certain ontology." For the midrashic relation to scripture from which Agnon takes inspiration is more than a way of reading. It implies precisely an entire modality of existence, as Rosenzweig, according to Levinas, would understand it. Thus Jewish liturgical or ritual life—note, as Levinas says, "in its wholeness *or* its disintegration"—also attests to an unrepresentable past "through the ritual that pervades the material gestures of existence that have been diverted from their natural ends toward the symbol. It is as if the land meant nothing but the promise of land, as if the body and its organs had been created to carry out the commandments . . . It is a life that, properly speaking, does not make up a world . . . Religion, or more precisely Judaism, would be the way in which a de-substantiation of being is of itself procured, an excluded middle in which the limits between life and nonlife are erased. The symbolism of the rite, like the enigma of the Hebraic word, denucleates ultimate solidity beneath the plasticity of forms, as taught by Western ontology" (*NP*, 18).

This reading of Jewish ritual life comes close to the reflections Levinas offered in a series of essays begun twenty years before and collected in *Difficult Freedom*. As in that work, it is part of a complex hermeneutic of Judaism. For the ethical structures that Levinas retrieves in Judaism *go against* the dominant philosophical conceptuality of the West. The habitual tendency of the self seeks to suppress alterity; first of all and most of the time my tendency is murderous toward the other. This is precisely what the encounter with the face can be said to interrupt. Here, similarly, in the distinctive terms of his later work, Levinas presupposes what he understands by what Spinoza called the *conatus essendi*, namely, the essential tendency of a being to persist in its being. He necessarily presupposes the order of ontology and its attendant violences; he presupposes substantification, what he also refers to as "the solidity of the substratum," as the very way of the world. He must presuppose what he will describe to be interrupted.

Hence in order to critically retrieve the true significance of Judaic religion dissimulated beneath the negative and privative determinations that the West assigns it, he must go by way of a specifically "Greek" philosophical language of the phenomenon, being, and substance. (This is also to say the access to "Hebrew" writing and ethical thought is never immediately given.) This is why Levinas argues that Judaic religion represents a de-substantiation of being. This is why he says that the life that Agnon's writing depicts "does not make up a world," for world is always thought together with being. There is in the Celan essay a similar description of Judaism as an "expulsion from the mundanity of the mundane" (*NP*, 45), namely, as an expulsion from the very worldhood of the world.

Hence Levinas can assert that Judaism proposes "an excluded middle in which the limits between life and nonlife disappear." The Agnon story to which Levinas refers, "The Sign," written in 1962, begins with the words: "In the year when the news reached us that all the Jews in my town had been killed, I was living in a certain section of Jerusalem . . ."[14] In referring to this story, Levinas attends to a historical moment of destruction that marks Agnon's work (as well as his own) in a most intimate manner. Agnon's story revolves around a narrator who is constricted emotionally; he is unable to weep in the synagogue in the poetic form of a lament. The story shifts between past and present; it, too, is organized around the crossing of the values of life and death. As Levinas explains, in "The Sign" "life is in death, death in life. The festival commemorating the giving of the Torah is placed at the heart of a mourning without a name [*un deuil sans nom*]" (*NP*, 13), a phrasing that recalls "Nameless." The passage that Levinas cites from Agnon's "The Sign" reads:

> And as for me, I found myself in the middle of my town as if the time of the resurrection of the dead had come. Great is the day of the resurrection of the dead! I felt a taste of it that day as I stood among my dead brothers and my fellow townspeople (who have "gone to another world"). And they stood before me, as they were during their lives in all the synagogues and houses of prayer in my town . . . Standing there, feeling worried, I gazed at the inhabitants of my town, and there was no hint of reproach in their eyes due to the fact that *I was like this* and *they were like that*.[15]

Levinas comments that Agnon's narrator "sees the inhabitants of his town again in their absolute place":

> A place that is not a site, not a landscape into which human beings blend; a place that is their place in the synagogues of the vanished town, in which presence is elevation, in which place is already nonplace . . . There is equality between the dead and the living, except that "some are like this" and "some are like that." In their places, at their posts, beyond their own essences, no longer speaking in the first person yet still speaking to us. (*NP*, 13–14)

Hence when Levinas describes Judaism as "an excluded middle in which the limits between life and nonlife disappear," he does not mean a logic

14. Agnon, *A Book That Was Lost*, 378.
15. Ibid., 400.

of opposition. He means an ambiguity that allows for—and ultimately disallows—the opposition.

Agnon's achievement, in Levinasian terms, would be the desubstantiation of the very knot of substance (a desubstantiation which can be said to be already operative in rabbinic interpretation). It would be the denucleation of "the solidity of the substratum, of the statue," writes Levinas in a note (*NP,* 18n.1). Levinas points to another example from literary history, an example which is, in some ways, closer to home for Levinas, in order to elucidate Agnon's achievement of the desubstantiation of substance:

> [It] is completely different from the one that typifies another great poet of the surreal, Gogol, in whose works the Uncanny is incapable of shaking the solidity of the substratum. The extraordinary event of the Nose that posits itself *in itself,* in opposition to its own face (the petrified, self-satisfied face of Major Kovaleff) and rides in a coach dressed as a general, does not upset the normal course of events. (*NP,* 10)

Gogol's story shows just how distinctive Agnon's achievement is; it shows just how difficult is the denucleation of substance, how persistent is the *conatus essendi.* Gogol is in some ways closer to home because of Levinas's enormous love for Russian literature, above all, for Dostoevsky, whom he privileges as a writer who gives to think responsibility on an originary level. There is no question in Levinas's essay, however, that the excluded middle between life and nonlife—the community with the dead—that Judaism proposes is a place constituted by Jewish liturgy, in response to what Levinas calls in Agnon, and, indeed, in his own life, a "nameless mourning," that is, by the Jewish liturgical response to catastrophe which for Levinas recognizes in ethics a signification that is "stronger than death" (*NP,* 25).

IMPROPER NAMING

"The names of persons whose Saying signifies a face *[dont le dire signifie un visage]*" (*NP,* 4): these are writers who give to think the ethical. Levinas's preface opposes these proper names to "the common names" and the "commonplaces" of structuralism and poststructuralism (and the examples Levinas gives are the death of God, "the play of signifiers without signifieds," and psychoanalytic speculations), which he dismisses as "fashionable banter" (*NP,* 4). Then, in an argumentative move and with a question that can also be found in the 1970 essay "No Identity," Levinas asks: "But can't we see in the end of a certain intelligibility the dawn of another? The end of an intelligibility which reaches its apotheosis in the ultimate identity 'of the identical and the nonidentical,' affirmed by Hegel!" (*NP*, 5). (Again, as in "No Identity," the fact that Levinas seeks precisely to put into question the metaphysics of identity, affirms, despite his protests, the very convergence between the poststructuralist, or in this case the Derridean, critique of the presence of the present and his own thinking of the ethical.) This new intelligibility, Levinas states, "is not the consciousness of self, but the relation with the other." Not the Said *(le Dit)*, it is "the Saying which always carves out a passage from the same to the other *[le Dire qui toujours se fraye un passage du Même à l'Autre]*" (*NP*, 12).

The Said is the linguistic equivalent of the economy of the Same. The Saying and the Said is a correlative relation (exceeding correlation) that marks the difference between a conative speech, oriented toward its addressee, interlocutionary and ethical, and a speech oriented toward the referent, more like a speaking *about* than a speaking *to* the other. The Saying, key to and characteristic of Levinas's description of ethical language in the later work, especially in *Otherwise than Being*, is often evoked in Levinas's discussions of ethical poetry, literature, and art. As I have previously cautioned, however, we should not take for granted that we know what we mean by the Saying. This is precisely what is seized upon by Levinas's readers hoping to extend his positive evaluations of art to an ethical poetics. Can we ever be sure that we are in the presence of the Saying, any more than we can, in the terms of the earlier work, *perform* the ethical language for which so few examples are given? Levinas usually focuses on the opposite problem, frequently referring to the "Saying which *congeals* into the thematization of the Said" and the constitutive risk of this. Suffice it to note that here too it is a question of an orientation that should be mobile freezing up, an ethical signification that is neutralized.

Levinas's 1972 essay on Paul Celan situates Celan as a Jewish poet in the line of Buber and not Heidegger.[16] The basic claim of Levinas's essay is that "the poem in Celan goes toward the Other" (*NP*, 41), that there is in Celan's work an attempt to think transcendence (*NP*, 42). Celan's text "The Meridian" (his 1960 acceptance speech upon receiving the Georg Büchner prize) is said "to interrupt itself ceaselessly" (*NP*, 41). Interruption signals the putting into question of the totality, as when Levinas

---

16. "Are Buber's categories to be preferred then? Are they to be preferred to so much inspired exegesis to the benefit of Hölderlin, Trakl, and Rilke, that descends in majesty from the Black Forest in order to show poetry opening the world in Being, between heaven and earth, where man finds a dwelling place?" (*NP*, 42).

speaks in his 1971 essay on Jean Lacroix of "the interruption of coherent discourse" (*NP*, 80), or of the modality of the enigma (*EP*, 69). Self-interruption is the trope for a form of ethical discourse in which the interruption is not reabsorbed into thematization and totality, namely, an ethical discourse that *performs* its own putting into question. (For given the precarious nature of this interruption, given that "every contesting and interruption of . . . a discourse is at once related by discourse" [*OB*, 169], nonetheless, Levinas asks: "[T]he discourse which suppresses the interruptions by relating them, does it not maintain the discontinuity under the knots which retie the thread?" [*OB*, 170].) The specific achievement of Celan's poetry, for Levinas, is the way in which it "interrupts the *ludic* order of the beautiful, of the play of concepts and of the play of the world" (*NP*, 66).

The significance of this statement is apparent when we consider how crucial the concept of play is to the ontology of the work of art in traditional aesthetics. Levinas evokes this implicitly and polemically in "Reality and Its Shadow" when he conceives of the aesthetic state of mind as one in which "consciousness, paralyzed in its freedom, *plays*, totally absorbed in the playing" (*RO*, 4). Levinas consistently describes the effect of the work of art on its audience as a playing, a captivation, or a bewitchment, which produces in turn a passivity, a loss of initiative, a passage from oneself into anonymity. These are, I showed in Chapter 5, all of the terms that he generally uses for his polemic against what Lévy-Bruhl called participation, and its false transcendence that Levinas always opposes to ethical transcendence.

Throughout his work, Levinas's antiludic discourse is apparent: in the antitheatrical or antifigural discourse that doubles his discourse against (pre-)figural interpretation in his Claudel reading, in *Totality and Infinity*'s opposition between poetic rapture and the sobriety of ethical discourse (*TI*, 201–2), in its rejection of the poet whose imagination is caught up in the *play* of the same (*TI*, 37). In the "Trace of the Other" (1963), Levinas seems to go out of his way to distinguish what he calls the "total gratuity" of the one-way movement that is paradigmatic of the ethical both from "the games of art *[les jeux de l'art]*" and also from a Bataillian notion of expenditure (*T*, 347, 349). The antiludic references in *Otherwise than Being* (1974) are numerous: ". . . for sensibility does not play the game of essence, does not play any game" (*OB*, 56, 58, 169). The Celan essay's reference to the "play of the world *[jeu du monde]*" registers Levinas's reading of Eugen Fink, who was Levinas's colleague at the time of his studies under Heidegger in 1928–29. Fink's *Der Spiel als Weltsymbol*, in Levinas's summary, "sees the game as among the very conditions of the world" (*NP*, 76n.2). Levinas's reservations about Fink's thesis, and about what he perceives as the Nietzschean atheism implicit in the very concept of the "play of the world," are apparent here and elsewhere. He speaks appositively of "the freedom of evasion, freedom of the game, freedom of irresponsibility" (*NP*, 76). Hence for Levinas to interrupt the ludic order of the beautiful is to interrupt the self-sufficiency and the irresponsibility of aesthetic experience.

Levinas's 1966 essay on Roger Laporte ends with the extravagant assertion: "Language is the fact that a single word is proffered: God" (*NP*, 93). Note that the title of Laporte's book is a citation from II Kings, *Une voix du fin silence* (A small still voice), which seems to authorize a reading of Laporte's work in terms of transcendence. Second, Laporte's work follows closely the example of Blanchot, whose work for Levinas points to alterities which have an ethical significance, even if that significance is not made explicit (*SMB*, 23). Levinas compares Laporte's work to Blanchot's, to which he credits an opening function: "Maurice Blanchot opened literature to a new dimension, in which real characters consume themselves in a zone of high tension that is neither objective reality nor the field of consciousness" (*NP*, 91). Levinas also makes reference to Blanchot's (and his own) thinking of the alterity of the *il y a:* "In Blanchot, there occurs a kind of impersonal, neuter sifting of the same things again and again, an incessant sound of coming and going, an endless rocking, like a fundamental opacity that cannot even properly be called fundamental, since it founds nothing" (*NP*, 91).

At various junctures in *Proper Names*, in the preface, the Celan essay, and very prominently in the essay on Agnon, the structure of the Saying and the Said is evoked, and the literary authors (or proper names) are credited with resisting the immobilization of the Saying in the Said. Agnon's work will be described as "a prolongation of the Saying" (*NP*, 21). That the very literary authors who traffic in a figured sense of language are credited with the Saying is remarkable to the extent that the classical theory of metaphor, understood since Aristotle as an analogy between two objects based on their resemblance necessarily assumes that metaphor relies on a knowledge of essences. That would consign the *im*proper naming that is metaphor to the realm of the Said. But this is not the case here. Moreover, in these essays, Levinas's counterclaim that art, usually excoriated as a form of nonresponsibility, can be ethical, and ethical in his precise sense of the term—that is, not *an* ethics but an ultraethics, namely, an ethics that has an opening function—is remarkable in another way. It negotiates the incommensurability that prevented art from being originary enough in the first place to be ethical.

LEVINAS READING DOSTOEVSKY

It's a long way from Kierkegaard's "I am the most solitary" (*EK, 282*) to Dostoevsky's "I am the most responsible," the privileged passage from *The Brothers Karamazov* to which Levinas refers frequently in his work. It would seem to be the difference between the spasmodic cry of a solitary self, lacerated and despairing, and a limitless originary responsibility that does not initiate in the subject and its freedoms. In the idiom of Levinas's later writings, "I am responsible to all and for all, and I more than all the others," is the very paradigm for responsible subjectivity. Characterized by a radical humility, the model of subjectivity is what Levinas himself refers to as kenotic. "The I which says I is not that which singularizes or individuates a concept or genus" (*CPP, 168*); it is unique. That the "I" always has one responsibility *more* than the others emphasizes the nonreciprocity and the radical asymmetry between myself and the other. Subjectivity here is an originary or preoriginary responsibility or guilt. Not, then, the predication of attributes of an "I," "I am more responsible/guilty" is what constitutes and also deconstitutes the "I."

Hence while Dostoevsky is on the one hand a writer who can readily be associated with the ones who cry out, Kierkegaard and Rimbaud, and whose work gives meaning to and explores the very term, *laceration* or *nadryv*, not just as a tearing things apart but as a purposeful hurting of oneself,[17] he is also, for Levinas, a writer whose work has a paramount ethical significance. The citation of the phrase from the book occurs nearly a dozen times in Levinas's work: in the 1975 essay "God and Philosophy" (*CPP, 168*), in *Otherwise than Being* (*OB, 146*), and in the interviews with Levinas conducted in the 1980s (*EI, 105; IR*). In *The Brothers Karamazov*, the phrase is first articulated by Father Zosima's elder brother Markel on his deathbed, with regard to the recklessness that preceded his conversion. It is repeated by Father Zosima in his recounting of his own conversion. At the height of his own dissolution, he remembers his elder brother's words, and they become instrumental in Zosima's conversion. Zosima's conversion account is itself redacted and narrated by his spiritual disciple, Alyosha Karamazov in the section of *The Brothers Karamazov* entitled "Notes in the Life of God of the Elder Zosima." In sum, the phrase, iterated throughout Book Six, applies not only to Alyosha's own life, but it extends to those for whom he feels responsible, his brothers. Ultimately, each of the brothers, Dmitri, Ivan, Smerdyakov,

17. Edward Wasiolek, *Dostoevsky: The Major Fiction* (Cambridge, MA: M.I.T., 1964), 155.

and Alyosha himself, is guilty of the murder of Fyodor Pavlovich. "I am responsible to all and for all" functions in pendant to and in dialogue with Ivan's (also iterated) phrase "All is permitted," which has what Mikhail Bakhtin has described as an "intense dialogical life" relayed through various characters in the course of Dostoevsky's novel.[18] (This phrase, incidentally, is cited by Levinas in a reference to the Nazi era in "Nameless" [*NP*, 180].)

Here Levinas is in a particular affinity to aspects of the Russian spiritual tradition that Dostoevsky drew on in his depiction of kenotic saintly figures, namely, the diction and the literature of eastern orthodox Saint's lives. Zosima is such a figure, as is Alyosha, as are, elsewhere in Dostoevsky's work, the elder Tikhon and the holy fool Maria Lebyatkin in *The Devils*, Prince Myshkin in *The Idiot*, and Sonia Marmeladov in *Crime and Punishment*. Of this last figure Levinas writes:

> There is a scene in Dostoevsky's *Crime and Punishment* where Sonya Marmeladov looks upon Raskolniknov in his despair and Dostoevsky speaks of "insatiable compassion." He does not say "inexhaustible compassion." It is as though the compassion that goes from Sonya to Raskolnikov were a hunger which the presence of Raskolnikov nourishes beyond any saturation, increasing this hunger to infinity. (T, 351)

In this explicit allusion to *Crime and Punishment* from the 1963 "Trace of the Other," Levinas uses a dramatic and visual vocabulary in his reference to "a scene" in *Crime and Punishment*. Raskolnikov, the murderer, kneels before Sonia, the prostitute, immediately prior to confessing his murder to her. While Levinas is making a semantic point about how compassion is characterized, his reference is conventionally thematic. An implied simile or *comme* governs the entire allusion, which turns on the resemblance between the *Crime and Punishment* passage and the structure of metaphysical desire. This is, then, another instance of Levinas's using a text to illustrate a philosophical argument, thereby reducing it to its denotative terms, eliding its literary specificity. Would this not be a betrayal of Dostoevsky's text, an ingratitude of a kind that similarly was operative in Levinas's readings of the texts of Blanchot and Rimbaud, even when he would mark a debt to them? Yet within the double bind

18. Mikhail Bakhtin, *Problems of Dostoevsky's Poetics*, trans. Caryl Emerson (Minnesota: University of Minnesota Press, 1984), 89. I have also consulted with profit: Wasiolek, *Dostoevsky*; Margaret Ziolkowski, *Hagiography and Modern Russian Literature* (Princeton, NJ: Princeton University Press, 1988); Sven Linner, *Starets Zosima in the Brothers Karamazov* (Stockholm: Almqvist and Wiksell, 1975); Victor Terras, *A Karamazov Companion* (Madison: University of Wisconsin Press, 1981).

of the hermeneutics of respect that has been broached in this book's preceding pages—in order to "do justice" to a text that asserts an asymmetrical ethical imperative, one must be unjust to it—such a betrayal, even
when it is neither intentional nor explicit, may be constitutive.

In *The Brothers Karamazov*, "I am responsible to all and for all" articulates an ecstatic Franciscan spirituality, a universal responsibility that extends to the love of the earth, plants, and animals. While it combines
aspects of the German Pietist tradition, the love of nature and beautiful
feelings in an enormously seductive way, it is nonetheless close to being
an instance of "aestheticized" religion, and it occurs within a Christian
matrix and worldview of the life of temptation, within a series of exemplary conversions, a stereotypical patterning of sin to salvation, profligacy
to conversion. This is the economy of personal salvation that Levinas in
Difficult Freedom calls "egoistic" (*DF*, 26), the life of temptation that is
itself the temptation, as Levinas states in the talmudic readings and toward which he expresses such ambivalence.

On the one hand, there is a convergence between Dostoevsky's phrase
and Levinas's ethical emphasis on kenotic subjectivity (indeed, so much
so that the interpenetration of the voices of Dostoevsky and Levinas
would seem itself to be ethical in its structure, within the terms of what
Bakhtin himself terms his "philosophical anthropology").[19] Indeed, the
two concrete textual instances in which Levinas refers to Dostoevsky are
convincing enough to have been able to give rise to at least one full-
length "Levinasian" study of Dostoevsky, Jacques Rolland's *Dostoïevski:
la question de l'autre*. The character of Sonia, associated in the novel with
other victims of violence, with the insulted and the injured, here appears
as the figure of the disinherited, the stranger, the poor one, in short,
what Levinas calls the other. In the "scene" to which Levinas refers, she
is, Rolland suggests, "pure face," bearing, in Raskolnikov's words "all the
suffering in the world."[20] Indeed, so great is the affinity between the texts
of Dostoevsky and Levinas that Dostoevsky would seem to be the one
writer to whom Levinasian ethics (quasi-transcendental and incommensurable with any novelistic "world") could be "applied." But would this
be a case of applied Levinas or applied Dostoevsky? The question is
bound to arise, as it did in the case of Levinas's intertextual engagement
with Rimbaud, Who is reading whom?

On the other hand, Dostoevsky's phrase is located firmly in the hagio-

19. Tzvetan Todorov, *Mikhail Bakhtin: The Dialogical Principle*, trans. Wlad Godzich
(Minneapolis: University of Minnesota Press, 1984).

20. Jacques Rolland, *Dostoïevski: la question de l'autre* (Paris: Verdier, 1983), 47–50.

graphical section of *The Brothers Karamazov*. The problem is, as Bakhtin states very bluntly, the hagiographical sections of Dostoevsky's work are the sole parts of it that are *not* constructed according to the polyphonic structure of unmerged voices that elsewhere prevails: "The hagiographical word is a word without a sideward glance, calmly adequate to itself and to its referential object"; it is, in short, monological.[21]

In *Otherwise than Being* Levinas states that "there is in subjectivity's relationship with the other, which we are here striving to describe, a quasi-hagiographic style that wishes to be neither a sermon nor the confession of a 'beautiful soul' " (*OB,* 47). In the interview with André Dalmas about Blanchot, he says that Ivan's "everything is permitted" is totalizing, "not because of Dostoevsky's atheism, but because of his spirituality" (*SMB,* 154). He registers his ambivalence toward Dostoevsky in *Difficult Freedom*, when he speaks (somewhat self-mockingly) of "our taste for the pathetic, our sensibility nourished by Christianity and Dostoevsky" (*DF,* 65), and when he ironically privileges "the workers of the eleventh hour" (*DF,* 65). The workers of the eleventh hour are the New Testament's representation of the Christians (who heard the proclamation later) over and against the Jews who cling to the proclamation in its earlier and altogether dissimulated form. When this reference occurs, it is in the context of Levinas's criticizing Spinoza for seeming to adopt the Christian triumphalist reading of the "Old Testament" in his *Theologico-Political Treatise*. Levinas wishes to inscribe Spinoza as the eleventh-hour worker and himself as the one who worked all day. But suffice it to observe, within the context of Levinas's Russian-Jewish identity, that this is also Levinas's inadvertent reference to himself. In short, Levinas's intertextual relationship to Dostoevsky, and the particular intrication of Jewish and Christian traditions that nourish his work, complicates any simply Judeo-centered reading of Levinas's ethics.

THE EXAMPLE OF BLANCHOT

We cannot conclude a discussion of Levinas and literature without briefly considering the kind of example and the kind of exception that Maurice Blanchot represents for Levinas. Indeed, the topic of the intertextual relationship between Levinas and Blanchot should be a book in itself. The sixty-year friendship between the two, which began at the University of Strasbourg in 1923, includes a history of reading each other's texts. Two of Blanchot's critical works, *The Infinite Conversation* and *The Writing of*

21. Bakhtin, *Dostoevsky's Poetics*, 248–49, 25, 203.

the Disaster, are written, as it were, under the sign of Levinas. During the war, while Levinas was incarcerated in a labor camp for French Jewish prisoners of war, Blanchot saved Levinas's wife and daughter (*IR*). In the interview with Poirié, Levinas remarks that Blanchot provides the highest example not only of a moral kind but of a quality of thought. He serves as it were as a literary example in his narrative prose, and especially as a literary critical example in his sustained meditations on the ontology of the literary work of art in *The Space of Literature* and in other critical prose works. I will focus on two of Levinas's four essays on Blanchot, collected in the volume *On Maurice Blanchot*.[22]

At the culminating point of his 1975 essay on Blanchot's *The Madness of the Day*, Levinas writes: "The other—the sole point in which an outside is opened. He plants a knife in my flesh . . . the transcendence of the intersubjective is oppression par excellence" (*SMB*, 169). Levinas is referring to one of two violent blows that the narrator of *The Madness of the Day* has suffered, the first when, as he matter-of-factly recounts, "someone ground glass in my eyes," and the second, when a madman in the asylum (where the narrator is incarcerated) stabs him in the hand, then begs his forgiveness and wishes to be his friend. Insofar as *The Madness of the Day* is a narrative in which, as Derrida observes, the value of an event (and its narration) is itself placed into question,[23] it is notable that here and elsewhere in Blanchot's text Levinas finds the incursion of otherness.

Another reference to the other which Levinas finds is in the only place in the narration where there occurs what the narrator calls "a real event." The "brief scene" that the narrator witnesses, and that, he recounts, excited him "to the point of delirium," appears to be that, in front of a door, a man steps back to let a baby carriage through. Levinas comments: "A man cedes his place *[cede le pas]* to a baby carriage . . . One person withdraws before another. One *is* for the other" (*SMB*, 165). Within Blanchot's narrative, this "event" is puzzling in its very inconsequentialness and inconspicuousness. But to take the terms that Levinas uses elsewhere, it can be understood as a kind of "ontological courtesy" (*IR*), the self's relinquishing of its own place in the sun—its imperialism—ceding its place to the other in a putting into question of the self that, since *Totality and Infinity*, he has described as ethical. He also assigns it the ethical meaning of substitution specific to his later work.

---

22. In chapter 4 of *Blanchot: Extreme Contemporary* (London: Routledge, 1997), Leslie Hill offers a nuanced account of this intertextual relationship.

23. Jacques Derrida, "The Law of Genre," *Glyph* 7 (1980). Maurice Blanchot, *The Madness of the Day*, trans. Lydia Davis (New York: Station Hill, 1985).

The Madness of the Day would seem to be an instance in which a literary work is genuinely commensurable with the level of Levinas's ultraethical discourse. There is a certain circularity here. Because Blanchot's text has no doubt relayed itself through Levinas's ethical philosophy, it is not surprising that nearly the sole, and the most resourceful interpretive explanation, is an ultraethical one. Of course, Levinas had always characterized Blanchot's work as "fundamental," or "more fundamental" (*smb*, 127), even though the alterity of the *il y a* "cannot properly be called fundamental, since it founds nothing" (*np*, 97). With such characterizations, Levinas thereby directed attention to the relation between the levels of their respective post-Heideggerian discourses and their possible commensurability.

This is why when Levinas proposes a reading of *The Madness of the Day*'s "someone took my hand and planted a knife in it" as illuminating the fact that "the transcendence of the intersubjective is oppression par excellence," this reading serves to illuminate in turn the irreducible *in*equality of the relation to the other, or what Levinas calls metaphysical asymmetry. One should add, as regards Levinas's interpretation of "the event" that the narrator witnesses, that the man who cedes his place to the other "works" as an example of ontological courtesy because it is one of the very few examples for the ethical that can be adduced on the basis of Levinas's texts. Like other examples for the ethical (tearing the bread from one's mouth, turning the cheek to the smiter, clothing the naked and feeding the hungry), ceding one's place to the other would seem to be located at the intersection between the transcendental and the empirical.

Another of Levinas's essays on Blanchot, "The Poet's Regard," appeared in 1956, one year after the publication of *The Space of Literature*. There Blanchot develops a phenomenology of reading in which he deploys the technical terms of solitude, death, pathos, exile, fascination, image to describe the literary work of art. Taking place neither in the world nor in any area where *pouvoir* or possibility reigns, the essence of the work of art, for Blanchot, is its nonessential character. These assertions are all put to the test in *The Space of Literature* in a series of exemplary close readings of Hölderlin, Mallarmé, Valéry, Rimbaud, Kakfa, Dostoevsky, and others.

Levinas acknowledges very precisely the possible convergence and the limits of such a convergence between the alterity of the ethical and the alterity of the literary when he describes the literary work of art in Blanchot as "an impersonal speech, without a 'you,' without interpellation, without vocative, and at the same time distinct from 'a coherent discourse' manifesting a universal Reason, both discourse and

Reason belonging to the order of the Day" (*SMB*, 131). This is to say that at issue in the literary work of art in Blanchot's analysis is not an ethical speaking but nonetheless a kind of speaking that is distinct from the totality. It is the outside or an exteriority that speaks. This is why Levinas also will say later in the same essay that "the literary space to which Blanchot directs us . . . abstains from ethical preoccupations, at least in an explicit form" (*SMB*, 137). It is as if this abstention were itself ultraethical.

Insofar as Blanchot's work also constitutes a dismantling of classical and Romantic aesthetics—especially around the concepts of work, its structure of completion and its "tone," the author and his expression, the relation of work to "world"—one may wonder how, exactly, Levinas would understand his own 1948 descriptions of the ontology of the work of art in relation to Blanchot's. To what extent has Blanchot's "more originary" interrogation of literature influenced his own? Such a question would have to go by way of Blanchot's reflections on two terms, *fascination* and *the image*, developed at the end of *The Space of Literature*'s first chapter, "The Essential Solitude," published originally in 1953 in *Nouvelle Revue Française*, and in one of the book's appendices entitled "Two Versions of the Imaginary," first published in 1951 in *Cahiers de la Pléiade*. The terminological overlap between Blanchot's statements about art and those which Levinas had deployed in "Reality and Its Shadow" is considerable: *shadow, double, image, magic, passivity*. Levinas's 1956 essay about Blanchot's literary criticism, "The Poet's Regard," suggests that he has accepted Blanchot's tacit or implicit response to and restatement of his own earlier theoretical position. For example, while in 1948 Levinas tends to emphasize the violence of the image so fundamental to the work of art, in 1956 he writes:

> Literature for Blanchot presupposes the regard of the poet, an original experience in both senses of this adjective: fundamental experience and experience of the origin. All artistic "disinterestedness" with regard to things has already been this experience. We do not go from the thing to the poetic image by a simple neutralization of the real, nor from everyday language to "the image of language" which would be poetic speaking—by diminution. What is required, after Blanchot (although he does not utilize the term), is a prior transcendence *[une transcendance préalable]* in order that things may be apperceived as image and language, as poetry. The image precedes, in this sense, perception. (*SMB*, 129–301)

Even though this "prior transcendence" still has much in common with what Levinas, after Wahl, had called "transdescendence," namely, the negative transcendence associated with the *il y a*, it is as if both Levinas and Blanchot are seeking in common what Libertson calls "the latent condition for phenomenality and retention which is precisely fascination" (*PRX*, 249). The polemical vehemence with which Levinas had earlier characterized the image is no longer apparent in this summary of Blanchot's subsequent understanding of the image. This suggests that, on the basis of reading Blanchot, Levinas has modified somewhat his understanding of the work of art, not so much as regards its ontology than as regards its possible relation to ethics. But any question of how much Levinas may have learned from Blanchot in the interim must also acknowledge that Levinas remains unconvinced about the capacity of art to signify transcendence. Nevertheless, what this book has explored, in following out the largely unaccented responses to literature in his texts, are literary dimensions in Levinas which have everything to do with the force of his ethical discourse.

FROM EXISTENTIALISM TO THE PRIMACY OF ECONOMY
BY GEORGES BATAILLE

The following books are reviewed in this Essay:

1. Emmanuel Levinas, *De l'existence à l'existant*, Collection "Exercice de la Pensée," edited by Georges Blin (Paris: Fontaine, 1947).

2. Jean Wahl, *Petite histoire de "l'existentialisme," suivie de Kafka et Kierkegaard: Commentaires* (Paris: Club Maintenant, 1947).

3. Guido da Ruggieri, *Existentialism*, edited and introduced by Rainer Heppenstall, translated by E. M. Cocks (London: Secker and Warburg, 1946).

4. Julien Benda, *Tradition de l'existentialisme, ou les philosophies de la vie* (Paris: Grasset, 1947).

No one today refuses existentialism a dominant place in the philosophical sphere. This doctrine, which is, in general, badly known, has benefited for some time from an exceptional vogue. But the dominant place is not the effect of this superficial vogue: it is nothing, apparently, in contemporary philosophy, that can be opposed to the works of a school that would pretend to renew the notion we have of ourselves and of the world.

This precedence naturally enough has been a source of irritation for some. It irritates many Marxists, who take it for the expression of a decadent class. It irritates the survivors of idealism whose positions are directly targeted. But the opposition between existentialism and Marxism is quite different from the opposition of each doctrine to idealism.

First of all, the minor position of contemporary Marxism is misleading. It is true that recent works that represent it do not have the attraction of newness: for all their notoriety, the general character of the great existentialist works is missing from them. But even among those who are adept at it, philosophy does not win out: Marxism acts. And if *in the philosophical sphere* it does not hold the place of existentialism, it is infinitely more influential.

On the other hand, the Marxist position is not exactly the opposite of the existentialist one. The primacy of life over thinking is common to both doctrines. Karl Löwith[1] has shown that each of them is opposed to Hegel's idealism: he has called attention to common traits between Kierkegaard, Marx, and Nietzsche. But evidently, of the three, Marx distanced himself least from Hegel, and in all ways the primacy of life is more real for Marxists. Existentialists are hardly faithful to their point of departure: they philosophize, and Marxists live. For them, as for Marx, it is a matter not of understanding the world but of changing it.

Curiously enough, Julien Benda associates existentialism and Marxism (which he nonetheless omits naming). The pure idealist, indifferent enough to the lot of men, who is drawn toward "the hatred of all that exists," attributes modern philosophy to "the crowd *[la foule].*" "To be attached to a thinking in its opposition to life is proper to men—exceptional and few in number—who are generally solitary, proud, and who are, let us say, of an aristocracy. It follows from this that with the revolution of the nineteenth century, *philosophy, which up till now was aristocratic, became popular.* Once more the Word was made flesh" (*Tradition de l'existentialisme*, p. 24; emphasis mine). For him, "Bergsonism, Nietzscheanism, existentialism" are "popular philosophies." This does not make a lot of sense, but let us leave Bergsonism aside: it is a matter of subversion, of the first object of Julien Benda's hatred. Subversion in effect is in accord with a side of people that is animal and proud, the primacy of life is subversive—it contests the *law*—and the crowd is par excellence opposed to the primacy of thought (or at least to the primacy of the stability that founds it).

It is evidently bizarre (but of little importance) that having this opinion of the philosophy of the nineteenth century, perceiving that in its most lively aspect it was oriented toward life, Julien Benda passes over Marxism

---

1. "L'achèvement de la philosophie classique par Hegel et sa dissolution chez Marx et Kierkegaard," in *Recherches Philosophiques* 4 (1934–35).

in silence. In all ways, his paradox helps [us] to grasp the irresistible movement of thinking which is prolonged among us, which is the refusal to
posit thinking as the end of thinking. Must one say that to resist this
movement, as Benda does, with an arrogant platitude, in truth is to serve
the cause one attacks?

Older, pre-Hegelian idealism is no doubt the form of philosophy
which is the strangest to our barbarous and impatient spirits. It is impossible to love its hypocrisy. At the same point of time within Marxism and
existentialism, a brusqueness lacking all respect and a "resolute decision"
bring us into opposition to eternal ideas. It is not always beautiful: a
flaccid need for anguished emotion, a sentimental bad taste has made a
vogue of existentialism. "Existentialism," according to the expression of
the Italian idealist Guido da Ruggieri, "places us in existence as if in a
detective novel" (*Existentialism*, p. 19). But the idealist anger is not aimed
at this heavy frivolity, it intends the relative nihilism and the ease in pene-
trating "life's muddy waters."[2]

The moment arrived, in the nineteenth century, in which the intelligence of man, carried to its high degree of acuity, ceased to take itself
for the center and the completion of the world. A feeling of infinite dignity was succeeded by one of distress and abandon. Irony undermined
dignity; hunger and passion rendered it detestable. Knowledge's content-

2. But between the work of the Roman professor and that of Julien Benda the rap-
prochement is limited to the subject and to the idealist point of view of the authors. It is
apparent that Julien Benda has only the vaguest idea of what he is talking about. He limits
himself to the vulgar argument: "But this is as old as the world!" Guido da Ruggieri gives
a short exposé, but it is nourished by and is clear concerning the so-called existentialist
philosophy—in the persons of Kierkegaard, Heidegger, Jaspers, and Gabriel Marcel. And
once it is understood that the English translated this little book in the guise of an introduction to a doctrine basically unknown to them: the hostility of the author has a more negative
effect on his readers than on the philosophers whose thought is summarized. The preface
by Rainer Heppenstall marks the extent to which the "existentialist adventure," which I
understand to be the sudden development of the French School and the hubbub around
it, is unintelligible from the outside. Its author, who writes in November 1945, draws his
principal information from an article of Mme Claude Edmonde Magny. For my part I
regret being personally placed among the French existentialists. In my understanding, the
whole business is an unhappy one, a generalized confusion sustained by a journalistic excita-
tion. Rainer Heppenstall seems to be, similarly, in doubt: "Certainly Kierkegaard was
known in England even later than in France. Then came so-and-so and so-and-so, but we
understood their meaning badly." What Mme Magny says about the books of Sartre, Ca-
mus, Blanchot, and myself (one single existentialist out of four) seems harrowing enough:
it is not what one was waiting for out of France after the silence of the occupation. And
he voluntarily cites a judgment of Benedetto Croce saying that the philosophy of existence
"encumbers the world with spirit," that it is "overexcited, poisoned, perverse, a sort of
inflammation of the groin."

ment is turned into its contrary, even if *I know* that I am hungry, beyond any hunger that could be appeased, a limitless desire will torment me. The primacy of life over thinking takes these two forms: Marx affirms the primacy of needs; the primacy of a desire which goes further than the satisfaction of a need is Kierkegaard's position. I will first speak of the primacy of desire (having to show that it, like need, is reducible to economic givens).

For philosophers in general and for Hegel, knowledge was the search for the object: this implied furthermore an adequation of subject (of man, of philosopher) to the object (that which is, the world, God, or the absolute Idea). This object was immutable, eternal, and "universal truth valid for all time." The fortuitous subject, his needs and his desires, were forcibly submitted to this truth, crushed by it. Hegel, it is true, posited the object as a totality of which each subject was a part: every individual, every act of thinking, was a moment of universal becoming, of a system of the world. But the subject knew himself to be reduced in the end to being but "a paragraph" of the ensemble—of a system. He could only fall into an abyss, destroy himself in the knowledge of a totality of becoming, of a *completed becoming*, of an *immutable becoming*. He could be only on one condition: knowing that "he" *was not*, that is, he was nothing but a subordinated piece of an immense and necessary ensemble, a "utility," and, if he believed himself to be autonomous, he was an error. Desire in Hegel is resolved thus in a knowledge that is absolute, that is a suppression of the subject, relative, who knows. *One exists no longer* in these conditions; history, first of all, is supposed to be completed, and so must be even the life of an individual subject. Never, if one thinks about it, has anyone conceived of anything more dead: the multiple life was the immense game and the immense error that the achievement of this death necessitated. Toward the end of his life, Hegel no longer posed the problem to himself: he repeated his lectures and played cards.

Against an inhuman philosophy, Kierkegaard elevated the protestation, the cry of a suffocated existence. To the satisfaction of the eternal idea he opposed the intensity of an individual sentiment and this chance of the possible—which may or may not be, and which leaves us suspended in anguish. He himself was an *existent:* even if existence, as he believed, was sin, he wished it within himself to be exacerbated, strained, and suspended. The God before whom he existed was not the immutable truth in himself, but this unknowable and unjustifiable existent that reason cannot attain to, which is the God of Abraham.

From this starting point, he cannot have philosophy, strictly speaking, but rather the cry, which, I have said, is the expression of an existence, of a subjectivity. This expression can be the fact of a man who is conversant in the problems of philosophy, which, for all that, will still not become a system. In this sense, Jean Wahl, according to whom "one cannot define in a satisfying way the term existentialism" (*Petite histoire*, p. 12), compares Kierkegaard to Rimbaud, indeed, to Van Gogh. The expression given to it by Rimbaud, which he lived, would have an interest on the same level as do the books of Kierkegaard. A pathetic existence expressed with force would be substituted for the position of philosophical truth. The role of a philosopher would be limited to showing how philosophy is resolved in the position of existence. Jean Wahl spoke of philosopher-poets who would be, if I understand him correctly, philosophers by origin but only in order to liquidate a heritage. They would endlessly resolve the tension of philosophical research in poetic effusion.[3] In sum, it is very natural, starting from Kierkegaard, to rediscover the attitude of a religion for whom the myths and the rites have no more interest than philosophical, indeed dogmatic, knowledge (in this respect we should even assimilate the older myths to these privileged experiences which surpass thinking).

I have given here but a first movement by which existentialism is, in the mind of Kierkegaard, detached from classical philosophy. It is still the case that the term existentialist when applied to Kierkegaard is superadded. Jean Wahl does not want this term for his own thinking, which voluntarily opposes Kierkegaard to modern existentialism.

With respect to this position, modern existentialism is a compromise. There is certainly opposition between this philosophy and philosophy in general. The latter is in principle the search for an immutable essence. And existentialism affirms (it is its school definition) that existence *precedes* essence. [Yet] it does not research essence any less than does the existence which precedes it. It is not entirely clear, but Heidegger, Jaspers, or Sartre speak of *existents*, of men *in general*. To this slippage corresponds elsewhere a hypertrophy of the intellectual enterprise. It is still a matter of *feeling* existence, of *living* before knowing (without this, existence could not precede essence). But knowledge, the professorial exercise, overflows (above all in Sartre). It is no longer the subjective life of

---

3. There are the greatest differences interior to the existentialist world. The systems of contemporary existentialism are altogether contrary to this position. A literature *illustrating* a system just withdraws from it all the more. The position of Kierkegaard was romantic; that of Heidegger who appeals to Hölderlin is romantic also, but Sartre has resolutely broken with it: he is a stranger to poetry. (Trans. note: This note was deleted in the two "corrected offprints" from Bataille's 1947 papers which were used as the basis for the *Oeuvres complètes*. I follow the 1947 *Critique* text which Levinas no doubt read.)

the individual who poses the questions but the very exigency of thinking. Doubtless it is for this reason that Jaspers, as Jean Wahl repeats, said that existentialism was the death of the philosophy of existence. One could contend rigorously (as Emmanuel Levinas does) that professorial existentialism has revealed Kierkegaard, that it has situated him exactly within the history of philosophy. If this is so, the existentialism of our day is comparable to the older sacrificer who revealed the truth of a victim by killing him.

This denial is bizarre, as if moral powerlessness came from an excess of intellectual power. The language of this philosophy is laborious, it is gluey. There is, it seems to me, a hesitation at its basis. Existentialist thinking is always fleeting but never achieves in itself the annihilation of thinking. Just as a child impelled by a need dances in place and cannot decide what to do, this thinking escapes without dying, sick with a morose virtuosity. All the elements vacillate: the nothing of Heidegger becomes being . . . I am astonished that at this point of development, *several* spirits are necessary to produce the cacophony of divergent possibilities: discoursing on time and being, a single one of them could represent ten ways of talking nonsense. If we cannot attain "a truth universally valid for all time," the only thing we do, philosophizing positively, is to proceed with a joke. A truth valid for one's time is but a commodity, in this case it is referred to action or is but a moment of the eternal truth to which it refers, or is but a manner of leaning dreadfully over the void.[4]

If one wishes indeed to see it, these brilliant developments of contemporary philosophy are murky. Heidegger forces admiration for his successful synthesis of traditional religious experience and the philosophy of a school associated with atheism; his teaching proceeds from the most meaningful investigation that has been made of the spheres of the profane and the sacred, the discursive and the mystical, the prosaic and the poetic.[5] But if one puts the account on the sacred, which Heidegger more generally names the *authentic*, one would wish to guard oneself from

4. Hegel constructs the successive truths of different times (the history of philosophy) as necessary moments of the absolute Idea. Kierkegaard, relying on an unintelligible revelation, affirmed the right of a subject against an objective position of necessary truth. Marx had action in view. Nietzsche spoke in the night of an absolute non-knowledge, announced the absence of revelation and of truth, the absence of God. Heidegger attains a neighboring position. Overtly Sartre would limit himself to saying the truth of his time. I have trouble believing this: How could a *philosopher* in such a case step beyond the limit without making of the limit that is encountered the object of a fundamental reflection?

5. One accuses him on the political level and perhaps one forces it: between that which is held to be unspeakably foul and the pardonable error, there are but differences in degree. (Trans. note: This sentence was deleted in *Oeuvres complètes.*)

emitting a value judgment: it is the open door (as it has been commonly in history) to all *viable* folly (and the margin of error is great); it is but a remedy: to oppose formally the authentic and the viable, not to take anything for authentic life but an intense consummation, deprived of sense and rigorously useless (the passion and the outburst cannot be subordinated to practical ends—there is no nonservile sovereign life except in the refusal to direct, to subject oneself: it is the morality of Sade). On this point, the misery of this philosophy seems to me dependent on its essence: the authenticity of Kierkegaard is inapplicable to a world, it was a consummation of life so intense that it left the development of knowledge in the background. One has trouble seeing in Heidegger that which responds to the passion which is truly mad and cried out by Kierkegaard. In Heidegger the authentic appears as a consciousness of the authentic, it is apparently no more than the nostalgia for rare authentic moments, which occur in a life of professorial studies, given over to the *knowledge* of the authentic. This life does not seem to be dominated by a terrible passion: one cannot be surprised by a slippage, which is not necessary but possible, from the authentic to Hitlerism. What dominated Heidegger was doubtless the intellectual desire to reveal being (being and not existence) in discourse (in philosophical language).[6] Jean Wahl says justly that "the knowledge of the existentialist, and even his existence" risks becoming disturbed (becoming a disturbance, I would say). He continues: "Does not the existentialist risk destroying the very existence that he wishes above all to preserve? It is a matter of knowing whether or not existence is something that should be reserved for solitary meditation" (*SH,* 33). But he needs neither Christ nor myth, the silence of the discourse that Wahl designates has no limit but the cry of a useless passion, and cannot fail, if it avoids the return to phrases which link us to other men (thus depriving us of solitude), to consume life to the limit of death.[7] There is no emphasis there: the experience of the void, of solitude, of presence as an unintelligible violence of world, both within oneself and outside of oneself, is not *less* but *more* pathetic than that of a religious person before the cross. To be devoted in principle to this silence and at

---

6. One knows of Heidegger's hostility to the word *existentialism:* if he responds by a concern for the authentic in the initial movement of Kierkegaard, he separates himself from it in the search for the meaning of being. Even if he does not admit, as does Jaspers, the name "philosophy of existence": he says "philosophy of being."

7. Jean Wahl's vocabulary seems to me unfortunate: "meditation" is a weak word, "to preserve" existence, to be afraid of "destroying it," could rigorously be understood in the opposite sense he intends (it is necessary "to lose" one's life in order "to find" it, "to consume" it, to no longer "preserve" it, in order not to be frustrated within it).

the same time to philosophize, to speak, is indeed disturbed: the slippage without which the exercise would not be is thus the very movement of thought. And if one dreams that this immense effort, that all this is destined to the discordance of different philosophies, which can claim to be a truth only relatively, to the absence of truth, a labor so great emerges that one knows nothing suspect, cowardly, empty-headed, inasmuch as it excites by a prodigious richness of views.

To consider this effort of hesitation, this vacillation, this incessant slippage of thinking, it is necessary to come to the position of Hegel which was given at the beginning of the argument.

It is strange today to apperceive that which Kierkegaard could not know: that Hegel, like Kierkegaard, understood the refusal of subjectivity before the absolute idea. One would have imagined in principle that Hegel's refusing would be a matter of a conceptual opposition: on the contrary. The fact is not deduced from a philosophical text but from a letter to a friend, to whom he confides that, for ten years he feared becoming mad. The reason for this was the necessity to renounce in himself the individual (representing to himself the necessity of being no longer himself, the particular being, the individual that he was, but rather the universal Idea, to fall into the divine impersonality, as it were—in a word, to become God, he felt himself becoming mad). This did not last for a single night, or for two days, but for ten years. In a sense, the rapid sentencing of Hegel had perhaps a force that even the long cry of Kierkegaard did not have. The rapid sentencing is no less given in existence—which trembles and exceeds—than is this cry. But Hegel is opposed to Kierkegaard in that the exigency of the universal is not given to him from the outside. It is a matter, *and this is more grave*, of a necessity at once impersonal and interior but immanent to the spirit that it imposes, articulated with rigor, leaving no way out. Kierkegaard had the leisure of arguing with or of subtly escaping from the argumentation of the other (of misunderstanding him). Hegel could not but obey his own reason—or lose it.

To read the *Phenomenology of Spirit* or to look at the portrait of the aged Hegel, one cannot miss being gripped by an impression of an icy achievement in which all possibilities are put together. This phenomenology is not an intellectual construction, it is the apparition of subjectivity in the world, it is the immense sequel of lacerations, of efforts, of labors, of errors, of falls, of revolts which lead subjectivity into an exhausting epic of the particular of the subject to the universality of the object, to the consciousness of self as a universe. That is the real history of the human genus, reduced to the changes which accomplish in the struggle the edifice necessary for the spirit which finally embraces totality by knowledge. This movement proceeding from a world in ruins, from a grinding of the teeth and from death, cannot be reduced to tragedy: but the fact that man is measured continually by death is the origin and the resource of it. The spirit which carries in itself like a mobile mirror, this unfolding of the history of subjectivity across wars and oppression, anguish and sweat, can be appeased: its appeasement is no less to the measure of an unbound immensity. The hard truth of the *Phenomenology* is that spirit is the same thing as history, that its tension and its repose are reduced to a distant effect of a thankless struggle for which the earth was the site. At stake in this stirring birth (whose rhythm is given in rapidity—a thousand times real— of the arrow piercing the heart) is, at the same time as the positing of the Individual (whom death individual-izes by the anguish he has before it, for the reason that no one can die in his place), is the reduction of the individual to the universal, that an-guish rivets to particularity. But this appeasing reduction is not at all the effect of a gentle wisdom. It is a destruction that scandalizes, that suffo-cates, even though reason requires it and renders an account of it. And the ravaged appeasement that appears on the features of the aged Hegel, the aspect of which both overpowers and reassures, is not at all the forget-ting of the impossibility whence it issues, but is more precisely the image of it: an image of death and of completion.

What is striking, if one envisions, on the contrary, the maintenance of subjectivity, of the individual in the cry, is that subjectivity is not saved either: it is only strange to that which destroys it (that which destroys appears to it in a transcendence). But the experience of a profound subjec-tivity has always one condition: it destroys the one who has it. The choice that Jean Wahl makes of Rimbaud, of Van Gogh is significant; it is a matter of spirits so strained that they do not survive. Kierkegaard con-sumed himself rapidly. But those who, on the condition that they disap-pear, express existence in intensity are not destroyed by a necessity of which they are conscious. They themselves do not attain to the universal: only the commentaries and the effect of their works—and of their life—on others render their particularity universal. But an illusion is main-tained: in the value attributed to the work, one does not know that the intensity of feelings which renders the work attractive also founds a uni-versal, by the destruction of the author of whom it is the promise. One separates *A Season in Hell* from the silence of Rimbaud; but one fails to discern the silence that is already in the cry, the cry still in the silence. If I return to my analysis on the subject of Kierkegaard: Kierkegaard did not know, when dying (but death here counts little, it is the failure, the nonsatisfaction and the laceration), that he would ultimately give to his reader of one hundred years later, Hegel's achieved satisfaction (but linked, immanently, to its opposite): nevertheless, the reader, in general, would not have a clear conscience about this. He would put the accent on the cry (on the protestation of the individual), not on the silence, even while a feeling of calm desolation already impregnates it. There are opposed possibilities which touch each other and are linked. The tragedy, ultimately, belongs to the moment when the actors and the audience have left the theater. Memory falls behind when it is time to grasp something that cannot be grasped: Kierkegaard himself grasped this the day when he noted in his journal: "I have an empty head like a theater after a performance."

What lures us is that individuality has humanly become the condition of the universal. Only a rich individuality, demanding intensely of subjectivity to be that which it is not, namely, universal, accedes to the true universality, which is not an interior entity, to which Kierkegaard opposes himself, which "maintains in destroying" and which "goes beyond" (in German Hegel used a single word, *aufheben*) subjectivity. But Kierkegaard could not see that the intensity of his refusal departed in no way from the Hegelian completion, that his very *blindness* and refusal were the condition of completion. One has said that Kierkegaard cannot be understood without Heidegger; it is arguable; but Hegel, doubtless, cannot be understood entirely without Kierkegaard. One wouldn't know how to give enough sense, in particular one wouldn't be able to avoid giving a pathetic sense to this necessity in us to carry individuality to the extreme of tension in order to destroy it. Propositions like "We are nothing without subjectivity" or "Subjectivity is nothing if it is not a universal" impose themselves on us in their contradictory evidence. But these propositions themselves are nothing if one has not seen in this contradiction precisely: what is at stake in human life and, more precisely and in a fundamental way, what is at stake in the laceration of this life can only be at stake in lacerating itself. Philosophy is evidently no stranger to this, its ownmost question, and existentialism has precisely the sense of having posed it, as I stated, by an error without which it would have been badly posed: the question in effect is never better posed than with an excess within the affirmation of a feeling which leads to refusing the question.[8]

Of course, without even speaking of its pathetic position, this problem

8. How to situate, how to define *existentialism* otherwise? But the word is decidedly annoying. It is convenient. It has even become inevitable to employ it in order to designate a given movement in the history of philosophy, going from Kierkegaard to Sartre. But there can be no *living* sense (I am so little existentialist in a sense that I detest writing *existential:* has it not displaced the usage of a pedantic word in order to designate what one

of the universal and of the particular is the central problem of philosophy, where it has taken numerous forms. For Emmanuel Levinas, the contribution of Heidegger's philosophy "consists in distinguishing between Being and entities, and in transporting relation, movement, efficacy, that hitherto resided in the existent, into Being."[9]

Whatever be the importance and the position of the problem in Heidegger,[10] Levinas, who was his student, but who very sensibly detached himself from him, has done so in a little work published under the title *De l'existence à l'existant*. The opposition between existence and existent does not differ from that of being-becoming. Existence is impersonal, it is the universal. The existent is the individual. It is the substantive of which existence is the verb: existence is for Levinas a "pure verb" of which the passage to the substantive is hypostasis.

What Levinas envisions leads in a direction distant from the perspectives that I have given: he is interested in the factical link between the universal and the particular, as if it were given once and for all in a static relation of existence to existent. He doesn't study the reversals and the lacerations that result from a relation. He is concerned with the possibility of hypostasis independent of its history. The difficulty of the task is felt: the animal is himself an existent in existence, and modern man is separated from the animal by the successive apparition of very different forms of subjectivity. But a recourse to historical givens is very removed from the methods of modern existentialism, which voluntarily closes itself up in present subjectivity. The little book of Emmanuel Levinas has nonetheless a remarkable interest, and its static analysis leads one to better see the givens of the drama that unfolds concerning the relation of the individual, who thinks, to the instant, which is the universal in him but which thinking, the search for the universal, cannot attain.

In a sense (if the expression designates a solidary group that Sartre, Simone de Beauvoir, and Merleau-Ponty exemplify), Emmanuel Levinas

---

thus wants to say? The impasse of modern existentialism is there) except on the condition of apperceiving in Sartre an attenuated aspect, a distant enough repercussion of a movement. In the order of things it is elsewhere. By nature existentialism cannot be affirmed by a determined name without repugnance (cf. *sh,* 33). In order for it to name itself, it would have to be a little more dead.

9. I am citing Levinas's intervention in a discussion given at the end of Wahl's *Petite histoire* (*sh,* 49).

10. Ruggiero (*Existentialism,* 49) gives the position of Jaspers and Heidegger a different interpretation. "One tells us . . . that existence is never a predicate, always a subject." And he complains about how easy it is to confuse "existence" with the "existent." But it is possible

is situated outside of "French existentialism." His philosophy has little relation with that of Sartre. A long captivity in Germany, in which he was a military prisoner, even prevented Levinas from reading *Being and Nothingness* before finishing his book. But he was one of the first in France to make known the thinking of Heidegger, under whom he studied and to which his own thinking, while being opposed to it, is linked: "If at the beginning our reflections are in large measure inspired by the philosophy of Martin Heidegger . . . , they are also governed by a profound need to leave the climate of that philosophy, and by the conviction that we cannot leave it for a philosophy that would be pre-Heideggerian" (*EE*, 19). On a slippery slope it would be difficult to say in precisely what way Levinas is opposed to his teacher. He links anguish to being, and no longer to nothingness. But is not Heidegger's nothing finally being? Between the two manners of thinking, there is, nonetheless, two sensible differences of *climate*, which a diametrical opposition of terms underscores. For Heidegger, the human being is unto death. Levinas (like Sartre) criticizes the representation of "being-unto-death." But this opposition is constructed: it is that of "the fear of being to the fear of nothingness." We read: "While anxiety, in Heidegger, brings about 'being-unto-death,' . . . the horror of the night 'with no exits' which 'does not answer' is an irremissible existence. 'Tomorrow, alas! one will still have to live'— a tomorrow contained in the infinity of today" (*EE*, 63). It is not death that frightens Levinas, but "the impossibility of death" (*EE*, 61). And to give voice to that which oppresses him, he cites the suffocation of Phaedra, moaning:

> The sky, the whole world's full of my forefathers. Where may I hide? Flee to infernal night. How? There my father holds the urn of doom . . . (*EE*, 63)

By way of the sentences of Levinas, one gets the sense of empty and irrational suffering, that only the death howl of a dog would not alter by a displaced intelligibility: it is still necessary on this occasion to refuse the popular (and superficial) idea that associates death with the expression of the impossible. Levinas writes:

> When the forms of things are dissolved in the night, the darkness of the night, which is neither an object nor the quality of an object, invades like a presence. In the night to which we are riveted, we are not dealing with anything. But this nothing is not that of pure nothingness. There is no longer *this* or *that*; there is not "something." But this universal absence is in its turn a presence,

---

that the interpretation articulated so precisely by Levinas takes into account that which makes Ruggiero's interpretation incomplete.

an absolutely unavoidable presence. It is not the dialectical counterpart of absence, and we do not grasp it through a thought. It is immediately there. There is no discourse. Nothing responds to us but this silence; the voice of this silence is understood and frightens like the silence of those infinite spaces Pascal speaks of. (*EE*, 58)

I myself introduce an equivocation in opposing the impenetrable howling of a dog in spite of, or better, on account of its absence of sense, to the intelligent terror of thinking (but the dog, apparently, is closer to the empty feeling of Levinas).

> What we call the I is itself submerged by the night, invaded, depersonalized, stifled by it. The disappearance of all things and of the I leaves what cannot disappear, the sheer fact of being in which one participates, whether one wants to or not, without having taken the initiative, anonymously. Being remains, like a field of forces, like a heavy atmosphere belonging to no one, universal, returning in the midst of the negation which put it aside, and in all the powers to which that negation may be multiplied. (*EE*, 58)

Nothing is less human than this; a disturbed animal, losing the elementary sense of animality, is, as it were, closer to responding correctly to the exigencies of his condition.

Levinas names the *there is*, "this impersonal, anonymous, yet inextinguishable 'consummation' of being" . . . The *there is*, according to him, "transcends inwardness as well as exteriority; it does not even make it possible to distinguish them" (*EE*, 57). *There is* is neither subject nor object: to subjects and objects it is opposed as existence (in general, universal) to existents (individual beings, particular things). If one wishes, in the situation of the *there is*, the existent is dissolved into existence.

Of course this situation is common, and if the clear and distinct knowledge of exterior objects and of the interiority of the I removes this situation, it is never possible that the knowing eliminates its return. The intelligence itself accedes to it in the end, by an operation that completes a system of procedures, all linked to precise objects, in the form of one total procedure, in which the preceding operations are dissolved. But common and coherent discourse only appears to accede to this dissolution. It speaks about it and cannot accomplish it, in that what discourse enunciates is always a meaningful proposition, the meaning of which is necessarily limited. Even if its coherence were absolute, there would be no isolated sentence that truly expressed dissolution, because discourse would then have to undo itself. Ultimately, the discourse that does not wish to oppose to the *there is* a sentence that speaks about it (which would distance it, due to the very fact that once enunciated, discourse limits the one who enunciates it to the clear world), ceasing to speak of it, therefore, in order to reach it, translates an inability not to betray its intention by a mortal disorder. Levinas says of some pages of *Thomas the Obscure* that they are a description of the *there is*. But this is not exact. Levinas describes and Blanchot cries—as it were—the *there is*.

> He descended into a sort of vault whose obscurity was complete . . . In front, in back, overhead, a hard stone wall barred his route; and this wall was not the greatest obstacle for he had also to reckon on his will which was fiercely determined to let him sleep there in a passivity exactly like death . . . Thomas's first observation was that he could still use his body, and particularly his eyes; it was not that he saw anything but that that on which he gazed disdained his gaze, without permitting him to look away. This eventually placed him in contact with a nocturnal mass which he vaguely perceived to be himself and in which he was bathed . . . by means of which he believed himself to be in contact with an intelligence his glance or his hand could touch; he was overtaken by a feeling of fright that he did not succeed in mastering. The night seemed soon to him far more somber, more terrible than any other night, as though it had truly issued from a wound of thought which no longer thought itself, of thought taken ironically as object by something other than thought. It was night itself. Images which constituted its obscurity inundated him, and his body transformed into a demoniacal spirit, tried to imagine them. He saw nothing, and, far from being distressed, he made this absence of vision the culmination of his sight. Useless for seeing, his eye took on extraordinary proportions, developed beyond measure and, stretching out on the horizon, let the night penetrate its center in order to create for itself an iris. Throughout this void, it was the look and the object of his look which mingled together. Not only did this eye which saw nothing apprehend something, it apprehended the cause of its vision. It saw as an object that which prevented it from seeing. *(Thomas l'obscur)*[11]

11. I have cited most of this passage in *Inner Experience* (trans. Leslie Anne Boldt [Albany: State University of New York Press, 1988], 101). Sartre bases his critique of that work on a sentence of this citation in which he grasps the "trickery" performed by Blanchot and myself: "He saw as an object that which prevented him from seeing." According to Sartre, there would be a substantification of nonknowledge, a hypostasizing of a pure nothingness. I say personally: "I know nothing, absolutely nothing. I cannot know *that which is*. Being unable to relate *that which is* to the known, I remain on the wrong path in the unknown." *Inner Experience* expresses entirely this situation, which is that of the *there is* of Levinas, and to which the sentence in question in Blanchot gives an accomplished expression. In opposition, Sartre's critique helps to grasp Levinas's thinking, which does not differ, it seems to me, from Blanchot's and from mine. Sartre himself avers that if I "substantify nonknowledge, it is with prudence, in the manner of a movement [not a thing]" ("Un nouveau mystique," in *Situations* I [Paris: Gallimard, 1947], 182). But, above all, Levinas's position helps to show what is misleading about the critique of Sartre, to whom the meaning of Blanchot's sentence is closed, and who is held within a proposition that is the perfect negation of poetry: "For me nothing is but that which I know."

Here the indifference to formal definition effectuates an inhibition of a will to insert in the sphere of objects of thinking that which has no place except outside. Levinas defines as an object, *by a formal generalization* (in other terms, by discourse) that which, in the *literary* text of Blanchot, is purely the cry of existence. The principle to which Levinas is held (that of existential philosophy) leaves its approach incomplete; if he generalizes (in consequence, if he imagines an object), then he is no less linked to the individual, to the intimate, to the subjective. Reciprocally, he had to engage life, which he experiences, in this generalization, and to experience it as a knowledge, within the very mode in which objects are distinctly *known* to us.[12] In this way, the existentialist *philosophy* changes us into things more profoundly than does science, which at least leaves *intimacy* unchanged. The scholar can, if he wishes to remain unreasonable, imagine the world as if the intimacy in it had the meaning of exterior phenomena, of which intimacy would be the effect. But if he mostly limits his life to knowing exteriorly, if he abandons intimacy, if practically he suppresses it, he cannot even *alter* it a little bit. He cannot even integrate it, as does the existentialist, hesitant only halfway, to the discursive projection of knowledge. The religious man himself admitted this projection, he himself altered intimacy, to the extent that he expressed it by discourse, he has doubtless introduced elements into it which are not reducible to it. The *revealed* and the *sacred* maintained the primacy of life over knowledge; that which escaped the operations of intelligence dominated from on high the lowness and humility of discourse. Existentialism itself cannot escape through the ritual precaution just described, by poetic freedom, from being put on the same level of things known. Moreover, it associates with knowledge a hesitation and a slippage. The epithet *existentialist* signifies that a man is neither saint nor poet, that he has attempted in vain—"in vain" is a critique, but even more, a reserve to critique—to detach knowledge from exteriority. Decidedly, he has become a "man of knowledge."

Levinas deliberately accentuates the description of the *there is* in the sense of horror and suffocation. The *there is* is that from which time, or the insertion of existence in time, delivers him. This intimate character—individual and painful—of an experience maintains, in a way of expression proper to it, the value of a cry, but at the same instant it maintains the value of a non-sense (if experience does not generally have that very

---

12. Levinas insists on the position of existence, or precisely the *there is* as "pure verb" in opposition to hypostasis, to the object which is known in its exteriority. If he speaks of it, nevertheless the accent is put on the intellectual operation, and not on a suppression—by ecstasy or poetry—of discursive knowledge.

same sense). For all that, Levinas introduces the notion of the *there is* by an analysis of the "materiality" of being. In his eyes, the suppression of the interest in the object in modern painting, the accent placed on the naked sensation of form and color, independent of intellectual interpretation, discovers the "materiality" of objects (a represented package of tobacco no longer has the virtue of evoking the reality in which it is found, of creating by association the values of symbol or usage. It is the sensation given by forms and colors, as free of sense as are sounds in music). Art, according to Levinas, tears forms away from the world, one could say, from the sphere of activity, in which each object assumes an altogether defined meaning. It has generally the virtues of exoticism. Said otherwise, if we see things, each one of them expresses an idea. It is not the thing's materiality that we see but the thing that expresses the idea. Thus art— say, poetry—destroys the meaning of the thing, it freezes the thing, and, in its manner, returns it to the last silence: that which it reveals is matter and "matter is the very fact of the *there is*" (*EE*, 57).

One has nothing to reply to Levinas's analysis if not that it reaches its object from the outside. The style of the analysis is doubtless existentialist ("[T]he research into modern painting in its protestation against realism" would proceed from a "sentiment of the end of the world"); and this pathos truly refers it to intimate feeling, to the author's horror of being. But from the fact of the objectivity of painting, the reference cannot take place solely in meaning. The tearing away from the world effectuated in artistic creations cannot be objectively separated from attraction, which is its *raison d'être*. Determined from the outside, the *there is* no longer has the limited sense that it, grasped from the inside, uniquely had.

Continuing to elaborate on the *there is*, Levinas is led to found it upon other objective facts, which are at least claimed as such, borrowed from French sociology. The "mystical participation" of Lévy-Bruhl exemplifies an absence of the object linked to the absence of the subject:

> In Durkheim if the sacred breaks with profane being by the feelings it arouses, these feelings remain those of a subject facing an object . . . The situation is quite different in Lévy-Bruhl. Mystical participation is completely different from the Platonic participation in a genus: in it the identity of the terms is lost. . . . The participation of one term in another does not consist in sharing an attribute; one term is the other. The private existence of each term, mastered by a subject that is, loses this private character and returns to an undifferentiated background; the existence of the one submerges the other, and is thus no longer an existence of the one. We recognize here the *there is*. The impersonality of the sacred in primitive religions, which for Durkheim is the "still" impersonal God from which will issue one day the God of advanced

religions, describes on the contrary a world where nothing prepares for the apparition of a God. The notion of the *there is* leads us, rather than to a God, to the absence of God, the absence of any being. (*EE*, 60–61)

A passage is effectuated from the representation of Durkheim, for whom the sacred is an object, to that of Lévy-Bruhl. In Lévy-Bruhl, participation is apparently founded on the objective error of the participant, who would take himself to be the same thing as the animal or the rain. The passage from Durkheim to Lévy-Bruhl does not remove us, as it first seems, from an experience founded on an observation from the outside. The notion introduced by Levinas, far from leaving participation to the error of the subject, itself helps to found its objective value. In this perspective, it is of no importance that the *there is* is at once the absence of subject and object. We cannot know it clearly, except from the outside, in the constancy of its formal effects, if knowledge is common and communicable, as knowledge wishes to be.

The problem introduced by the little work of Levinas is exactly that of the communication of an ineffable experience. The *there is* is, apparently, the ineffable of mystics: although Levinas *has spoken* about it, nevertheless he has expressed it exactly only through the channel of formal effects (modern painting, surrealist art, Lévy-Bruhl's participation).[13] The rest is intimacy, which cannot be communicated under the heading of clear knowledge, but solely in the form of poetry. If you will, knowledge is necessarily something other than effusion, and "knowledge-effusion" lacks force. It has neither the force of effusion nor that of knowledge. To the extent that "knowledge-effusion" is effusion, it has the value of poetry (which can be the material for knowledge); to the extent to which it is knowledge, it has the value of formal consistency which draws it away from poetry. Poetic effusion and the positing of objective forms both have the ability to reach intimacy but not the slippage from one to the other.

The impotency of thinking is given in the sterility of the slippages: poetry obscures knowledge, knowledge tames poetry, but neither poetic knowledge nor intellectual poetry[14] are up to man. Humanity is the exigency of an extreme possibility: both the domains of science and poetry tolerate neither failure nor compromise. (But poetry is sovereign and never can be subjugated: the extreme knowledge requires, on the contrary, the recognition of poetry, which is never the means of its autonomous activity, but remains the end of the one who knows—and the end

---

13. Levinas clearly alludes to the intentions of surrealism.
14. This is Lautréamont's "blot of intellectual blood."

of knowledge, to the extent that knowledge pushed to the extreme is the dissolution of knowledge.) In truth knowledge cannot escape from its impotency; it cannot escape from its power.

Existentialism wanted to flee . . . This is not important anymore. There is no knowledge except that of the general, and in general knowledge there are but two ways, the Hegelian one, of a cohesion of all possible thoughts, and that of science, proceeding in particular points according to precise approaches. Furthermore, from the very beginning, each of them engages an equivalence of their completion with its contrary: there is no knowledge but that which makes itself. But a total knowledge (dialectical or scientific) is also total night. An accomplished knowledge is but the most advanced point of knowledge. But if there were no longer anything unknown beyond this most advanced point, the least unknown thing could in its turn become known, that which was previously unknown being decidedly related to the known, the known would become in this completion in its entirety the unknown. There is no global cohesion of oppositions of thinking that does not imply in advance this opening unto the impossible, and there is no lucid science which does not experience, given our rough state of knowledge, the *supreme ignorance* of him who would extend the operations of science to the totality of elements.

But "total night" and "supreme ignorance" are not necessarily what they seem. The ignorance into which I fall, if I know that, in the end, knowledge knows nothing, does not have the same object as common ignorance. "Commonly" I do not know [*j'ignore "communement"*] the cause of a given effect or the effect of a given action, or I do not know about the unexpected death, recently, of someone: while the supreme ignorance has for an object that which is, all that which is, which is not a thing and which can be named *there is*. Commonly I do not know the *there is* (in the same way that I do not know a thing), when I know *this* or *that*, or when I do not know a cause or an effect. But on the other hand, in supreme ignorance, I wake myself up to it as to the poetry of an empty immensity, opening onto it the door that I imagined to give unto my room. The *there is* from the very fact that it is not *this*, which I can relate to *that*, as to a genus of which it is the example, cannot exist in me (before me) except in the form of ignorance. At the same time supreme ignorance necessarily reveals the nudity of *that which is*, reduces it to an unintelligible presence in which all difference is destroyed, to which the name *there is* belongs.

For that reason I can regard the night of nonknowledge as my deliverance: Is it not the fusion of the subject and the object, of spirit and matter?

And the necessities of my isolated existence—obliged to know *this* and *that*—are they not my servitude? But I cannot escape servitude by a trick that is knowledge without passion. The passion of knowledge—I mean passion without measure—alone has the force to lead knowledge to the moment in which it is dissolved; while knowledge without passion welcomes the infinite possibility of sentences.

The *there is* is for Levinas, the fact of being, independent of the object perceived and of the subject who perceives: it is the existence of impersonal being in general, opposed to the existent, to the isolated being who is the hypostasis of it. But the time proper to impersonal existence differs from that of the individual being. Impersonal existence lacks distinct instants and the possibility of rhythm. All the points of time are alike there, like the points of space in a black night. The position of a subject for whom the instant can cause an irruption in being would be necessary, Levinas writes, "so that this insomnia, which is like the very eternity of being, stops" (*EE*, 66). This is the I who exists isolatedly, who according to Levinas assumes the instant, stops in a sense in the contraction of an effort in which a domination of personal being is affirmed. The instant would only have graspable existence to the extent to which it is grasped in a substantive being, in which it is propriety, discerned and isolatable, of an isolated subject. But therefore he will no longer be the atomistic point of time that we customarily imagine. It would not be all of a piece; it would be, on the contrary, "articulated" (*EE*, 18), linking in the event the past and the present.

The instant is truly the philosopher's bottle of ink. The instant of Sartre "is not." The instant of another is eternal. Each chooses a sort of instant, like a dish in a restaurant, according to the affinity of a system. I can ask myself in jest the question: The instant "would it not be?" "Would it be eternal?" I will never be able to divide it but in jest. I cannot but order the cohesion of contradictory ideas in the perspective in which the necessities of an entire development would appear. What I have said up till now is referred to this cohesion (without exposing it); in every way a notion cannot be envisaged outside of the composition of perspectives that it opens in the spirit, which is the global possibility of language. But the passion of knowledge is not limited to this way, and the procedure of science, less ill at ease, is imposed on the elaboration of the last problem approached.

Can the sense of the present instant be determined by an assumed value in a quantitative game? Economy gives to the instant a precise signification, to which no interior view can be opposed. Economy is truly the major aspect that human existence has for science, the economic sense of the instant does not respond at all to the assumption of a subject, to which Levinas attends. He responds on the contrary with the sentiment of the *there is*. But without presupposing a necessary cohesion of contradictory notions, it is not without interest to imagine the sense of this affirmation within the framework of an analysis of material facts.

Economic science follows the courses of objects produced and consumed. It takes account of work—human and mechanical—insofar as it enters into these courses (then it assimilates to the work which is either directly or indirectly productive, the work that isn't, but which is paid for in the same way as the first one). It is not always sufficient. Production and consumption of objects does not represent the economic game in its entirety. And if it were necessary to say precisely the meaning of this game we would have to imagine as a foundation the physiological facts to which it responds. It appears thus that animal activity is at one time acquisition, at another time an expenditure of energy. The most humble movements represent an expenditure so appreciable that a farmer has interest if he can in maintaining a recumbent calf: the animal accumulates energy in the form of fat that it will have otherwise expended in comings and goings. But human activity has distinctly developed two chapters of opposed expenditures: productive (rudimentary for most animals), and unproductive. The first are means of acquisitions (which are not themselves ends but are means to second, unproductive expenditures). If one imagines the meaning of these operations in time, it is clear that the one of a productive expenditure—that is to say, from an economic point of view, from an acquisition—is given in its relation with the future; the one of an unproductive expenditure on the contrary is given in the present instant. One can say reciprocally: if economy imagines the future, the only activity that has a meaning is productive expenditure (work, or some such expenditure necessary to the production of work); and unproductive expenditure is a nonsense, even a countersense (so long as it does not become a habitual complement of productive activity). It would be necessary to add, but this is another story; if economy would imagine the present . . . in fact, economy never imagines it. This is the reason why economic science is so incomplete. If, all the same, I imagine in spite of economists, nonsense is thus productive activity, the unproductive alone has *value*.

It is only to a superficial gaze that an unproductive value would appear as a simple negation. It is indeed negation but of an already given negation. It negates the already effectuated negation of the present instant. On the contrary it is productive value that is essentially negative: for it negates *that which is*, the present, to the profit of the future, *which is not*. In fact, unproductive activity in general is always positive. It is, manifestly, a *loss*, but the meaning of this word is not really negative unless the lost substance is really lacking to him who lost it. It isn't like that. It cannot be that in sum. Living beings generally have at their disposition a super-abundance of energy: whatever might be the expenditure required for necessary work, given an average crossing of resources (means of production), there is too much energy to spend in the world. It was costly to produce it, but we cannot do anything about it: a given production cannot be limited to the furnishing of necessary energy to go on. Whatever be the energy engaged in this production, it is necessarily—in average condition—of less value than produced value. One cannot in fact organize an accumulation so rapid that it absorbs the totality of surplus, and if one did it the growth of tools of production would end shortly with a shifting of the used energy in relation to the volume of production. Thus the loss realized in unproductive expenditures is one, if you will, but not according to the negative value of the word: it can, here or there, slow down the desirable accumulation, but energy is lost *to the profit of the present instant—which is*, whereas the future *is not*.

The word *profit* is incongruent indeed if *the present instant* determines it, but this incompatibility reveals precisely that which rules the narrowness of economic sciences: it is the narrowness of the language of knowledge that does not have, in principle, the power to reckon with the present. In discursive language, the present is the poor parent (or the scapegoat): that which only has sense for the one who doesn't have any sense, which has value only for the one who is not useful. An immense state is given a sense: that of the decisive emancipation of man, but this seductive end makes it pass, in a privileged fashion, under the power of logic. The present instant, having sense only in inverse reason to logic, an entire people knows an accrued servitude, *which is*—which, in consequence, does not count, in the name of an emancipation *which is not*,—which in consequence is the meaning of servitude. To the rigorous effort which shakes the world no one of course would oppose the perfect impotency of the instant. I will limit myself to showing that unproductive expenditure, having the meaning of the instant, is rarely a waste as one imagines; as a general rule *it has the positive value of art*. Living beings are made so that in losing themselves their excess of energy shines. The effect is a spring, which attracts, beyond the satisfaction of a need. Art is precisely this positive squandering of energy: it is an economic fact, and economy gives it a value measurable in theory once it assumes the sense of the present time.

For Levinas art indeed is one of the ways of the *there is*. Art "tears objects away from the world," but that is exactly because in the world an object only has meaning in the future and because the meaning of art is in the present time. This object here, the piece of paper, has the quality of an object to the extent that I imagine its existence beyond this instant here, in view of the possibilities that belong to it (of the use it will have). If I limit my interest to the present instant it slides into the unintelligible materiality of that which is (and which art reveals according to Levinas). It dissolves itself in an awakening to the indistinct immensity. In this obscurity I myself am dissolved (I discern myself to the extent that the possibility of my duration is given in the future). Poetry, which deprives isolated beings of their position of subject or object,[15] is an intense consummation of life in the present time. Perhaps it is immediately incomprehensible: if I rapidly write a poem, if I wish, I can work immediately, but writing a burning poem engages life in a disorder that is not very productive, in a wasting of time and goods that are at hand. The irregularity and the complexity of effects, the difficulty of judging the authenticity of poetry does not authorize economic science to ignore it. The fact that a poem persists, brings money to its author, marks an endless possibility of communicating consummation (by the repetitions of language) and of inscribing on the author's account a part of the unproductive expenditure to which the reader is engaged: the meaning of consummation, each time, is no less given in the present instant: it is the contrary of work, the sense of which is limited to the future use of the product.

The fact that unproductive expenditure—poetry, art, and generally free consummation—tends toward the dissolution of the subject cannot escape economics either. The traditional study of productive economics requires the positing of subjects inscribed in duration. Productive economics is precisely the domain of the isolated subject. Its study engages those juridical conditions the attribution of values produced toward non-solidary persons. Reciprocally, the subject cannot be posited outside of the activity, the result of which is the personal enjoyment of a product. But all unproductive expenditure requires of a subject the provisional abandonment of this movement: the subject denies himself in a paradoxical fashion to the extent that he makes fun of appropriation and spends without hope of profit. If I take up the terminology of Levinas again, he is driven into existence and not into the existent. There is no longer the subject of the objective world, opposed to the object that he is not, that he appropriates usefully if he can. He gives up everything to the other without receiving anything in return, and even independently of appro-

15. "The poetry that overwhelms 'existents' in their positing" (*EE*, 82).

priating the other or a part of the goods of the other. This presupposes in the first place that *in the present time* he ceases to make a difference between himself and the other that itself signifies that ultimately he no longer distinguishes the world from his existence. The painter, modifying the canvas, no longer distinguishes it from himself; his creation is not other than himself, whether or not he has the intention of painting nature. The fact of the conservation and the sale of paintings changes nothing: it does not enclose the essential element of the painting, which is communicable movement going from the existent to existence. The importance of individual features of the author fools us: these traits are accentuated, but this is because in truth the suppression of a subject as such requires an accentuated individuality. And sometimes the authenticity of art, which wished for a sickly subjectivity, has denied it finally to the point of death.

If one follows this development, the content of apparently profound thoughts introduced by modern philosophers from an embarrassed subjectivity that passion does not consume right away and the enervated style of existentialism emerges. This content is expressed in facts of science. Such an operation is now regarded as an index of vulgarity. But we cannot remain honestly with judgments which do not imagine the decisive issue, and which, on the other hand, would be founded on the possibility of a compromise of knowledge and intimacy. The compromise, put to the test, appears contrary to the desires that commanded it. At the same time, it enervates the rigor of conscience and of passion, without which it is not interiority. If it appears in the last place that the objective analysis does not restrain a field of research at all, but substitutes the clear result to chance, hesitant approaches of a philosophy without unity, there is no avowable reason to oppose a prejudice to my ambitious attempt. A *general economy* (distinct from the traditional economy, the latter being restricted to the domain of production), ceasing to ignore the movements of exuberance, occupies a new place on the level of knowledge. It encompasses in its research—at the same time as work, the fabrication of products and accumulation—the unproductive usage of wealth . . . It puts an end to this manner of misrecognition in which economic theory has held the immense unproductive activity of men, in which idealism held the material conditions of life.[16] It does not raise up the necessity of a coherent composition of language, such that the plenitude of its developed possi-

16. This critique would not be able to address itself to the idealism of Hegel, whose *Phenomenology of Spirit*, in Marx's own avowal, does the work of the essence of man. The economic interpretation of history in the precise sense of the class struggle, is already given by Hegel.

bilities orders the meaning of each of them in relation to the other, and it reveals the nonsense, the perfect opacity, or, more precisely, the silence, of the ensemble. Precisely, this composition is the domain of philosophy: a science results from an agreement of minds on the method and the results, prior to the accord on first principles which found them. The sciences are in general opposed to mystical thinking from the fact of continual exchanges with techniques: the sciences have the truth of techniques that the necessities of life do not cease to put to the test.

One will find an appreciable advantage in passing from the vacillating approximations of the philosophers of existence to precisions objectively given in experience. Overtly or not, existentialism itself already rested on numerous affirmations about exterior observation (in Levinas openly). But the method itself leaves the door open to individual chance. Levinas defines the fact of being in describing the horror he experiences there. Another would have drawn from the same fact drunkenness, joy, or ecstasy. From an economic point of view, it suffices to show the relation of an experienced sentiment to the state of personal resources; it is often possible, if not easy. Ascesis slows down exchanges and reduces slowly the sum of energy necessary to the duration of the subject: the ascetic at the same time limits the usage of his resources to a slow ecstatic consummation, to the exclusion of expenditures precipitated by free existence. He can thus lose himself without trembling overly in a happy fusion, in which he loses the notion of himself and of the world. In any case, the happiness of ascesis is the formal constancy which limits the signification of anguish commonly experienced before the fact of being. Anguish itself cannot be imagined without taking account of an economic state: to presuppose a regime of exchanges that would be up to an individual, anguish has a place if the possibility of a desirable expenditure puts into play the continuation of the regime. It presupposes elsewhere the establishment of a compromise: anguish is also an expenditure, but habitually less onerous than if we were to respond to desire: besides, it is sometimes *the most onerous*. It consumes more profoundly than abandon would have: anguish by this detour has the audacity of Gribouille; sometimes even it reaches a degree of consummation more intense. The fact of remaining arrested before possibility is also a formal constancy of anguish, but the possibility in anguish is always a dangerous expenditure, which puts into question the prolongation of an adopted regime: sometimes expenditure itself does not seem necessarily unproductive; but it is to the extent that it can ruin the one to whom it gives anguish. Of course, vague anguish, where there is no longer a distinct object, is always in the background of any anguish. But this bottom of anguish cannot itself be entirely grasped except through superficial forms. The bottom of anguish is in effect the coincidence between an absence of a subject with an absence of an object, but it is a *possibility*, it is its ultimate possibility, the extreme temptation, which puts into play the opening without reserve unto an absence of meaning. It is not the most costly expenditure that is thus solicited but the most unjustifiable, that which does not have the least reason: it is achieved unproductivity, and it is the radical annulling of time to come. In fact it is, at the same time, rapture, but on a condition that, this possibility being posited, anguish robs the spirit of it: if not, the time to come would still be imagined, if not, temptation would have a meaning.[17] The movement from *anguish* to *ecstasy* is the end and the *key* of a general theory of economy, but for all that it doesn't enter into a claimed depth of thinking. Deep thinking is incomplete thinking. It lacks the quantitative basis without which one can follow nothing. There is no difference between the nature of elementary considerations on the daily uses of riches and these fundamental insights. But what may be surprising—the views of philosophers of existence are in no way diminished by the light. What I spoke of in the last place illuminates the mist of mystical theology, but the richness of this place is not touched. Only the presuppositions and the hypostasis (the mystical facts) are dissipated. Nothing remains that is up to reason, but reason no longer renders an account of the fact of a world up to reason. It is clear at the extremity of possible thoughts that the distant extremity is not different from the beginning (the world of the man of knowledge is no less rich than that of more simple religions) but meanwhile, like simple need, desire beyond need is expressed in terms of economy. For the ghosts of religion or for the existentialist clouds, this substitutes an unavoidable necessity. Economy draws a plentitude from these general views. The futile—and guilty—aspect of crucial moments is justified—and is affirmed *as a face*.

A second interest of this method has to do with the place of the domain studied in the ensemble of the sciences, as science in general is closed up in itself. That which it imagines does not open from itself any void in the fabric of laws and facts that it establishes. On the other hand, the general perspective of economy is established starting from a center which is the subject of knowledge or, more precisely, the intimacy of the subject. In other terms, general economy cannot avoid the consideration of the present instant, and all the lines of established perspectives con-

17. It is the dialectic of sense and non-sense, which destroys non-sense. The same feature is found in the passage from anguish to ecstacy, knowledgeably studied by Jamet in the mystical experience of a sick subject.

verge on this point. For this reason general economy could not have constituted itself before the development of a philosophy of interiority, but from the first it would have been necessary to put this philosophy on earth. Beyond a given limit, there is nothing more to wait for than the confusion of a method neglecting in principle the factical observation from the outside. The philosophy of existence has posited subjectivity, and it is to the extent that this positing necessarily implies the ruin of the subject posited that this philosophy is worthy of interest. Furthermore, it had to make part of the way itself. Already the existence of the philosophy of Levinas is no longer that of the subject. It is existence given independently of all subject and object, although still approached by the way of the subject. But the objective way introduces a decisive change: the servitude of the operations of knowledge—a substitution of the philosophy of known existence (of an intellectual approach) for naked existence—arises at the very moment in which *intimacy* comes into play. The method poses in principle the impossibility of *knowing* the instant with which intimacy is identified. The outside is only given to knowledge by the fact of the appurtenance of things to duration. Thus it leaves open a chance to experience: poetry, or rapture, supposes a downfall and the suppression of knowledge, which are not given in anguish. *It is the sovereignty of poetry.* At the same time a hatred of poetry—*because it is not inaccessible.*

Translated by Jill Robbins

INDEX